CHILDREN'S PLAY IN CHILD CARE SETTINGS

Action theory

SUNY Series,
Children's Play in Society

Anthony D. Pellegrini, Editor

CHILDREN'S PLAY IN CHILD CARE SETTINGS

Edited by
Hillel Goelman
and
Ellen Vineberg Jacobs

STATE UNIVERSITY OF NEW YORK PRESS

Production by Ruth Fisher
Marketing by Bernadette LaManna

Published by
State University of New York Press, Albany

For information, address the State University of New York Press,
State University Plaza, Albany, NY 12246

Library of Congress Cataloging-in-Publication Data
Children's play in child care settings / edited by Hillel Goelman and
    Ellen Vineberg Jacobs.
        p.   cm. — (SUNY series, children's play in society)
    Includes index.
    ISBN 0-7914-1697-6 (alk. paper). — ISBN 0-7914-1698-4 (pbk. :
alk. paper)
    1. Child care.   2. Play—Psychological aspects.   3. Day care
centers.   I. Goelman, Hillel, 1951-   . II. Jacobs, Ellen
Vineberg, 1946-   . III. Series.
HQ778.5.C54   1994
155.4'18—dc20   93-18083
                                                                     CIP

10   9   8   7   6   5   4   3   2   1

Contents

Introduction

Ellen Vineberg Jacobs

This book is about child care and play. The context for the collection of studies in this text is the child care setting—either a family day care home or a group day care center. The substantive focus of each of the papers is play. Child care has become an accepted aspect of childhood for a large percentage of North American families. Play, which is the essence of childhood, should be a quintessential feature of a child care program, particularly as the child may spend the majority of his/her waking hours in the child-care setting. If we believe that play is an essential part of childhood, then providing a forum for the presentation of research on the importance of play in the child-care setting is crucial. Therefore, we have undertaken the task of compiling studies that address the topic of play in the child-care setting from a variety of perspectives.

The introduction to this book is structured to provide the reader with definitional information about child-care and play. The relationship between child-care attendance and development is presented and the developmental issues associated with the quality of the care are discussed. Cognitive and social play categories are defined and the association between play and development is explored. Environmental influences on play such as the availability of materials, novelty, realism and types of materials are examined in depth, as is the influence of caregivers on children's play. The individual chapters are introduced and concerns about play issues in child-care settings are raised at the conclusion of the chapter.

In the current child-care context a wide variety of formal arrangements and options are available. For the purpose of this text we will confine the discussion to group care wherein a child is cared for in an environment other than his/her own home. The two most common forms of out-of-home group care are family day care and center care. In family day care the caregiver offers child care in her own home. He/she may look after a number of children within a wide age range. In most communities licensing regulations regarding family day-care homes usually stipulate that no more than five to six children can be cared for in the home and this number includes the caregiver's children. However, some homes are licensed to take twelve to fifteen children. Generally, there are no regulations regarding age grouping. One of the advantages of family day care is that the caregiver's hours of operation may be very flexible and he/she can offer the type of support that a parent on a variable schedule may require. The training and experience of these caregivers varies as does the physical environment of the indoor and outdoor space of the home. Consequently the daily activities and experiences of the children in this type of care arrangement will vary as well.

Group day-care centers are usually located in large public places such as community centers, schools, religious institutions, recreation centers and shopping centers. In some cases the day care is housed in a building constructed or renovated specifically for the day-care center. There are usually a number of children of approximately the same age and this permits the grouping of children by age. Licensing requirements vary from one locale to another, however, older preschoolers are usually assigned to groups of fifteen to twenty with a ratio of one caregiver for eight to ten children. Where infants are concerned the ratio may be one adult to three children and for toddlers it may be one adult to four or five children. The education and training of caregivers in this type of setting is usually stipulated in licensing procedures. The most stringent rules require one in three caregivers to have a university degree in early childhood education and all other caregivers in the center must have at least a college or junior college level certificate in early childhood education. These centers usually have well defined routines, organized programs for the children and a fixed operating schedule that is convenient for parents who work a regular eight to nine hour day. The fees vary in accordance with the facilities and services offered and the operating philosophy of the center. Nonprofit and for-profit centers may charge the same fees, however, the services and provisions will differ as the profit must be derived from the fees. The indoor and outdoor physical environment of each group center will depend upon location of the center and the equipment and materials available to the children. Some employers offer day care in the workplace and some schools offer after school care for children of all ages.

As more children participate in nonparental child-care arrangements, questions related to the effects of these arrangements on their development has become more pertinent. We know from the multitude of studies that have been conducted to date that we cannot point to simple, causal relationships between any aspect of day care and the child's development. Taken together, the studies allow us to discuss the relationship between child-care attendance and the particular aspects of development that have been researched.

For example, studies that examined social development found that day-care attendance was related to increased aggressiveness (Schwarz, Strickland & Krolick, 1974), more positive peer interactions (Vlietstra, 1981), less attentiveness and social responsibility (Schwarz et al., 1981), but more advanced perspective-taking skills, more operative behavior and more confidence in social interactions (Clarke-Stewart, 1984; Howes & Olenick, 1986; Ramey, McPhee & Yates, 1982; Rubenstein & Howes, 1979). In studies of children's cognitive development, day-care attendance was related to higher measures of cognitive competence (Andersson, 1989; Carew, 1980), more complex speech and higher Peabody Picture Vocabulary Test (PPVT) scores (Rubenstein, Howes, & Boyle, 1981).

It has been postulated that high quality care can make a difference in the experiences that children have in their child-care environment, but the question remains as to the definition of high quality care. Is it the aspects of the center that can be measured and regulated such as teacher-child ratios, group size, total population size within the center, teacher training, teacher experience and director education? Or, might quality be more dependent on global variables such as personal care routines, furnishings and displays for children, fine- and gross-motor activities, creative activities, language and reasoning activities, as measured by the Early Childhood Environmental Rating Scale (Harms & Clifford, 1980) or curriculum, adult-child interactions, relations between the home and program and the developmental evaluation of children as suggested by the Developmentally Appropriate Practice (Bredekamp, 1987)? Quality might actually be a delicate combination of these variables. It would seem likely that these elements of quality interact to create an atmosphere within the child-care environment that influence a child's behavior and development.

Studies have shown that children who attended high quality centers were rated as more confident in their social interactions, more cooperative and sociable and less dependent and displayed less nonsocial play behavior than children in low quality centers (Holloway & Reichhart-Erickson, 1988; Howes & Olenick, 1986; Owen & Henderson, 1989; McCartney, Scarr, Phillips, Grajek & Schwarz, 1982). Preschool children enrolled in high quality care as toddlers engaged in more social pretend play than preschoolers who had been in low quality care as toddlers (Howes, 1990). These findings which indicate that there is a relationship between quality of care and play behaviors are cause for concern. Play is one of the most frequent, naturally occurring behaviors of childhood and research studies have shown that there is a strong association between play and development. Prior to a discussion of this relationship, it is essential to define and explain what play is and how it is viewed by researchers and early childhood educators.

Play: Definitions and Examples

Play is an intrinsically motivated behavior that is determined by the child and is not controlled by the stimuli around him/her. In play, the child is an active participant and the activity that he/she is engaged in is the focus. Since there is freedom from externally imposed rules in play, the activity can take whatever form the child wishes without regard for an expected pattern of behavior. Play has an "as if" quality which enables the child to transform self, others, objects and situations and behave in accordance with these transformations. This aspect of play allows the child to escape from the rigors of reality and engage in pretense (Garvey, 1977a; Hutt, 1970; Rubin, Fein & Vandenberg, 1983; Vandenberg, 1978).

Parten (1932) categorized play from a social behavior perspective, while Piaget (1962) and Smilansky (1968) categorized it from a cognitive perspective. Parten's differentiations between social and nonsocial play behaviors resulted in three non-social and three social play categories. In the nonsocial play, *unoccupied behavior* is defined as the child wandering aimlessly without focusing on any activity; *onlooker behavior* refers to the child standing at the periphery of groups and/or activities, within hearing and speaking distance of the other children, making comments but not being actively involved; and in *solitary play* the child is involved in an independent activity without the company of any other children. In the social play category, *parallel play* is defined as the independent play of children who are in close proximity to other children and are playing with the same materials, but are not interacting with one another; the distinguishing features of *associative play* are active play together, the occurrence of conversations that concern a common activity and engagement in a similar activity; *cooperative play* involves group organization for the purpose of attaining a goal and there are differentiated roles and a sense of belonging to the group (Parten, 1932).

Studying play from a cognitive perspective, Piaget (1962) divided play into three categories—sensorimotor play, symbolic play and games with rules. Smilansky (1968), taking the lead from Piaget suggested that play might better be divided into four categories—functional, constructive, dramatic and games with rules. In *functional play,* there is simple, repeated motor action with or without an object, while in *constructive play* children use the materials to create other things; in *dramatic play* the children engage in pretense by assuming roles, engaging in the make-believe transformation of objects and situations and in *games with rules* children accept prearranged rules and conform to these rules while involved in the particular game (Rubin, Fein & Vandenberg, 1983).

Researchers have adapted and combined Parten's and Piaget/Smilansky's play categories and explored play behaviors from a socio-cognitive perspective (Rubin, 1977a, 1982b; Rubin, Maioni & Hornung, 1976; Rubin, Watson & Jambor, 1978; Smith, 1978). This has resulted in a recording format which provides early childhood educators and researchers with more substantial information about the relationship between play environments (peers, adults, materials, space, arrangement of furnishings) and the child's level of play.

Play and Development

Research indicates that there are strong correlational relationships between play and the development of cognitive, social and language skills. Several studies have shown that problem-solving skills are enhanced through play experiences (Simon & Smith, 1983; Pepler, 1979; Pepler & Ross, 1981). By playing with puzzle pieces and the form board for the puzzle, children were able to solve puzzles requiring convergent thinking, while playing with puzzle pieces without the form board led to better solutions of problems requiring divergent thinking (Pepler & Ross, 1981). In a study conducted by Smith and Dutton (1979), children who were given the opportunity to play with the materials required for the solution of the problem performed better on a task requiring innovative thinking than those who had been given specific training in how to solve a particular problem and those who had not had any experience at all with the materials.

Sociodramatic play, wherein children assume the role of another person, was thought to enhance children's perspective-taking abilities as they have to assume the identity of another person which requires the expression of the feelings and thoughts of that person. Studies conducted to date have confirmed this hypothesis (Connolly & Doyle, 1984; Rubin & Maioni, 1975). Those children who are frequent sociodramatic players tend to be more popular and are rated as friendlier and more cooperative than those who spend more time in functional and constructive play (Fein, 1981; Rubin & Maioni, 1975). Sociodramatic play is correlated with prosocial behavior; children who are involved in dramatic play exhibit sharing and other positive behaviors (Freyberg, 1973; Smilansky, 1968).

In a study of the relationship between explicit language and play, Pellegrini (1986) found that children tended to use more elaborated language in dramatic play than in block play. The research indicated that it was necessary for the children to make themselves clearly understood, particularly when they were referring to items that were imaginary and called for agreement as to the existence and inclusion of these items in the play episode.

In this chapter the quality of the child-care environment has been shown to be linked to the play behaviors that the children display while in child care. If the quality of the child care is determined by teacher training (regulatable issues) and the materials available to the children within the environment (global issues) then quality of care should have some relationship to the play observed in the child-care setting. Research studies have indicated that there is a relationship between play behaviors and environmental factors, personal factors, peer experiences, culture, socioeconomic status, and child-rearing factors (Rubin, et al., 1983). For the purpose of this introduction the discussion will be limited to the relationship between play behaviors and environmental factors, particularly those that are related to child-care settings.

Environmental Influences

The materials that are available to children in their environmental settings are seen to influence the type of play behavior that the children exhibit. The novelty, realism and types of materials are associated with the type of play behavior displayed. When children are given novel materials to play with, exploration seems to take precedence over play (Berlyne, 1960, 1969; Hutt, 1970). The child will manipulate the novel item in an effort to see what the object does and as the exploration of the object nears completion, the exploratory behavior diminishes and play behavior increases (Ross, Rheingold & Eckerman, 1972). The child's play interactions with the materials switches to an investigation of what he/she can do with the object rather than examining the object to see what it does (Hutt, 1966).

Once the child has had the opportunity to explore the play materials and begins to play actively with the materials, it becomes evident that certain materials are associated with particular types of play behaviors. Through observational research, investigators have been able to specify the social and cognitive levels of play associated with specific materials. Art materials are associated with solitary or parallel behavior and constructive play (Rubin, 1977a, 1977b; Shure, 1963). Most children engaged in cutting, gluing and painting do so seated side by side with a peer and are quite intent on producing a particular item. Verbal interactions may occur, however much of the focus is on creating, rather than communicating and engaging in group interactions. Housekeeping toys, dolls, dress-up clothes and vehicles encourage group dramatic play in which children assume roles and interact cooperatively with one another to enact the scenario successfully (Johnson, Christie & Yawkey, 1987). While beads, play dough and sand and water are usually used in solitary or parallel functional play (Rubin, 1977a, 1977b); blocks are associated with all levels of social play and constructive and dramatic cognitive play (Rubin & Seibel, 1979). In the Rubin and Seibel study (1979), the block play that was solitary in nature tended to be associated with constructive forms of play, while the block play that was group based was associated with dramatic play.

Realism of the play material is related to the content of the play (Pulaski, 1973). Children who are provided with highly structured toys such as the realistic food items (fried egg) designed by Fisher Price tend to use these props in an item-specific manner. The fried egg included in the play is just that and is not transformed into any other item.

The quantity of play materials available is also associated with the play behaviors that occur in indoor and outdoor play settings. When the amount of play materials is decreased, social interaction among the children is increased. This is true for both positive (sharing) and negative (aggression) interactions. An increase in the amount of play material is associated with a decrease in sharing and aggression (Bjorklund, 1979; Eckerman & Whatley, 1977, Smith & Connolly, 1980). The amount of play space is another issue which influences play.

We know that crowding (less than 25 usable square feet available per child) can lead to aggressive behavior. However, a reduction in play space that does not result in a crowded situation influences the type of play that is displayed in that environment in a different manner. Rough and tumble play and running tend to decrease with a decrease in space, while imaginative play and onlooker behavior increase (McGrew, 1972; Peck & Goldman, 1978; Smith & Connolly, 1976). The manner in which the available space is organized is also associated with children's play behaviors.

Decreasing the amount of large open space in the classroom by creating well-defined, smaller play spaces devoted to particular activities reduces rowdy behavior (Sheehan & Day, 1975). Making materials easily accessible to the children by placing them at the child's eye level and within the child's reach results in greater use of these materials (Pollowy, 1974). Organizing the space so that there is an unrestricted flow of traffic in the room reduces aggression as does the erection of low barriers which define and protect particular areas (e.g., blocks) from accidental intrusions (Kritchevsky, 1977). The classroom environment is not composed solely of materials and equipment, the human beings within the classroom also contribute to the total environment.

Research has shown that caregivers who have either university or post-secondary education are more likely to provide programs and activities for the children that are developmentally appropriate than caregivers who had only a high school diploma (Goelman & Pence, 1988; Ruopp et al. (1979) Whitebrook, Howes & Phillips, 1990). The Ruopp et al. study in particular indicates that there is a strong positive relationship between the caregiver's child-care related training and children's cooperative behavior, task persistence and gains in general knowledge. Another study revealed that those caregivers who had university level training which included courses related to child care and child development appeared to be less restrictive in their interactions with the children and encouraged independent behavior and verbal interactions (Berk, 1985). Adults have an effect on children's play and caregivers who interact with the child during most of the child's waking hours can have a powerful effect on the child's play and hence, the child's development.

Studies have shown that when adults who understand child development issues participate in children's play, the play episodes are longer-lasting and richer (Sylva, Roy & Painter, 1980; Dunn & Wooding, 1977) and the play is likely to be at a higher level (Bruner, 1980). Caregivers who have had specific early childhood training know how to set the stage for positive play experiences by providing the right amount of time for the play to evolve (Griffing, 1983); adequate and appropriate space within which it can occur (Segal & Adcock, 1981; Woodard, 1984); and appropriate materials to support the play. Given these attributes, caregivers in child-care centers seem to be able to determine the kind of play experiences that the children will have.

If caregiver education, different environmental arrangements and the provision of particular toys can "pull for" specific types of play behavior, it becomes obvious that the caregiver can manipulate children's play to a large extent. In so doing they can subject the child to an "environmental press" which "shapes the behavior and the development of the child in the setting" (Garbarino, 1989, p. 19). How acceptable is this action? Should we be manipulating the children's environment and to what extent? Would it be more "natural" to let play evolve in the day care setting?

The ten papers in this text have examined play from an applied, rather than a philosophical, perspective. All of the issues that the authors have addressed are pertinent to the development of young children. The topics examined in each paper are presented in an index format in Figure 1. It includes the age of the subjects, the environmental quality measure, observational measures of play behaviors, caregiver measures, and type of care studied.

Carollee Howes and Darlene Clements have written about the teacher's influences on the development of children's play with peers in child care. They used a longitudinal approach to study changes over time in teacher-child interactions in day-care settings and the extent to which teachers mediated peer contacts. The issue of age of entry of children into day care was also examined. The results indicated that teacher-child interactions did change over time in the direction of a decrease in the time that children spent close to teachers. They were surprised to find that teachers in their study tended to monitor the children's play for safety issues, but did little to mediate the peer contacts. These authors suggest that the teachers in this study might have believed that children ought to be free to interact with one another at will during unstructured periods within the day-care routine—e.g., free play and play time and therefore, they did not use the opportunity afforded by free play to manage peer contacts.

Michael Lamb, Kathleen Sternberg, Nan Knuth, Carl Hwang and Anders Broberg authored the chapter on peer play and nonparental care experiences. They focused on four issues in their attempt to understand the relationship between the quality of the care setting and the extent to which peer social skills were developed. The authors were interested in the possibility of obtaining reliable measures of the quality of children's peer play and the nonparental care setting; whether peer social skills are part of a broader social construct—sociability with others; to what extent a child's sociability is influenced by the quality of care at home and in the nonparental care setting; and whether children play with peers differently in the various out-of-home care environments. This chapter reports on several studies that were conducted to answer these questions. The conclusions that the authors offer are that reliable measures of the quality of peer play can be obtained; that individual differences in peer skills are good predictors of children's behavior in other nonparental care environments and that high quality care at home and in out-of-home care is associated with skilled interaction with peers.

Donna Wittmer and Alice Honig have addressed the issue of caregiver responses to toddlers and three year olds in specific activities within the day-care routine. The caregivers in this study did not display the same hands-off behavior as the caregivers in the Howes & Clements study did. In fact, positive peer interactions were associated with positive teacher-child interactions, whereas negative interactions with peers and play materials were not associated with positive shaping of children's play. They also addressed the issue of caregivers' different responses to children according to the age and sex of the child.

Ellen Vineberg Jacobs and Donna Romano White examined the relationship between day-care quality and play behavior of kindergarten children in a two-part study. The first study established the fact that there was a positive relationship between day-care attendance and the child's interest and participation in the kindergarten classroom. The ECERS was used to measure quality and there was no association between the quality of the day care attended and play behavior in kindergarten. The second study determined that there was a relationship between negative play behavior in the day-care center and apathy and withdrawal in the kindergarten. The authors explain that negative behavior was coded whenever the focal child was engaged in a negative or aggressive interaction either as an initiator or as a target. Thus, children involved in negative play situations may have learned to withdraw from social interaction in the classroom and may have carried this behavior with them into the kindergarten. The authors believe that the results of these studies indicate that there is a longitudinal relationship between child-care experiences and social behavior in the elementary school.

Tiffany Field described three longitudinal projects in which she studied the social behavior of children who had attended quality infant child-care centers. In these studies, Field attempted to deal with confounding influences which have typically plagued other studies of this nature. Thus, she designed her studies to eliminate differences between families who chose to place their infants in day care and those who did not, differences in children's age of entry into care, as well as length of time in care and stability and quality of care. The data from the three studies showed that at the preschool level children who had more years of quality care were not at risk and were actually more social. Those at the grade one level who had attended full time care in quality center-based infant care appeared to be more involved with peers, had more friends and were more assertive than those who had spent less time in infant care. Children in grade six who had spent more time in infant care actually had more positive results for academic, emotional and social well-being than those who had spent less time in infant care.

Nina Howe, Lora Moller and Bette Chambers have addressed the issue of dramatic play in the day-care curriculum. They examined the relationship between the design of dramatic play centers and children's play behavior; more specifically they compared the relationship between social and cognitive play of children and the theme, novelty and duration of traditional versus novel dramatic play centers. Their results indicated that different novel dramatic play centers were associated with different types of social play behaviors and that more dramatic play occurred in familiar, rather than novel dramatic play centers. The authors call for more teacher involvement in the planning and design of dramatic play centers so that children will be stimulated to engage in dramatic play at all social play levels.

Eliana Tobias examined the play behaviors of special needs children who were enrolled in four different types of preschool programs of varying environmental quality. The group composition within each of these programs differed. In segregated programs all of the children were handicapped; in the reversed mainstreamed setting, 50 percent had a handicap; and in community based day care and the nursery setting the special needs child might be the only one with a handicap. The results indicated that the developmentally delayed children engaged in high rates of solitary play in segregated and day care settings and in low rates of cooperative play. An analysis of the cognitive levels of play indicated that there was more constructive play in segregated, reversed mainstreamed and nursery school settings than in day-care centers where the special needs children displayed more functional play. It is interesting to note that dramatic play by the special needs child was infrequently observed in all settings. Tobias states that the play of the special needs children is not enhanced just by bringing them together with nonhandicapped children. She calls for teachers to set the stage for more enriching play experiences and to guide the children in their play within an environment that takes into account the needs of these children.

Miriam Rosenthal examined the social and nonsocial play of infants and toddlers enrolled in family day-care settings. On the basis of previous studies, Rosenthal hypothesized that (1) the quality of the family day-care environment would influence play behavior in terms of the levels of play with peers and with toys, (2) the quality of the family day-care environment would be a better predictor of children's play in the day-care settings than would be their home background and (3) spatial organization per se would have an effect on social play. The author used a time sampling observational technique to examine children's play with objects and peers, and used the same methodology to study the caregiver's spontaneous interactions with the children. Her findings indicated that age, sex and separation difficulties affected social play rather than play with objects. Even when family background effects were taken into account, the children's play behavior was mainly influenced by factors in the child-care environment.

Hillel Goelman and Alan Pence have explored play, talk and literacy in child development and the family day-care environmental context. They have focused on the association between symbolic play and the development of literacy and the relationship between the ecological features of child care and child language development. The authors used the Day Care Home Environmental Rating Scale (DCHERS) to obtain global measures of family day care homes and regulatable measurements as well. They found that both were positively associated with scores on language development and levels of interactive play.

Goelman and Pence analyzed the specific features of adult and child discourse patterns observed in play situations. In particular, they examined (1) relationships between levels of cognitive stimulation in the child's home and the family day care and levels of receptive and expressive language; (2) relationships between literate features of oral discourse in adult and child talk in home and family day care and the child's overall level of receptive and expressive language; and (3) similarities and differences between adult-child discourse in home and family day care. In summary, their findings indicated that the general level of cognitive stimulation was positively related to the children's receptive and expressive language test scores, and that the nature of the adult-child language interactions in terms of amount, style and content in home and family day care were positively related to outcomes on tests of expressive and receptive language. The authors state that high quality family day-care homes provide language experiences that are similar to and consistent with that which is available in high quality homes. They postulate that the two complement one another and offer the child a supportive environment for the growth and development of expressive and receptive language.

Jaipaul Roopnarine, Josephine Bright and Nancy Riegraf have addressed the topic of family dynamics and day-care children's peer group participation. Their research is focused on the relationships between mothers' and fathers' parenting skills, their personal well-being, martial relationship, job satisfaction, support networks and preschoolers' play behaviors and social activities in day care. The question which drives their research is "What behaviors are derived from and shaped in specific socialization systems?" In their study they assessed parent-child relationships, marital relationships and children's cooperative activities and sharing behavior with peers and found that parent-child relations were embedded within the larger social contexts in which development occurs. To obtain more specific information concerning these social contexts, they observed children's peer play interactions in the day care setting. The results indicated that maternal personal well-being and marital relations, but not parenting, showed significant associations with higher forms of children's cognitive and social modes of play. These findings are discussed at length in their paper and stimulate a number of interesting questions for further research.

Summary

The articles included in this text should provide a substantial amount of interesting information for adults who work with children in various types of day care arrangements and those who are involved in child development issues. Adults seem to have a rather influential role in children's development, either directly or indirectly, in their interactions with the children or by structuring the environments in which children function on a daily basis. Adult manipulation of play situations and play environments can have an effect on the play behaviors that the children display and these in turn are related to the young child's development. If adults structure the environment to pull for certain types of play behaviors are we likely to see "real" play? If adults refrain from engaging in this type of manipulation will children derive enough developmental value for the time invested in play, particularly in a day-care setting where there are so many hours that can be devoted to play experiences? Howes and Clements thought that caregivers would act as managers of children's play much the same way that mothers do when their children are engaged in interactions with peers. However, they found that caregivers made few attempts to mediate peer contacts for toddlers and preschoolers. They tended to station themselves at the periphery of the children's play and stepped in solely for safety reasons. Some play advocates would applaud this finding and the educators who have managed to convince caregivers to keep their hands off children's play. However, in this text there are indications that adult involvement in children's play is essential in specific instances.

Howe et al., implore caregivers to consider the dramatic play environment and to facilitate the development of higher levels of dramatic play by taking a more active role in setting up dramatic play spaces and providing the materials that "pull for" group, as well as solitary and parallel dramatic play. Tobias states that play for special needs children is not enhanced simply by bringing handicapped and nonhandicapped children together. These children need a carefully planned physical environment that will influence the complexity of play behaviors and stimulate participation in activities to encourage independence and social competence. Goelman and Pence state that adult-child communications during play episodes in the day care setting are linked to outcomes on children's language measures. These results should have an impact on the practices of caregivers who work with young children. A careful reading of the following chapters should provide interesting insights into children's play in various child-care environments and the importance of the adult's role in children's play.

	AGE OF SUBJECTS INF. TOD. PRE. EL.	QUALITY MEASURE INCLUDED	LONGITUDINAL PERIOD	PLAY OBSERVATION FORMAT	CAREGIVERS OBSERVED YES/NO	TYPE OF CARE FDC/CC/HC/NS
Field	Infant/Toddler	unspec.	12 yrs	Parten	no	CC
Goelman and Pence	Preschool (4.0)	HOME DCHERS	no	Modified Smilansky/Parten	yes	FDC
Howe	Preschool (2.6–5.0)	—	no	Smilansky/Parten	no	CC
Howes et al.	Toddler–Preschool (1.1–4.0)	ECERS	3 yrs	Social behaviors	yes	CC/FDC
Jacobs and White	Preschool (4.0–5.0)	ECERS	2 yrs	Parten/Dodge modified	no	CC
Lamb	Toddler (2.0–3.0)	HOME	3 yrs	Howes Peer Play Scale (1980) Peer Observation Technique	no	FDC/CC
Roopnarine et al.	Preschool	—	no	Smilansky/Parten	no	CC
Rosenthal	Toddler (2.0)	EQR ECERS	no	Rubenstein and Howes (1979), Howes (1980)	yes	FDC
Tobias	Preschool (4.0–5.0)	ECERS	no	Smilansky/Parten	no	CC/NS/SACC
Wittmer	Toddler–Preschool (2.0–3.0)	—	no	APPROACH (Caldwell and Honig)	yes	CC

REFERENCES

Adessky, R., & White, D. R. (1991). Child Care Experience Predicts Teacher Ratings of Aggression in Kindergarten Girls. Washington, DC.

Andersson, B. E. (1989). Effects of public day care: A longitudinal study. *Child Development, 60*, 857-866.

Berk, L. (1985). Relationship of educational attainment, child orientated attitudes, job satisfaction, and career commitment to caregiver behavior toward children. *Child Care Quarterly, 14,* 103-129.

Berlyne, D. E. (1960). *Conflict, arousal and curiosity.* New York: McGraw-Hill.

Berlyne, D. E. (1969). Laughter, humor and play. In G. Lindzey & E. Aronson (Eds.), *The Handbook of Social Psychology* (Vol. 3). Reading, MA: Addison-Wesley.

Bjorklund, G. (1979). *The effects of toy quantity and qualitative category on toddlers' play.* Paper presented at the meeting of the Society for Research in Child Development, San Francisco.

Bredekamp, S. (1987). *Developmentally Appropriate Practice in Early Childhood Programs Serving Children From Birth Through Age 8.* Washington, DC: National Association for the Education of Young Children.

Bruner, J. (1980). *Under five in Britain.* Ypsilanti, MI: High/Scope.

Carew, J. (1980). Experience and the development of intelligence in young children. *Monographs of the Society for Research in Child Development,* 45 (12, Serial No. 183).

Clarke-Stewart, A. (1984). Day care: A new context for research and development. In A. Collins (Ed.), *Minnesota Symposium on Child Psychology.* Hillsdale, NJ: Erlbaum.

Clarke-Stewart, A. (1987). *In Search of Consistencies in Child Care Research.* Washington, DC: National Association for the Education of Young Children.

Connolly, J., & Doyle, A. B. (1984). Relation of social fantasy play to social competence in preschoolers. *Development Psychology, 20,* 797-806.

Dunn, J., & Wooding, C. (1977). Play in the home and its implications for learning. In B. Tizard & D. Harvey (Eds.), *Biology of play.* London: Heinemann.

Eckerman, C. D., & Whatley, J. L. (1977). Toys and social interaction between peers. *Child Development, 48,* 1645-1656.

Fein, G. G. (1981). Pretend play: An integrative review. *Child Development, 52,* 1095-1118.

Freyberg, J. (1973). Increasing the imaginative play of urban disadvantaged kindergarten children through systematic training. In J. L. Singer (Ed.), *The child's world of make-believe.* New York: Academic Press.

Gabarino, J. (1989). An ecological perspective on the role of play in child development. In N. Block & A. D. Pellagrini (Eds.) *The Ecological Context of Children's Play.* Norwood, NJ: Ablex Publishing Corporation.

Garvey, C. (1977a). *Play.* Cambridge, MA: Harvard University Press.

Goelman, H., & Pence, A. R. (1988). Children in three types of day care: Daily experiences, quality of care, and developmental outcomes. *Early Child Development and Care, 33,* 67-76.

Griffing, P. (1983). Encouraging dramatic play in early childhood. *Young Children,* 38(4), 13-22.

Harmes, T., & Clifford, R. (1980). *Early Childhood Environmental Rating Scale.* New York: Teachers College Press.

Hutt, C. (1966). Exploration and play in children. *Symposium of the Zoological Society of London, 18,* 61-81.

Hutt, C. (1970). Specific and diverse exploration. In H. Reese & L. Lipsett (Eds.). *Advances in child development and behavior.* New York: Academic Press.

Holloway, S. D., & Reichart-Erickson, M. (1988). The relationship of day care quality to children's free-play behavior and social problem-solving skills. *Early Childhood Research Quarterly, 3,* 39-53.

Howes, C. (1980). Peer play scale as an index of complexity of peer interaction. *Developmental Psychology, 16,* 371-372.

Howes, C., & Olenick, M. (1986). Family and child care influences on toddlers' compliance. *Child Development, 57,* 202-216.

Howes, C. (1990). Can age of entry into child care and the quality of child care predict adjustment in kindergarten? *Developmental Psychology, 26,* (2), 292-303.

Johnson, J. E., Christie, J. F., & Yawkey, T. D. (1987). *Play and Early Childhood Development*. Glenview, IL.: Scott, Foresman & Company.

McCartney, K., Scarr, S., Phillips, D., Grajek, S., & Schwarz, J. C. (1982). Environmental differences among day care centers and their effects on children's development. In E. Zigler & E. Gordon (Eds.), *Day Care: Scientific and social policy issues* (pp. 126-151). Boston: Auburn.

McGrew, W. C. (1972). *An ethological study of children's behavior*. London: Academic Press.

Owen, M. T., & Henderson, V. K. (1989). *Relations between child care qualities and child behavior at age four: Do parent-child interactions play a role?* Paper presented at the Biennial meeting of the Society for Research in Child Development, Kansas City, MO.

Parten, M. B. (1932). Social participation among preschool children. *Journal of Abnormal Psychology, 27,* 243-269.

Peck, J., & Goldman, R. (1978). *The behaviours of kindergarten children under selected conditions of the social and physical environment.* Paper presented at the meeting of the American Education Research Association, Toronto.

Pellegrini, A. (1986). Play centres and the production of imaginative language. *Discourse Processes, 9,* 115-125.

Pepler, D. J. (1979). *Effects of convergent and divergent play experience on preschoolers' problem-solving behaviors.* Unpublished doctoral dissertation, University of Waterloo.

Pepler, D. J., & Ross, H. S. (1981). The effects of play on convergent and divergent problem-solving. *Child Development, 52,* 1202-1210.

Phillips, D., McCartney, K., & Scarr, S. (1987). Child-Care Quality and Children's Social Development. *Developmental Psychology, 23* (4), 537-543.

Piaget, J. (1962). *Play, dreams and imitations in childhood.* New York: Norton.

Pollowy, A. M. (1974). The child in the physical environment: A design problem. In G. Coates (Ed.), *Alternative living environments.* Stroudsburg, PA: Dowden, Hutchison, and Ross.

Ramey, C., McPhee, D., & Yates, K. (1982). Preventing developmental retardation: A general systems model. In L. Bond & J. Joffee (Eds.), *Facilitating infant and early childhood development: Vol. 6.*

Primary prevention of psychopathology. (pp. 343-401). Hanover, NH: University Press of New England.

Ross, H. S., Rheingold, H. L., & Eckerman, C. D. (1972). Approach and exploration of a novel alternative by 12-month-old infants. *Journal of Experiment Child Psychology, 13,* 85-93.

Rubenstein, J., & Howes, C. (1979). Caregiving and infant behavior in day care and homes. *Developmental Psychology, 15,* 1-24.

Rubenstein, J., Howes, C., & Boyle, P. (1981). A two year follow-up of infants in community based day care. *Journal of Child Psychology and Psychiatry, 22,* 209-218.

Rubin, K. H. (1977a). The play behaviors of young children. *Young Children, 32,* 16-24.

Rubin, K. H. (1977b). The social cognitive value of preschool toys and activities. *Canadian Journal of Behavioral Science, 9,* 382-385.

Rubin, K. H. (1982b). Nonsocial play in preschoolers: Necessarily evil? *Child Development, 53,* 651-657.

Rubin, K. H., Fein, G. G., & Vandenberg, B. (1983). Play. In P. H. Mussen (Ed.) *Handbook of Child Psychology,* Vol. 4. New York: John Wiley & Sons.

Rubin, K. H., & Maioni, T. (1975). Play preference and its relationship to egocentrism, popularity and classification skills in preschoolers. *Merrill-Palmer Quarterly, 21,* 171-179.

Rubin, K. H., Maioni, T. L., & Hornung, M. (1976). Free play behaviors in middle and lower class preschoolers: Parten and Piaget revisited. *Child Development, 47,* 414-419.

Rubin, K. H., & Seibel, C. (1979). *The effects of ecological setting on the cognitive and social play behavior of preschoolers.* Annual meeting of the American Educational Research Association, San Francisco.

Rubin, K. H., Watson, K., & Jambor, T. (1978). Free play behaviors in preschool and kindergarten children. *Child Development, 49,* 534-536.

Ruopp, R., Travers, J., Glantz, B., & Coelen, C. (1979). *Children at the centre.* Final report of the National Day care Study. Cambridge, MA: Abt Associates.

Schwarz, J. C., Strickland, R. G. & Kroblick, G. (1974). Infant day care: Behavioral effects at preschool age. *Developmental Psychology, 10,* 502-506.

Schwarz, J. C., Scarr, S. W., Capafulo, B., Furrow, D., McCartney, K., Billington, R., Phillips, D., & Hindy, C. (1981, August). *Center, sitter and home care before age two: A report on the first Bermuda infant care study.* Paper presented at the meeting of the American Psychological Association, Los Angeles.

Segal, M., & Adcock, D. (1981). *Just pretending: Ways to help children grow through imaginative play.* Englewood Cliffs, NJ: Prentice-Hall.

Sheehan, R., & Day, D. (1975). Is open space just empty space? *Day Care and Early Education, 3,* 10-13.

Shure, M. E. (1963). Psychological ecology of a nursery school child. *Child Development, 34,* 979-994.

Simon, T., & Smith, P. K. (1983). The study of play and problem solving in preschool children: Have experimenter effects been responsible for previous results? *British Journal of Developmental Psychology, 1,* 289-297.

Smilansky, S. (1968). *The effects of sociodramatic play on disadvantaged preschool children.* New York: Wiley.

Smith, P. K. (1978). A longitudinal study of social participation in preschool children: Solitary and parallel play reexamined. *Developmental Psychology, 14,* 517-523.

Smith, P. K., & Connolly, K. J. (1976). Social and aggressive behavior in preschool children as a function of crowding. *Social Science Information, 16,* 601-620.

Smith, P. K., & Connolly, J. K. (1980). *The ecology of preschool behavior.* Cambridge, England: Cambridge University Press.

Smith, P. K., & Dutton, S. (1979). Play and training in direct and innovative problem solving. *Child Development, 50,* 830-836.

Sylva, K., Roy, C., & Painter, M. (1980). *Childwatching at playgroup and nursery school.* Ypselanti, MI: High/Scope Press.

Vandell, D., & Corasaniti, M. A. (1988). The relation between third graders after school care and social, academic, and emotional functioning. *Child Development, 59,* 868-875.

Vandenberg, B. (1978). Play and development from an ethological perspective. *American Psychologist, 33,* 724-738.

Vlietstra, A. G. (1981). Full-versus half-day preschool attendance: Effects in young children as assessed by teacher ratings and behavioral observations. *Child Development, 52,* 603-610.

Whitebrook, M., Howes, C., & Phillips, D. (1990). *Who cares: Child care teachers in America.* Final report of the national Child Care Staffing Study. Oakland, CA: Child Care Employee Project.

Woodard, C. (1984). Guidelines for facilitating sociodramatic play. *Childhood Education, 60,* 172-177.

1

Adult Socialization of Children's Play in Child Care

Carollee Howes and Darlene Clements

Introduction

There is a persistent assumption in the literature on the development of children's relations with their peers that adult socialization is an important aspect of these processes of development. According to a framework suggested by Parke (Parke, MacDonald, Beitel, & Bhavangari, 1986), adults shape peer relationships directly through various socialization techniques and processes, and indirectly through the security of the child's attachment to the caregiver. In this chapter we will be concerned with adult socialization of peer relationships. Specifically, we will examine child care teacher's influences on the development of children's play with peers in child care.

The parents of most toddler and preschool children in the United States and Canada work outside the home. Many of these children spend their days in the company of unrelated peers supervised by an adult who is not their parent. Therefore, the children develop their relations with peers largely in the context of child care and the child care teacher. According to a socialization model of the influences of adults on children's peer relationships, child care teachers should be important influences in the children's social development. Despite their theoretical importance there is little literature focused on the child care teacher's influence on development of relations with peers (Howes, 1986; Mize & Ladd, 1986).

There is a tradition in child care research of using relations specified in the parent child literature to guide the child care research (see Howes, 1992 for a review). Thus if the parent-child literature identifies warmth and sensitivity as important attributes of mothers the child care researcher examines the role of teacher warmth and sensitivity. In most cases this technique has been productive. For example, responsive teachers as well as mothers are linked to more optimal child development. We will follow in the steps of this tradition by reviewing literature on parental socialization of peer relations and speculating on its applicability to child care teachers. We will then present observational data on teacher's behaviors from two longitudinal studies of children's development of peer relationships within child care.

We appreciate the data collection efforts of Kristin Droege, Annette Groen, Claire Hamilton, Catherine Matheson, Lisabeth Mayers, Jacqueline Moore, Leslie Phillipsen, and Fang Wu.

Adults as Socializers of Peer Contacts

The socialization literature suggests three pathways for studying adult influences on peer relations: (1) Adults as gatekeepers, or the role of the adult in creating access to peers; (2) Adult style of interacting with children; and (3) Adult direct Management of peer contacts.

Adults as Gatekeepers

Parents function as gatekeepers when they arrange peer contacts. Parents are implicitly making decisions about their children's peer relations when they select child care for their children. A parent who selects an arrangement with no available peers places a different value on peer relations than a parent who deliberately selects a child care arrangement that includes agemates for the child. Some parents make elaborate arrangements and compromises to keep their child with their friends in child care while others move the child with little or no attention to the stability of the peer group. Some parents consider the child's contacts with peers within child care to be sufficient while others arrange out-of-school play dates for their children.

Few studies have directly explored the role of these variations in children's development of social competence with peers. Longitudinal work by Howes (1988) suggests that a stable peer group is beneficial for the development of social competence with peers. In that study preschool-age children who changed child-care centers with familiar peers appeared more competent than those separated from peers.

Ladd and colleagues (Ladd & Golter, 1988; Ladd, Hart, Wadworth, & Golter, 1988) have explored relations between preschool children's peer contacts in- and out-of-school and the children's social functioning in school. In one study (Ladd et al., 1988) preschool children who played with peers outside of school were more socially competent in school. In a second study (Ladd & Golter, 1988) preschool children with more out-of-school peer contacts had a larger range of playmates and more consistent play companions in school. These studies suggest that parents by their selection of child care and by their ability and willingness to make social connections between child care and home will influence the child's social competence with peers within child care.

Teachers may serve as gatekeepers within the child-care context. Often teachers determine or influence children's placement in activity groups throughout the day. In elementary schools children placed by the teacher in ability groups are likely to form friendships (Halligan & Sorensen, 1985). Teachers also usually decide which children will move to different classrooms within the child care center. Often these decisions are made on the basis of age and/or maturity rather than on friendship patterns yet separation from friends can be a negative influence on social competence with peers (Howes, 1988).

Adult's Interactive Style

Researchers have measured adult-child interactive style either by paper and pencil questionnaires designed to elicit parent beliefs about their child rearing styles or by direct observation of adult-child interaction. The classic study of adult-child rearing styles is the Baumrind study (1967, 1971, 1973). Baumrind identified and studied in longitudinal fashion three groups of families: authoritarian (high control and low warmth), authoritative (high control and high warmth) and permissive (low control and low warmth). The authoritative parents were most likely to have socially successful children. More recently Hinde and Tamplin (1983) in a study of preschool children reported that authoritarian mothers tended to have hostile children who were unfriendly to peers while authoritative mothers tended to have children high in friendliness to peers. Roopnarine (1987), also studying preschoolers, reports that mothers high in involvement with their children and who used reasoning as a disciplinary technique were associated with children who were positive towards peers. Thus, we can conclude that parents who are warm rather than detached and who provide guidelines and boundaries for appropriate behaviors with peers will be more successful in eliciting competence with peers.

To understand exactly what authoritative as opposed to authoritarian or permissive adults are doing with children we must turn to the literature that directly observes adult-child interaction. While there is a large observational literature on mother-child interaction, there is a relatively small literature that directly examines links between adult-child interaction and peer interaction. Lamb and Nash (1989) recently reviewed this literature and found that while friendly and sociable infants tend to have harmonious interactions with both parents and peers there was little evidence for general and linear relations between parents socialization practices and behaviors with peers.

A recent strategy in the literature linking parents and peers has been to identify, using sociometric techniques, children who have different social status classifications within their peer groups. The researchers then compare parent-child interaction across status groups. Using this technique Putallaz (1987, 1991) reports that parents of first graders with higher sociometric status were more competent in their interaction with adult peers, more positive and focused on feelings and less disagreeable and demanding when interacting with their own children than parents of lower status children. MacDonald (MacDonald & Parke, 1984; MacDonald, 1987) used the classification into status group technique with preschoolers. He found that fathers of neglected boys engaged in less affectively arousing, physical play than did fathers of popular and rejected boys but that fathers of rejected boys were more likely to either over stimulate or avoid stimulating their sons during play than fathers of popular boys.

Few researchers have examined teacher influences on children's play with peers. In fact one researcher in this area (Harper & Huie, 1987) classifies children attending child care as either adult or peer oriented, arguing that interactions with peers and adults are alternative social options for child-care children. Other researchers have examined links between teacher behaviors and play with peers. In one such recent study children rated as more competent with peers were also the children who engaged in more responsive interactions with teachers (Whitebook et al., 1990).

Thus, it appears that children more sociable with parents and teachers may also be more sociable with their peers. These studies are primarily correlational. We can not assume that the adults are necessarily producing the children's behavior. We will now turn to studies that attempt to measure the adult's role in managing peer contacts.

Adults as Managers

Parents and teachers are managers of children's peer contacts when they get involved in the child's play with peers. There is a small literature that describes what adults actually do and how such behaviors relate to the child's competence. Extant studies have relied on parent reports (Ladd & Golter, 1988) or have watched mothers in laboratory settings (Finnie & Russell, 1988; Parke & Bhavnagri, 1988). Very little is known about differences between the social mediation behaviors of parents and teachers or their relative influence on the child. Casual observation suggests that the two groups may have very different socializing techniques, e.g., parents may ignore or encourage hitting back while teachers forbid it.

Parents appear to change their management techniques depending on the age of the child. Lollis and Ross (1987) and Halverson and Waldrop (1970) have observed that when toddler age children are playing mothers intervene fairly often, but only in conflict situations and most often when their own child is the aggressor. Ladd and Golter (1988) in studying preschool children found that mothers often used indirect supervision of peer contacts. They were aware of the children's activity but were not consistently present or involved. School age children receive even less direct supervision (Bryant, 1985).

Several studies have linked parental management techniques to children's social skills. Parke and Bhavanagri (1988) report that toddler age children were more socially competent with peer play when mothers were present than when the children were alone. Bhavnagri (1987) extended this research to preschoolers. She reports an age difference in parental influence. Younger children (2 to $3^1/_2$ years old) were more competent in their mothers' presence but older children ($3^1/_2$ to 6) were able to maintain their levels of interaction when maternal intervention was removed. Similarly Ladd and Golter (1988) report that those preschool children who were more frequently rejected by their classmates in school and were rated as more hostile towards peers by their teachers were more often directly than indirectly supervised by parents. In this study direct supervision was defined as the parent remaining physically present when the child was playing with a peer. Finally, Finnie and Russell (1988) compared maternal management style in two groups of preschool children: high and low social status. Mothers were asked to help their children enter a play group. Mothers of high status children used behaviors such as assessing the groups frame of reference and encouraged the child to integrate into the play without changing the nature of the play. In contrast mothers of low status children avoided the task, were hostile and intrusive or asked questions that disrupted the ongoing play. Thus, mothers of high status children tended to coach their children in successful techniques while mothers of low status children suggested techniques known to be unsuccessful in the peer culture.

We know of only one study of teacher management of children's peer contacts. An early child care study (Rubenstein & Howes, 1979) reported that toddler teachers had low frequencies of intervening in peer contacts. The only studies that link teacher behaviors to social competence with peers are intervention studies. In these studies (see Berndt & Ladd, 1989 for reviews of this literature) children having difficulty with peers are targeted for special social skills training programs. These programs are beyond the scope of this chapter except to illustrate the point that direct teacher intervention into children's behaviors with peers appears to be influential.

Changes Over Time in Teacher Socialization of Peer Contacts

In our own work we are concerned with the development of children's social competence with peers in child care settings. We are using two longitudinal samples to investigate children's relationships with peers and adults and the relations between peer and adult influences. One sample includes children who all entered group child care settings as infants. The second sample of children were first assessed as infants but varied in their age of entry into child care. In each sample we have assessed at regular intervals the teacher-child interaction and teacher mediation of the child's peer contacts. In the following section we will examine changes over time in teacher-child interaction and teacher mediation of peer contacts. We also will explore differences in teacher-child interaction and teacher mediation when the children entered child care at different ages.

Method

Sample

Children

Study 1. Seventy-two children (32 girls) and their teachers initially participated in study one. Approximately two-thirds of the sample were middle-class and one-third working class. The sample was 61 percent Euro-American, 14 percent African-American, and the remainder Hispanic and Asian-American. All of the children were enrolled as infants in either child-care centers or family day-care homes. All but 13 children changed their child care arrangement over the course of the study. Over the three year course of the study we lost twenty-five children reducing our longitudinal sample size to 47 (23 girls). Children left the study because they moved out of the geographic area or because they no longer attended child-care arrangements that included peers. Children remaining in the study were no different in terms of ethnicity or family background than children not remaining in the study.

Study 2. Ninety-eight children (47 girls) and their teachers participated in study two. The children were almost 100 percent Euro-American and middle class. All of the children were recruited into the study as infants and participated in an initial session unrelated to the purposes of this chapter. As toddlers 42 (17 girls) of the children were enrolled in child care arrangements that included peers. An additional 42 children (19 girls) enrolled in child care arrangements with peers in the next year, as three-year-olds. Fourteen more children (7 girls) enrolled in child-care arrangements with peers as four-year-olds.

Child Care Arrangements

In order to describe the child care arrangements of the children the observers recorded the number of children and adults present and completed the Early Childhood Environmental Rating Scale (ECERS) (Harms & Clifford, 1980) on each child care visit. The ECERS provides a comprehensive assessment of the day-to-day quality of care provided to children. Individual items can be rated from a low of 1 to a high of 7. A rating of 3 on these scales indicates minimally acceptable quality while a 5 indicates good quality. The ECERS is widely used and has predicted optimal child outcomes in a number of studies (Phillips, 1987). Two subscales of the ECERS were used based on factor analytic work with a much larger number of very diverse centers (Whitebook, Howes, & Phillips, 1990). One subscale, *appropriate caregiving* describes adult-child interaction, teacher supervision, and discipline. The second subscale, *developmentally appropriate activities*, describes materials, schedule, and activities.

The child care arrangements of the children in studies one and two were somewhat different. Descriptive information on the child care arrangements is in Table 1.1. The children in study one were initially more likely to be enrolled in full day center based programs whereas the children in study two initially were more likely to be enrolled in family day care homes and subsequently in half-day center care. Except for the time one ratios in study 2 all of the adult-child ratios were within limits accepted by child care experts. The ECERS scores indicate that on the average child care quality was good but not excellent.

Table 1.1   Child Care Arrangements

	STUDY 1 AVERAGE AGE OF CHILD				
	18m.	24m.	30m.	36m.	42m.
number of children	72	63	58	53	47
child care form					
center	61	52	47	52	50
family day care home	11	11	9	1	0
hours per day	5.2	8.0	8.0	7.9	7.9
hours per week	20.7	32.2	37.8	38.5	38.6
number of children	6.6	9.1	15.2	14.2	17.5
adult:child ratio	3.2	3.4	4.1	5.0	6.1
ECERS					
caregiving	—	4.0	4.0	4.1	4.2
activities	—	3.8	3.7	3.8	3.9

	STUDY 2 AVERAGE AGE OF CHILD		
	21m.	36.7m.	50.6m.
number of children	42	42	88
child care form			
center	10	38	84
family day care home	32	4	4
hours per day	6.1	3.9	4.4
hours per week	23.5	12.2	14.6
number of children	7.3	13.9	14.5
adult:child ratio	4.6	5.5	6.2
ECERS			
caregiving	—	4.1	4.7
activities	—	3.7	3.6

Procedures

Child Care Visits

The child care observational procedures were identical in the two studies. Each child was observed in the child care setting on two separate days by each of two observers. Each visit lasted an hour. Visits were scheduled at times when the child was free to interact with both adults and peers.

During each one-hour visit the observer coded three 5-minute time samples of the social behaviors of the child. The time samples were spaced evenly throughout the observation period; that is the child's behavior was coded approximately every 20 minutes. Each 5-minute time sample was broken into fifteen 20-second intervals. Behaviors were coded as present or absent within each interval.

Schedule of Child Care Visits

Study 1. Each child was initially seen between the ages of 13 and 24 months. Four more visits were made to the child. Each visit was scheduled approximately six months after the previous visit.

Study 2. Each child was initially seen in child care during his or her first year of enrollment. Thirty-seven of the 42 children who enrolled in child care as toddlers and 37 of the 42 children who enrolled in child care as three-year-olds were again seen in child care as four-year-olds.

Measures

The measures were identical in the two studies. A total of 62 adult and child social behaviors were coded during the child care observations. In this chapter we will discuss measures of adult engagement and of adult mediation of peer play. Within each 20 second interval the child's proximity to the adult was coded. The child was considered to be in proximity if he or she was within three feet of the adult. If the child was in proximity the adult-child's interaction was rated. The adult involvement scale (Howes & Stewart, 1987) was used to rate the intensity of the adult-child interaction. The scale points of the scale are presented in Table 1.2. Four measures of adult-child interaction were used: *Percent of the observation period in which the child was in proximity to an adult; Percent of time in adult proximity the child was ignored; Percent of responsive adult involvement* (levels 3, 4, and 5) and the *Mean level of adult involvement.* The mean level of adult involvement was computed by weighing the frequency of involvement at each level by the scale point, summing the weighted frequencies and dividing them by the total frequency of involvement.

Adult mediation of peer play was coded when adults attempted to manage peer contacts. Four types of positive mediation were coded: *place*—the adult moves or verbally guides the child so that she or he is in a good physical position for peer interaction; *interpret or comment*—the adult explains the peer's behavior to the child; *set up*—the adult initiates a peer contact for the child; and *step back*—the adult removes herself from the interaction and monitors the peer contact. Four types of negative mediation were coded: *interrupt*—the adult

Table 1.2   Adult involvement Scale

LEVEL 1—ROUTINE CAREGIVING

The caregiver touches the child for routine care but makes no verbal responses to the child. For example, a caregiver may pick up a child and carry her to a changing table or a caregiver may place the child at the snack table.

LEVEL 2—MINIMAL CAREGIVING

The caregiver touches or talks to the child in order to discipline the child, to move the child away from another child, to answer direct requests for help, or to give verbal directives with no reply encouraged. For example, a caregiver says to a group of children "Time to come inside, put away the bikes" or a caregiver pulls a child over to her by the arm and says "you are in time out for throwing sand" or a caregiver ties a child's shoe.

LEVEL 3—SIMPLE CAREGIVING

The caregiver answers the child's social bids but does not elaborate or extend them. The caregiver does not give positive physical contact. For example, a child says, "Look at my picture," the caregiver says, "Yes," or the caregiver smiles back to the infants smile.

LEVEL 4—ELABORATED CAREGIVING

The caregiver engages in positive physical gestures, maintains close proximity to the child, acknowledges the child's social bids and responds but does not restate the child's statements, engage the child in conversation, play interactively with the child, or suggest material to structure the child's play. For example, the caregiver reads a book to a small group of children or sits near children playing with playdough.

LEVEL 5—INTENSE CAREGIVING

The caregiver holds or hugs the child to provide comfort, restates the child's social bids, engages the child in conversation, plays interactively with the child, suggests materials to structure the child's play, sits and eats with the child providing a social atmosphere. For example, while changing a diaper the caregiver blows on the infant's tummy, waits for the infant to laugh and then tickles her again or a caregiver sits on the floor with children playing with legos talking with them about their building and working with them to solve construction problems.

---

removes the child from the peer contact with no comment on the peer interaction; *intervene*—the adult tries to remediate a peer conflict; *separate*—the adult explicitly tells the children that they may not play together; and *punish*—the adult reprimands a child for an action directed to a peer.

Inter-observer reliability was established to an 82 percent agreement for all behaviors in an interval prior to each data collection period. Inter-observer reliability was re-established at monthly intervals through the entire data collection period. Median kappa reliability scores from these reliability checks for the measures used in this analysis ranged from .88 to .94 (median = .92).

Results

Comparison of Adult Child Interaction Over Time

The children in our two studies spent approximately one-quarter to one-half of the observation period in proximity with the teacher and the children were engaged with teachers approximately two-thirds of the time they were in proximity. See Table 1.3 for descriptive data.

Study 1. We used multivariate repeated measures analysis of variance and planned contrast techniques to compare adult-child interaction over time. Forty-seven children constituted the longitudinal sample with data at every time point. There were significant differences in teacher-child interaction over time (Pillais F (16, 608) = 10.40, $p<.0001$) Children decreased over time the time they spent in the proximity of the teacher (F (16,608) = 14.91, $p<.001$). Teachers decreased the percent of time they ignored the child between eighteen and twenty-four months (F (16,608) = 39.01, $p<.001$), decreased their responsive play between 24 and 30 months (F (16,608) = 3.68, $p<.01$), and decreased their average level of play between 30 and 36 months (F (16,608) = 4.78, $p<.001$).

Study 2. We also used two sets of multivariate repeated measures analysis of variance to compare children's behavior with teachers over time in study two. One set of tests used children who entered child care as infants. The other used children who entered child care as three-year-olds. Teacher behaviors with children changed between toddlerhood and preschool for the children who entered child care as infants (Pillais F (4,33) = 14.36, $p<.001$). Children spent more time in proximity to teachers as toddlers than as preschoolers (F (4,33) = 51.98, $p<.001$). Teachers were less likely to ignore children as preschoolers than they were when the children were toddlers (F (4,33) = 8.33, $p<.007$). There were no significant differences in teacher engagement.

Table 1.3   Comparison of Teacher Engagement Over Time

	STUDY 1 AVERAGE AGE OF CHILD				
	18m.	24m.	30m.	36m.	42m.
n of children	72	61	56	53	47
Teacher engagement					
percent time					
child in adult					
proximity	38	34	29	23	16
percent child					
ignored	37	32	35	33	33
percent responsive					
engagement	78	78	71	685	68
level of play	3.30	3.46	3.26	3.06	3.03

	STUDY 2 AVERAGE AGE OF CHILD		
	21m.	36.7m.	54.9m.
n of children	42	42	88
Teacher engagement			
percent time			
child in adult			
proximity	27	24	17
percent child			
ignored	38	33	26
percent responsive			
engagement	75	79	75
level of play	3.30	3.39	3.41

NOTE: NUMBERS IN TABLE REPRESENT MEAN SCORES

Teacher-child interaction also changed for the children who entered child care as three-year-olds (Pillais F (4,33) = 22.08, $p<.001$). There was only one significant univariate F. Children spent less time in teacher proximity as four-year-olds (F (4,33) = 62.84, $p<.001$) than as three-year-olds.

Comparison of Teacher-Child Interaction in Children
Who Entered Child Care at Different Ages

We used one way multivariate analysis of variance to compare as four-year-olds three groups of study 2 children: children entering child care as infants, as three-year-olds and as four-year-olds. There were no significant differences in teacher-child interaction between the groups.

Comparison of Teacher Mediation of Peer Contacts Over Time

The teachers in our studies had very low frequencies of mediating peer contact (Table 1.4). Teachers spent only 1 to 2 percent of the observation period mediating peer contact. Because of the low frequencies of mediating behaviors we created two composite measures: positive mediation behaviors and negative mediation behaviors.

Study 1. We used multivariate repeated measures analysis of variance techniques to compare teacher mediation of peer contacts over time in study 1. There were no significant changes over time.

Study 2. We also used two sets of multivariate repeated measured analysis of variance to compare teacher mediation of peer contacts over time in study two. Teacher mediation of peer contacts changed for the children who

Table 1.4   Comparison of Teacher Mediation of Peer Play Over Time

| | STUDY 1 | | | | |
| | AVERAGE AGE OF CHILD | | | | |
	18m.	24m.	30m.	36m.	42m.
number of children	72	61	56	53	47
Teacher mediation					
Place	.4(16)	.5(8)	.4(7)	.4(15)	.2(6)
Interpret	.3(14)	.2(7)	.4(5)	.1(4)	.3(6)
Set up	.8(20)	.6(16)	.8(16)	1.0(18)	.5(11)
Step back	.1(4)	.2(6)	.1(1)	.3(9)	.0(1)
Comment	.2(4)	.4(11)	.1(8)	.2(8)	.4(12)
Positive mediate	1.7(23)	1.8(30)	1.3(28)	2.0(30)	1.4(26)
Interrupt	.8(20)	1.2(33)	.7(27)	1.6(33)	1.3(32)
Intervene	1.6(33)	2.0(42)	1.7(41)	2.0(36)	.9(28)
Separate	.1(4)	.1(3)	.1(2)	.2(7)	.1(2)
Punish	.0(0)	.0(0)	.0(0)	.0(0)	.1(3)
Negative mediate	2.0(33)	3.4(44)	2.2(46)	3.6(40)	2.4(34)

Table 1.4   Comparison of Teacher Mediation of Peer Play Over Time
(continued)

	STUDY 2 AVERAGE AGE OF CHILD		
	21m.	36.7m.	54.9m.
number of children	42	42	88
Teacher mediation			
Place	1.6(24)	.4(7)	.4(9)
Set up	.6(13)	1.3(12)	.2(7)
Step back	.1(2)	.1(4)	.0(0)
Comment	.5(7)	.3(6)	.4(10)
Positive mediate	2.8(29)	2.1(20)	1.0(23)
Interrupt	.8(16)	.7(16)	1.6(34)
Intervene	2.7(29)	1.1(18)	.6(12)
Separate	.2(5)	.0(0)	.0(0)
Punish	.1(2)	.0(0)	.0(0)
Negative mediate	3.8(46)	1.8(44)	2.2(33)

NOTE: NUMBERS IN TABLE REPRESENT MEAN FREQUENCIES (NUMBER OF CHILDREN RECEIVING MEDIATION BEHAVIOR)

entered child care as infants (F (2,33) = 15.98, $p<.001$). They received more positive (F (2,33) = 20.46, $p<.001$) and more negative (F (2,33) = 20.31, $p<.001$) teacher mediation of peer contacts as toddlers than as four-year-olds. The children who entered child care as three-year-olds received similar amounts of teacher mediation of peer contacts as three and four-year-olds.

Comparison of Teacher Mediation of Peer Contacts in Children Who Entered Child Care at Different Ages

We used one way multivariate analysis of variance to compare as four-year-olds three groups of study 2 children: children entering child care as infants, as three-year-olds and as four-year-olds. There were no significant differences in teacher mediation of peer contacts between the groups.

Discussion and Summary

Our review of the literature suggests that adult socialization of peer contacts occurs as adults serve as gatekeepers, as managers, and less directly in the style of adult-child interactions. We were unable to examine the role of teachers as gatekeepers in our work. However, the parents of the children in our studies in their gatekeeper roles arranged a variety of peer based child care experiences for their children. In particular, the parents of the children in study 2 varied greatly in the age that they enrolled their child in a regular peer group experience. Teacher-child interaction and teacher mediation of peer contacts were similar for children enrolled at different ages. Future research with this sample will examine differences in children's behaviors with peers in children who began child care at different ages.

We did directly investigate the manager role of teachers. The most noteworthy finding is how little teachers attempt to mediate peer contacts. Our informal observations suggest that teacher's belief systems may work against teacher management of peer contacts. Teachers used free play and outdoor times in the child care center to step back and visit with their own peers. They tended to monitor peer play only for safety believing that children learn best when they solve their own peer problems.

It is interesting that the one significant difference in teacher mediation of peer contact was between the study 2 toddlers and preschoolers. The majority of the study 2 children enrolled in child care as infants were cared for in unlicensed informally arranged family day care homes. Although we have called the adults in these family day care homes teachers they identified themselves as mothers who were staying home with their own children and helping out a friend. As mothers they were less reluctant to mediate peer contact than the preschool teachers who cared for the children as four-year-olds.

Teacher-child interaction did change over time in these studies. The most striking difference was the decrease in the time the child spent close to the teacher. Other research suggests that with age children spend more time with peers and less with teachers (Holmberg, 1980). Although the teachers in study 1 did change their responsiveness to the child, becoming less responsive, all of the teachers in the two samples were generally responsive to the children and engaged them in fairly high levels of play. These findings support our notion that the teachers viewed the peer system as relatively autonomous of the teacher-child system. When the children were with peers they were primarily ignored, when the children engaged with the teacher, the teacher was responsive and sensitive. An interesting future research direction would be to directly interview teachers in order to determine if the belief system we have inferred from their behavior is in existence.

In conclusion, the literature suggests that children benefit from parental socialization of peer contacts. Our observations suggest that sensitive and responsive teachers do little mediation of peer contacts. In future work with these samples we will explore whether individual differences in teacher behavior are related to individual differences in children's play with peers.

NOTES

1. There is no universal nomenclature to describe the adult who cares for children in child care. She may be a family day care mother or provider, a caregiver, or a teacher. In this chapter we will use the term teacher to mean any caregiver in child care.

REFERENCES

Baumrind, D. (1971). Current practices of parental authority. *Developmental Psychology Monograph, 4* (1, Pt. 2)

Baumrind, D. (1967). Child care practices anteceding three patterns of preschool behavior. *Genetic Psychology Monographs, 75*, 43-88.

Baumrind, D. (1973). The development of instrumental competence through socialization. In A. D. Pick (Ed.), *Minnesota Symposium on Child Psychology* (Volume 7) (pp. 3-46). Minneapolis, MN: University of Minnesota Press.

Berndt, T., & Ladd, G. (1989). *Peer relationships in child development.* New York: Wiley.

Bhavnagri, N. (1987). *Parents as facilitators of Preschool Children's Peer Relationships.* University of Illinois at Champaign-Urbana, Unpublished doctoral dissertation.

Bryant, B. K. (1985). The neighborhood walk: Sources of support in middle childhood. *Monograph of the Society for Research in Child Development, 50* (3, Serial No. 210).

Finnie, V., & Russell, A. (1988). Preschool children's social status and their mothers' behavior and knowledge in the supervisory role. *Developmental Psychology, 24*, 789-801.

Halligan, M. T., & Sorensen, A. B. (1985). Ability groupings and children's friendships. *American Educational Research Journal, 22*, 485-499.

Halverson, C. F., & Waldrop, M. F. (1970). Maternal behavior towards own and other preschool children: The problem of "ownness." *Child Development, 41*, 839-845.

Harper, L., & Huie, C. (1987). Relations among preschool children's adult and peer contacts and later academic achievement. *Child Development, 58*, 1051-1065.

Harms, T., & Clifford, R. (1980). The early childhood environmental rating scale. New York: Teachers College Press.

Hinde, R., & Tamplin, A. (1983). Relations between mother-child interaction and behavior in preschool. *British Journal of Developmental Psychology, 1*, 231-257.

Holmberg, M. C. (1980). The development of social exchange patterns from 12 to 42 months. *Child Development, 51*, 448-456.

Howes, C. (1992). Caregiving environments and their consequences for children: The experience in the United States. In E. Melbuish & P. Moss (Eds.), *Daycare and the young child: An international perspective*. London: Tavistock.

Howes, C. (1986). Children's social competence with peers: Contributions from child care. *Early Childhood Research Quarterly, 2*, 155-168.

Howes, C. (1988). Peer interaction of young children. *Monographs of the Society for Research in Child Development, 53* (1, Serial No. 217).

Ladd, G., & Golter, B. (1988). Parents' management of preschooler's peer relations: Is it related to children's social competence? *Developmental Psychology, 24*, 109-117.

Ladd, G. W., Hart, C. H., Wadworth, E. M., & Golter, B. (1988). In Salzinger, Antrobus, & Hammer (Eds.), *Social networks of children adolescents and college students*. New Jersey: Erlbaum.

Lamb, M., & Nash, A. (1989). Infant-mother attachment, sociability, and peer competence. In T. J. Berndt & G. W. Ladd (Eds), *Peer relationships in child development,* (pp. 219-245). New York: Wiley.

Lollis, S., & Ross, H. S. (1987, April). *Mothers' interventions in toddler-peer conflicts*. Paper presented at the biennial meeting of the Society for Research in Child Development, Baltimore.

MacDonald, K., & Parke, R. (1984). Bridging the gap: Parent-child play interaction and peer interactive competence. *Child Development, 55*, 1265-1277.

MacDonald, K. (1987). Parent-child physical play with rejected, neglected, and popular boys. *Developmental Psychology, 23*, 705-711.

Mize, J., & Ladd, G. (1986). Promoting positive peer relations with young children: Rationale and strategies. *Child Care Quarterly, 14*, 221-237.

Parke, R. D., MacDonald, K. B., Beitel, A., & Bhavnagri, N. (1986). The role of the family in the development of peer relationships. In R. J. McMahan (Eds.), Marriages and families. New York: Brunner.

Parke, R. D., & Bhavnagri, N. P. (1988). Parents as managers of children's peer relationships. In D. Belle (Ed.), *Children's social networks and social supports*. New York: Wiley.

Phillips, D. A. (Ed.) (1987). *Quality in child care: What does research tell us*? Research Monograph of the National Association for the Education of Young Children.

Putallaz, M., & Heflin, A. H. (1991). Parent-child interaction. In S. R. Asher & J. D. Coie (Eds.), *Peer rejection in childhood*. New York: Cambridge University Press.

Putallaz, M. (1987). Maternal behavior and children's sociometric status. *Child Development, 58*, 324-340.

Rubenstein, J., & Howes, C. (1979). Caregiving and infant behavior in day care and homes. *Developmental Psychology, 15*, 1-24.

Roopnarine, J. L. (1987). Social interaction in the peer group: Relationship to perceptions of parenting and to children's interpersonal awareness and problem-solving ability. *Journal of Applied Developmental Psychology, 8*, 351-362.

Whitebook, M., Howes, C., & Phillips, D. (1990). *Who cares: Child care teachers in Americ*a. Final Report of the National Child Care Staffing Study. Oakland, CA: Child Care Employee Project.

2

Peer Play and Nonparental Care Experiences

**Michael E. Lamb, Kathleen J. Sternberg, Nan Knuth,
Carl Philip Hwang, and Anders G. Broberg**

Children in nonparental care arrangements have a number of experiences that are unique to them and are not shared by agemates who receive exclusive parental care. Among the most important of these experiences are increased exposure to adults and peers. Children in alternative care interact with multiple adults with different personalities, behavioral styles, and expectations. In contrast to parents, these adults have often had some formal training and are paid for taking care of children. In a study of Swedish children in alternative care settings, for example, we recently found that the children were exposed to between three and nine different adults in the alternative care setting in the average week (Unpublished findings). In addition, nonparental care arrangements almost invariably permit more and different kinds of contacts and interactions with peers than are typically experienced by children remaining at home with their parents. In the same study, we found that the children spent an average of eight hours per day in the alternative care settings, with 48 percent of the time spent in "free play" and 52 percent in "adult planned activities."

The purpose of this chapter is to examine the relationship between alternative care and the quality of peer play experiences. We accomplish this by reviewing the context in which this research was initially conceptualized and then summarize the results of two studies that we have undertaken on this topic. Our focus is on four questions. First, is it possible to obtain reliable measures of the quality of children's peer play and the quality of the alternative care setting? Second, are peer social skills part of a broader construct—sociability with others? The third question concerns the relationship between the quality of care and the quality of peer play: To what extent is children's sociability influenced by the quality of care both at home and in the alternative care setting? Finally, do children play with peers differently in different out-of-home-care environments?

Why Study the Association Between Peer Play and Nonparental Care?

Over the last two decades, there have been at least three waves of research on nonparental care and its effects (Belsky, 1984; Lamb & Sternberg, 1990). During each of these waves, a different underlying hypothesis or question has guided researchers. In the first phase, there was widespread popular concern that nonparental care, particularly during the early years of life, was likely to have harmful effects on children. During this era most research was focused on the question: Is daycare good or bad for children? and a minor variant of this question, Must alternative care always be bad for children? Over time it became clear that this orientation was much too simplistic, particularly in light of accumulating research findings indicating that most children were not adversely affected by the experience of nonparental care. There then began an era in which the underlying question became, In what circumstances is alternative care good or bad for children? and Are there particular types of children for whom it is more or less likely to be harmful? In this era, researchers began attempting to examine the way in which alternative care experiences were integrated into the wider network of formative experiences that children had. This orientation permitted the emergence of the latest phase in which researchers have begun seeking to identify the aspects or components of alternative care that make it a beneficial or undesirable experience for children.

It became clear that in the single-minded focus on the effects of repeated parent-child separations, researchers often overlooked the fact that children in regular nonparental care arrangements experienced a number of events that were unique to them and were not shared by peers—notably an increased exposure to adults and peers. Being exposed to many different adults may make children more empathic by forcing them to recognize the variety of perspectives that adults bring to relationships. Similarly, experiences with peers are also likely to be influential, particularly in light of the finding that nine-month-olds who played together for 50 minutes on each of 10 sessions over a three week long period were later more oriented toward interaction with peers and engaged in more interaction, even with unfamiliar age mates, than did infants who were deprived of these supplementary experiences (Becker, 1977). Not surprisingly, therefore, other researchers working with infants, toddlers, and preschoolers have confirmed that children enrolled in regular nonparental care settings engage in more interactions with their peers than do those without such experiences (Field & Roopnarine, 1982; Harper & Huie, 1985).

When researchers undertake studies such as these, comparing the propensities of children in two or three groups (distinguished on the basis of nonparental care histories, for example), their focus is on differences between the group means, and as a result, the reliability of individual measures is not critical. Increasingly, however, we and other researchers wish to examine the correlates of individual differences in the adaptation to nonparental care, and this makes it essential to examine the psychometric properties—especially the reliability—of observational measures of peer social skills. Stated differently, our substantive goal was to understand the relationship between the quality of the care setting and the extent to which peer social skills were developed. We wanted to determine whether peer social skills were likely to be enhanced more when children experienced care of high quality than when they experienced care of lower quality. Issues of measurement must be addressed first, however. Do measures of peer play quality taken at one time predict scores that would be obtained if the same children were observed at another time or in another setting? Exactly the same question must be asked of observational measures of the quality of care. Unless these measures are reliable indices of both quality of care and peer social skills, they are unlikely to be useful to us as we attempt to understand the relationship between quality of care and developing peer social skills.

Quality of peer play has been operationally defined by measuring the frequency with which certain behaviors are directed toward one another by peers as well as by tabulating the amount of time spent in play of a more sophisticated quality. The reliability of these measures is unknown, however. In addition, although reviewers have frequently proclaimed the beneficial effects of high quality care, this term has been defined with any clarity only in the last few years. Researchers have come to distinguish between two aspects of quality (Howes, 1991). First, there are some easily quantifiable indices of the *structural quality*, including the number of children in the care of each adult, group size, the age range of children in each group, the stability of both children and adults within each group, the dimension and appointments of the physical setting, the amount of training and experience teachers or careproviders have had, and so on. These structural measures provide readily quantifiable indices of factors that seem likely to improve the ability of adults to provide sensitive growth-promoting experiences for children. However, even the most experienced and best trained adults attending to small numbers of children in well-provisioned centers do not necessarily provide growth-promoting experiences for children because the structural indices of quality only affect children's experiences if they are translated into differences at a dynamic or interactional level. Consequently, researchers such as ourselves have attempted to develop measures that tap *dynamic aspects of the quality of care*. These involve attempts to directly measure the sensitivity of the adults, the extent to which they promote interactions with and between the children, and the extent to which they facilitate interested engagement rather than disinterest and boredom. The goal of the first study described below was to assess the reliability of our dynamic measures of quality, just as we explored the reliability of the measures of peer social skills.

The Salt Lake City Family Day-Care Study

This study involved 18 children (half boys) who ranged in age from 24 to 36 months (M = 29 months) when they were enrolled in the study. All children came from middle class, two parent families. Subjects were recruited by contacting family day-care providers in Salt Lake City, Utah. Care providers who agreed to participate in the study then asked the parents of one of the children in their care if we could contact them to describe the study and solicit their participation. To qualify for participation in this study, children needed to have been in the care of the current family day-care provider for at least six months. To maximize the range of family day-care settings sampled, only one child was recruited from each day-care home.

These children were observed 5 or 6 times over a several week-long period in the naturalistic context of the family day-care homes. During the observations, careproviders were asked not to deviate from their daily routines. The target child was unaware that he or she was the focus of our study because he or she was observed while playing with other children and the observers tried to be as unobtrusive as possible while following the children around playgrounds, backyards and careproviders' homes. During the observations, the observers systematically alternated the order in which the three observational measures—the Belsky and Walker (1980) checklist, the Howes Peer Observation Scale, and our Peer Observation technique—were administered in order to eliminate any order effects. Each measure was completed three time during each 2 to 3 hour long visit. Additional information was gathered by interviewing careproviders either in the evenings or after observations had been completed. The parents of the target children were interviewed in their homes after the children had gone to bed.

The quality of alternative care was assessed using: (1) the range of ages of children in alternative care; (2) the number of children in the family day-care home; (3) an index of the careproviders' education and training; (4) Caldwell's HOME inventory, completed in the family day-care home (Caldwell & Bradley 1979); and (5) the Belsky and Walker Checklist. This checklist includes 13 positive and 7 negative events and the observer noted whether each occurred at least once during a 3-minute spot sample unit. The positive events were: positive regard by careprovider, verbal elaboration by careprovider, heightened-exaggerated emotional display by careprovider, careprovider empathizes, routine made into learning experience, careprovider engaged with more than one child, careprovider engaged while doing routine maintenance, careprovider engaged in nonstructured attention focusing, careprovider facilitates peer relations, careprovider on floor involved, careprovider distant involved, child explores nontoy object, and child happy. The negative events were: child crying, careprovider prohibits some child action, child in restrictive device, children waiting, careproviders in nonchild conversation, child uninvolved-aimless, and routine as routine. The scores from three spot observations made during each visit were summed and subsequently averaged and standardized across visits to yield one negative event score and one positive event score.

The quality of children's play was measured using: (1) the Howes Peer Play Scale and (2) our own Peer Observation Technique. The Howes (1980) scale involves observing a target child in a time sampling procedure for twenty minutes (20 seconds of observation and 10 seconds of recording) and noting the highest level of play observed during the 20 second unit. On the Howes scale, which has Guttman-scale qualities, 0 is scored when no play is observed, 1 when the children are engaged in noninteractive parallel play, 2 when there is parallel play with mutual regard, 3 simple social play (one child directs a social bid to the other), 4 complementary and reciprocal play with mutual awareness, and 5 complementary and reciprocal social play. Further details are provided in the Howes (1980) coding manual. Scores from the three observations per visit were summed for analytic purposes.

Our Peer Observation Technique is a time-sampling procedure in which the observer recorded a variety of positive and negative peer behaviors directed by and to the target child during a 10-minute period. For each visit the total number of positive and negative peer play behaviors were calculated. The positive peer-related behavior score was the sum of the observed instances of initiate play, imitate, vocalize, touch, proffer, accept, and laugh or smile. The negative peer-related behavior score was the sum of the observed instances of reject bid, turn away, take away toy, take toy from, have toy taken from, throw, defensive struggle, offensive struggle, strike-hit, and cry. These scores were averaged and standardized across visits to yield a positive and negative peer outcome score. Scores from the three observations per visit were summed for analytic purposes.

Is It Possible to Obtain Reliable Measures of Children's Peer Play Quality and the Quality of Alternative Care Settings?

With respect to reliability of measurement, our analyses showed that all but one of the observational measures were highly reliable even though the assessments were conducted over a six-week period. Table 2.1 shows that the multiple assessments of the quality of care using the Belsky and Walker checklists were fairly reliable (Alpha = .67 and .54 for the positive and negative scores respectively). As shown on Table 2.2, the Alpha coefficient for the Howes peer play scale was .71. Alpha coefficients were also high for the measures of the number of positive peer play behaviors (.70). Only the number of negative peer-directed behaviors varied widely from day to day, resulting in a low coefficient of internal reliability (Alpha = .20). With the exception of this measure, our results suggested surprisingly good stability from day to day in both the quality of care and the quality of the children's peer play.

Table 2.1   Reliability of Belsky and Walker Measures of Alternative Care

BELSKY POSITIVE

	Corrected Item-Total Correlation	Alpha If Item Deleted
Time 1	.55	.65
Time 2	.70	.56
Time 3	.75	.53
Time 4	.43	.69
Time 5	−.04	.80

STANDARDIZED ALPHA = .67

BELSKY NEGATIVE

	Corrected Item-Total Correlation	Alpha If Item Deleted
Time 1	.02	.42
Time 2	.27	.27
Time 3	.23	.47
Time 4	.59	.20
Time 5	.30	.28

STANDARDIZED ALPHA = .54

When both observational and structural measures of the quality of alternative care were considered, there were several interesting findings. When the age range of the children in the alternative care setting was more narrow, the scores on the Belsky Positive ($r = -.45$; $p = .031$) and the Caldwell HOME scales were higher ($r = .52$; $p = .03$) and the Belsky negative scores were lower ($r = -.66$; $p = .005$). The extent of careprovider training was negatively correlated with the Belsky positive score ($r = -.61$; $p = .008$). Careprovider education was unrelated to any of the other measures of alternative care quality. The multiple measures of quality thus appeared to tap a common dimension, although some expected associations were not statistically significant.

Overall, the results of this study showed that measures of children's peer play quality and measures of the quality of alternative care were both reliable.

Table 2.2   Reliability of Peer Play Measures

HOWES PEER PLAY

	Corrected Item-Total Correlation	Alpha If Item Deleted
Time 1	.64	.58
Time 2	.61	.59
Time 3	.12	.78
Time 4	.60	.60
Time 5	.41	.68

STANDARDIZED ALPHA = .71

PEER PLAY POSITIVE

	Corrected Item-Total Correlation	Alpha If Item Deleted
Time 1	.72	.68
Time 2	.62	.72
Time 3	.52	.76
Time 4	.52	.76
Time 5	.46	.77

STANDARDIZED ALPHA = .79

NEGATIVE PEER PLAY

	Corrected Item-Total Correlation	Alpha If Item Deleted
Time 1	.14	.00
Time 2	−.18	.30
Time 3	.14	−.05
Time 4	−.03	.22
Time 5	.30	−.15

STANDARDIZED ALPHA = .20

Our results indicated that even brief observations of toddlers playing with their peers could yield reliable information about individual differences in social skills, and that similarly brief observations of their interactions with careproviders provided reliable indices of the careproviders' behavioral tendencies.

The Göteborg Childcare Study

In 1982, the Göteborg Childcare Study began with 145 Swedish children, averaging 16 months of age. All of the children had been home with one or both of their parents from the time of their birth until they were enrolled in the study, and all of the parents had registered their children for placement in day care facilities. At the time, however, there was a shortage of such facilities in the city of Göteborg. Consequently, only a portion of the families who agreed to participate in the study were actually able to obtain out-of-home care for their children. Fifty-three of the families were offered and accepted places in center day care, and these became our center care group. Another 33 were placed in family day care homes. Finally, 54 children were not assigned to places in either center or family day care settings and so remained home in the care of their parents.

All of the children were observed in their homes prior to beginning regular nonparental care. During this initial observation we assessed the children's peer skills by observing the children interacting for 30 minutes with a familiar peer of the parents' choice. During this observation, we used the procedures developed in the first study to obtain measures of the total number of peer directed positive behaviors, the total number of peer directed negative behaviors, and the total number of units during which the rating on the Howes scale was 3 or higher. During the same phase, we assessed the quality of home care using Caldwell's HOME and the Belsky and Walker (1980) checklists, and we interviewed the parents about their social support network and their family backgrounds. The children's sociability with unfamiliar adults was also assessed upon the observer-interviewer's arrival at the child's home, using a procedure developed and more fully described by Stevenson and Lamb (1979; Thompson & Lamb, 1983). The child's response was rated in each of eight contexts: initial reaction to stranger and reactions to offer of toy, to attempted initiation of game, when given floor freedom, to offer of toy when on floor, to attempted initiation of game, to attempted pick up, and to stranger's departure. Rating was on a 5-point scale, with 1 indicating a fussy, unfriendly response and 5 indicating an outgoing, positive response. In addition, the observer recorded her or his overall impression of the child's sociability on a 9-point scale. All ratings were then added to yield a measure with a possible range of 9 to 49. Stevenson and Lamb (1979) reported significant correlations (r = .46) with sociability in a test situation, as well as significant test-retest reliability between multiple assessments in both the same (r = .73) and different (r's = .49, .40) contexts over a 2-week period. The children's experiences diverged when approximately two thirds of the children began out-of-home care roughly six weeks later. These children were observed in their out-of-home care settings so that their developing peer social skills could be assessed in that context, and so that we could gather information on the quality of the alternative care they experienced.

One year after the initial assessment, the children, their parents, and their careproviders were visited again (Phase II). Parents were interviewed, the quality of home care and the quality of alternative care were assessed once again, and the children were again observed interacting with their peers both at home and in the alternative care setting. The same procedure was followed one year later (Phase III). The phase II sociability assessment procedure was altered to accommodate the increased age of the children. The child's response was rated in each of five contexts: initial reaction, response to request to approach, reaction to initiation of turn-taking game, response to verbal query, reaction to stranger's attempt to pick up and read to the child. Rating was on a 5-point scale similar to that used in phase I. In addition, the observer recorded his or her overall impression on a 9-point scale. When the ratings were summed, the possible range was 6 to 34. In phase III, the sociability measure was again changed to accommodate the increased age of the children. On this occasion, a single 9-point rating, measuring the observer's overall impression, was employed.

For the purposes of this chapter, we summarize the findings concerning peer social skills during the first three phases that were presented in more detail elsewhere (Broberg, Hwang, Lamb, & Ketterlinus, 1989; Lamb, Hwang, Broberg, & Bookstein, 1988; Lamb, Hwang, Bookstein, Broberg, Hult, & Frodi, 1988). In the first analyses, we focus only on measures of the peer social skills observed at home because this was a context that was similar for all children in the study regardless of their out-of-home care experiences. The determinants of individual differences in peer play and sociability with unfamiliar adults was assessed using the technique of "soft modeling" to permit empirical assessments of the associations among multiple constructs each indirectly measured (for a description of Partial Least Squares (PLS), or soft-modelling techniques, see Bookstein, 1986, and Ketterlinus, Sampson, Bookstein, and Lamb, 1989).

Are Peer Social Skills Part of a Broader Construct—Sociability with Others? Is Peer Social Skills Influenced by the Quality of Care Received?

PLS analyses showed that the measures of peer play and sociability were related to the same predictor latent variables and thus should be considered as a single outcome latent variable, which we called "social skills." The relevant model for the social skills outcomes is depicted in Figure 2.1. The net R for the combined prediction was a respectable .64. Inspection of the figure indicates that the quality of home care, the quality of out-of-home care, social skills at time II, and gender all contributed to the prediction of observed social skills in Phase III, whereas background (primarily social class) and support had modest associations. Children who were more sociable and playful with both peers and strange adults came from homes receiving higher scores on Caldwell's HOME and had less-involved fathers. They also spent more time in out-of-home care facilities characterized by low scores on both the positive and negative scales of the Belsky and Walker checklist. Girls were more sociable than boys.

The prediction by gender, quality of home care, and quality of alternative care remained substantial (net R = .57) even when prior social skills were not included in the model. As the figure shows, prior social skills were the best predictors of individual differences in social skills at time III. This indicates that the stability in successive measures of social skills is substantial but that knowledge of prior social skills does not much enhance the degree of prediction achieved using the other predictor variables alone. Presumably this is because scores on the earlier

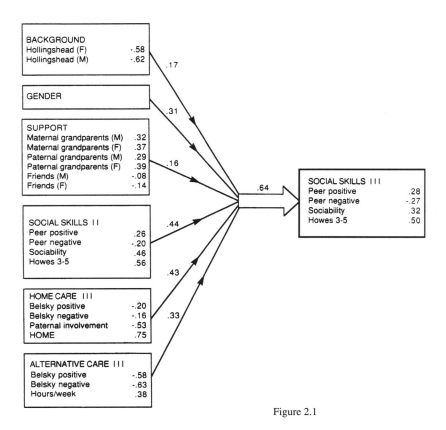

Figure 2.1

measures of child social skills are themselves determined by variations in child gender, the quality of home care, and the quality of alternative care.

When the model was computed again using the large subsample (n = 115) of children who had remained in the same group through the first two phases but may have changed care arrangements between Phases II and III, the coefficients were very similar (net R = .63), although the relative importance of the hours per week measure within the quality of alternative care latent variable decreased from a coefficient of .38 to .10, the gender latent variable had a coefficient of only .16, and the coefficient for support rose to .21. In neither model did group assignment have any impact on the social skills III latent variable.

In further analysis, several structural indices of the quality of care were added to the latent variable tapping quality of alternative care: absolute group size, the child/caregiver ratio, the age range of the children in the alternative care setting, and the proportion of children in an alternative care setting whose ages were within 12 months of the target child's. As in the previous analysis, we found that peer play and sociability as assessed in the home were related to the same predictor variables (see Figure 2.2). The net R for the social skills outcome was quite high relative to the net R yielded in Study 1 (.77 vs. 64). The best predictor of the social skills III latent variable was the quality of alternative care in Phase III. The three next most important predictors (all Phase II latent variables) made approximately the same contribution to the prediction of Phase III social skills; they were quality of home care II, quality of alternative care II, and social skills II. (When the latent variable for social skills II was removed, the net R was reduced to a very respectable .71.) The measure of parental SES contributed a much smaller proportion of the predictive power of the model than the other four latent variables depicted.

Substantively, these results show that children who were, in Phase III, more sociable and playful attended high quality alternative care facilities, had more involved fathers, and were from homes that had both high HOME scores and low scores on the Belsky positive checklist. Highly sociable children attended out-of-home care facilities in both Phases II and III that had a narrower age range and a more homogeneous age mixture and were characterized by the occurrence of fewer negative events. By Phase III the child/caregiver ratio became the most important component of the quality of alternative care latent variable. Facilities that had few children per caregiver had children who exhibited more age-appropriate social skills.

These results from the Göteborg Childcare Study show that peer social skills are quite stable over time: The best predictors of children's social skills were measures of their social skills assessed at the previous phase. Like the results of the Salt Lake City Family Daycare Study, these results suggest that peer social skills are stable dimensions of individual functioning. Second, our results suggest that peer social skills form part of a broader constellation of measures tapping sociability. Children who were sociable and friendly with peers were

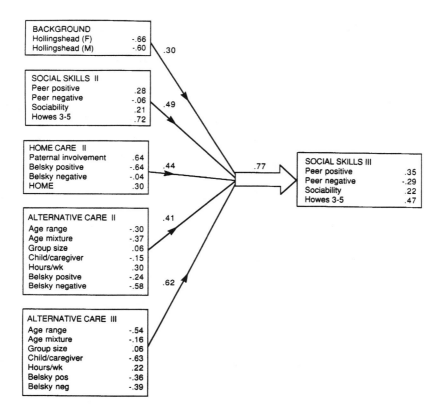

Figure 2.2

also sociable and friendly with the investigators, and for purposes of prediction, sociability with peers and adults appeared to be a single dimension. Third, our results demonstrated that the degree of sociability manifested by the children was influenced to a substantial extent by measures of the quality of care received both at home and in the out-of-home care facilities. Interestingly, we found that the dynamic measures of quality were among the least consistent predictors of peer social skills. Thus even though these measures appeared to be at least moderately reliable, their relationships with the measures of sociability were not particularly high, and their coefficients varied from analysis to analysis, suggesting that they did not provide a clear index of the quality of care. The structural measures of quality appeared to be more useful, as did Caldwell's HOME index, a measure that was used in the Göteborg study only to assess quality of the children's care at home.

Of course, peer social skills were not only influenced by the quality of care. The children varied in their sociability with peers and adults at the onset of the study, with some children being more inhibited with their peers and with strange adults than others were (Broberg, Lamb, & Hwang, 1990). These individual differences may have an organismic basis and might to a certain degree underlie longitudinal stability in measures of social skills.

Do Children Play with Peers Differently in Different Out-of-Home-Care Environments?

There has been little research on the effects of the social setting on the quality of children's interactions with peers, and most attempts to assess the effects of out-of-home care on children's peer social skills have involved observations in a single context. In order to address this question, we analyzed the play of Swedish children observed both at home and in the alternate care settings at ages 1-2 (n = 86), 2-3 (n = 67) and 3-4 (n = 48). As in other analyses of data from the Göteborg Childcare Study, the play was measured using the positive peer-related behavior score (initiate play, imitate, vocalize, touch, proffer, accept and laugh or smile), the negative peer related behavior score (reject bid, turn away, take away toy from, have toy taken from, throw, defensive struggle, offensive struggle, strike, hit and cry), level of play (summing the number of intervals in which the children exhibited play at levels 3, 4, or 5 on the Howes scale) as well as the frequency of withdrawal (lack of proximity, standing aimless).

As mentioned previously, there were no differences between center daycare and family day-care children when observed in the home setting. As shown in Table 2.3, however, differences emerged in the alternative care setting. In the first two phases, the family day-care children showed more positive behavior and play of higher quality than did the children in day-care centers. While these differences were no longer apparent at 3 to 4 years of age, the children in the daycare centers showed more withdrawal than did children in family daycare at this age.

Why did the children in family day care appear more socially skilled than center-care children when observed playing in the alternative care settings? One explanation for these findings is that the family day-care setting is more conducive to social play. The number of children in family day care homes is lower, and this may make it easier for children to play with one another without interruption. In addition, the family daycare setting is more likely to permit cross-age interaction, in which slightly older children may promote high quality social play through a form of scaffolding (Rogoff, 1990).

Table 2.3   Mean Proportion of Time That Play Behavior Occurred in the Family Day Care and Day Care Setting

	1–2 YEARS		2–3 YEARS		3–4 YEARS	
	Family Day Care	Day Care	Family Day Care	Day Care	Family Day Care	Day Care
Peer Positive	34.4+	23.9	46.6+	33.8	49.6	40.5
Peer Negative	3.8	3.5	2.1	2.7	2.0	3.6
Peer Withdr.	28.7	30.3	16.5	21.7	11.8	21.6*
Howes 3–5	7.4*	4.2	32.6*	18.4	24.5*	14.0

*p < .01,
+p < .05

Conclusion

Overall, the results of these two studies suggest that, even with children as young as 16 months of age, reliable measures of the quality of peer play can be obtained in observations as brief as thirty minutes long. Our results also show that these individual differences in peer skills are good predictors of the children's subsequent behavior in similar contexts. Third, our studies show that children who experience high quality care both at home and in out-of-home care settings benefit in a variety of ways; among other things they become more skilled in interaction with peers. At least at younger ages, furthermore, the family daycare context may facilitate peer social skills better than the center care context.

REFERENCES

Becker, J. M. T. (1977). A learning analysis of the development of peer oriented behavior in nine month old infants. *Developmental Psychology, 13,* 481-491.

Belsky, J. (1984). Two waves of day care research: Developmental effects and conditions of quality. In R. Ainslie (Ed.), *The child and the daycare setting* (pp. 1-34). New York: Praeger.

Belsky, J., & Walker, A. (1980). *Infant-toddler center spot observation system.* Unpublished manuscript, Department of Individual and Family Studies, Pennsylvania State University.

Bookstein, F. L. (1986). The elements of latent variable models: A cautionary lecture. In M. E. Lamb, A. L. Brown, and B. Rogoff (Eds.), *Advances in developmental psychology* (Vol. 4, pp. 203-230). Hillsdale, NJ: Lawrence Erlbaum Associates.

Broberg, A. G., Hwang C. P., Lamb, M. E., & Ketterlinus, R. D. (1989). Child care effects on socioemotional and intellectual competence in Swedish preschoolers. In J. S. Lande, S. Scarr, and N. Gunzenhauser (Eds.), *Caring for children: Challenge to America* (pp. 49-75). Hillsdale, NJ: Lawrence Erlbaum Associates.

Broberg, A., Lamb, M. E., & Hwang, C. P. (1990). Inhibition: Its stability and correlates in 16- to 20-month-old children. *Child Development, 61,* 1153-1163.

Caldwell, B., & Bradley, R. (1979). *Home observations for measurement of the environment.* Little Rock: University of Arkansas, School of Education.

Field, T. M., & Roopnarine, J. L. (1982). Infant-peer interaction. In T. M. Field, H. C. Quay, L. Troll, and G. E. Finley (Eds.), *Review of human development.* New York: Wiley.

Harper, L. V., & Huie, K. S. (1985). The effects of prior group experience, age, and familiarity on the quality and organization of preschoolers' relationships. *Child Development, 56,* 704-717.

Howes, C. (1980). Peer play scales as an index of complexity of peer interaction. *Developmental Psychology, 16,* 371-372.

Howes, C. (1991). Caregiving environments and the consequences for children: The experience in the United States. In E. Melhuish and P. Moss (Eds.), *Day care and the young child: International perspectives* (pp. 185-198). London: Routledge.

Ketterlinus, R. D., Sampson, P., Bookstein, F. L., & Lamb, M. E. (1989). Partial least squares analysis in developmental psychopathology. *Development and Psychopathology, 1,* 351-371.

Lamb, M. E., Hwang, C. P., Bookstein, F. L., Broberg, A., Hult, G., & Frodi, M. (1988). Determinants of social competence in Sweden's preschoolers. *Developmental Psychology, 24,* 58-70.

Lamb, M. E., Hwang C. P., Broberg, A., & Bookstein, F. L. (1988). The effects of out-of-home care on the development of social competence in Sweden: A longitudinal study. *Early Childhood Research Quarterly, 3,* 379-402.

Lamb, M. E., & Sternberg, K. J. (1990). Do we really know how day care affects children? *Journal of Applied Developmental Psychology, 11*, 359-371.

Rogoff, B. (1990). *Apprenticeship in learning.* New York: Oxford University Press.

Stevenson, M. B., & Lamb, M. E. (1979). Effects of infant sociability and the caretaking environment on infant cognitive performance. *Child Development, 50*, 340-349.

Thompson, R. A., & Lamb, M. E. (1983). Security of attachment and stranger sociability in infancy. *Developmental Psychology, 19*, 184-191.

3

Family Dynamics and Day Care Children's Peer Group Participation

Jaipaul L. Roopnarine, Josephine A. Bright, and Nancy Beth Riegraf

Despite two decades of research on the impact of extrafamilial care on children's social and cognitive development, only recently have we begun to focus attention on the links between parental interpersonal functioning and children's adjustment to and their development in day care. The expanded emphasis in day care research has gained momentum, in part, because of the vehement and persistent efforts of some developmental psychologists (e.g., Belsky, 1984; 1990; Bronfenbrenner, 1986) who have called attention to the complex and often interrelated social systems in which families and children exist. This has led to major reconceptualizations of the manner in which we approach the study of families and children and to vigorous attempts to identify proximal and distal sources of influences on children's development. As a result, there is a growing body of work that highlights the importance of intrapersonal and interpersonal adult functioning for children's social and personality development (see Belsky, 1990, for a review).

In this chapter, we use the human ecology framework as a guide in our discussion of specific aspects of parents' intrapersonal and interpersonal functioning and their relationship to children's play behaviors and general social activities in daycare. Of particular interest to us are the relationships between mothers' and fathers' parenting skills, their personal well-being, marital relationship, job satisfaction, support networks, and preschoolers' play behaviors and social activities in day care. Before we summarize our own work, the presentation would benefit tremendously from a discussion of the theoretical/conceptual basis of our research, and a treatment of related research on the links between parental functioning and children's social participation with parents and peers.

The Breadth of Day Care

As several authoritative reviews (e.g., Belsky, 1990; Clarke-Stewart, 1989) have explicitly pointed out, the complex ecology of human development must be considered if we are to accurately assess the effects of daycare on children's development. Two sets of theoretical propositions are central to our discussion. The first suggests that parenting is directly influenced not only by adults' intrapersonal functioning and child characteristics, but also by forces emanating from the larger social context within which parent-child socialization occurs. Three factors have been suggested as important in influencing parenting and childhood development: marital relations, social support, and occupational experiences. Although Belsky's complete model is yet to be tested, he asserts that marital relations, as a context of stress/support, may exert the greatest influence on parenting because of the emotional investment and time spent in a marriage. But, the primacy of marital relations for parent-child relationships and extended and extrafamilial care would most certainly vary by family constellation variables and ethnic group. Nevertheless, regardless of which proximal or distal interpersonal factor exerts the greatest impact on parenting and childhood development, the cognitive-emotional orientation within the home environment is likely to become integrated into children's experiences in daycare.

This essential link, then, between the home and day care environment guides the second set of conceptual advances. Two competing models as to how the peer and parent-child socialization systems are related have been articulated. The *single process* models suggest that children's social competencies are primarily shaped within the parent-child system with modifications and extensions occurring in the peer group (Hartup, 1979). If we view the family as providing the day care child with salient role models, as the chief supplier of the child's affectional needs, and the overriding disciplinary force, then children in supplemental care would rely on the vicissitudes of the parent-child system to guide their day care experiences. By contrast, the *dual process* models suggest that specific social skills are learned within the parent-child or peer system (Hartup, 1979).

That children enter day care during the first few months of life raises interesting questions as to the role of the family as the primary domain of early influence. It has become imperative that we critically examine what behaviors are derived from and shaped in specific socialization systems. Furthermore, the perspective on the burgeoning role of extrafamilial socialization agents could pose problems in terms of conveying dominant cultural-familial views and regulating children's behaviors. Quite possibly, multiple caregiving tendencies do not always intermesh and may lack continuity.

Considering the complex nature of children's social worlds and the potential interlocking relationships among a constellation of social systems and subsystems espoused by these models, we draw attention to three general issues that are relevant to children's day-care experiences: (a) parents' marital relations and parenting and children's development; (b) parents' social support networks and job satisfaction and parenting and children's development; and (c) the degree of concordance between the parenting/marital system and peer group relations. Accordingly, we contend that for intact two-parent mainstream ethnic families, the marriage would be the first order support system for parenting and through parenting affect children's daycare experiences. Job satisfaction and social support are more likely to affect marital relations directly, with less noticeable indirect effects on childhood development, unless in cases where families are psychologically stranded and are unemployed or living in poverty.

The Parent-Child/Marital System and Day Care

A diverse body of work documents the association between marital relations and parenting. For example, high levels of parental involvement has been linked to marital communication (Belsky, Gilstrap, & Rovine, 1984), supportive husbands tend to influence maternal behavior (Pedersen, 1982), mothers who are likely to nag and scold their sons reported being less warm and affectionate toward their husbands (Sears, Maccoby, & Levin, 1957), and spousal interpersonal relationship that is marked by anger and underarousal is associated with angry and cold parenting (Gottman & Katz, 1989), while persistent marital conflicts and marital disruption have been linked to childhood behavior disorders (see Emery, 1982). It appears, therefore, that marital problems in particular can throw the family into a disorganized state, which can translate into inadequate parenting behaviors and ultimately to antisocial behaviors and low levels of play in children (see Gottman & Katz, 1989; Patterson, DeBaryshe, & Ramsey, 1989).

In the case of day care experience and marital relations, the two are possibly connected in four interdependent ways: (a) the quality of supplemental care does affect children's development which, in turn, could evoke positive/negative feelings and attitudes in parents, thereby influencing parenting and marital relations since the two exist side by side; (b) spousal support and regard for maternal employment aspirations and economic viability could influence spousal relationships and hence parenting behaviors and may have lag effects on how children behave in the peer group; (c) the influence of marital discord on children's development, depending on the degree of family disorganization and family management techniques, may be attenuated by quality center care; and (d) parents' emotional adjustment to placing their young children in day care could affect their ability to monitor and meet the emotional and cognitive needs of their children which, then, could affect marital communication (Lamb, Owen, & Chase-Lansdale, 1979). The paucity of data in this area makes it difficult to address these propositions fully.

Personal Well-Being and Personality Attributes

It is well established that personality attributes and the personal well-being of parents affect their children's developmental outcomes. Parents who display a good deal of warmth, sensitivity, and receptiveness are providing their children with some of the functional determinants of healthy personality development (see Belsky, 1990). High levels of nurturance have been shown to promote achievement orientation and the extension of cooperative and friendly bids to adults and peers (Baumrind, 1967, 1971). Similarly, high levels of interpersonal trust, and good parental coping style are linked to the display of warmth, helpfulness, acceptance, and low levels of disapproval when interacting with children (Mondell & Tyler, 1981). Conversely, depressed mothers provide a hostile, disruptive, and rejecting home for children (Weismann & Paykel, 1974). If we extend these findings to support the argument that the sociobehavioral and emotional tendencies of parents form the early basis for children's interactions with other adults and peers (see Easterbrooks & Lamb, 1979), and given the concordance noted between the peer and parent-child systems (Putallaz, 1987; Roopnarine, 1987; Roopnarine & Adams, 1987), one cannot help but think that interpersonal functioning variables may have an overarching influence on various aspects of parents' functioning and such influence may extend beyond the parent-child dyad itself. Adults who are unable to work through their own interpersonal difficulties from childhood, run the risk of employing undesirable socialization techniques that are more prone to undermine the mental health of young children (see Belsky, 1990). Under these conditions children's interactions with peers may be negatively affected, irrespective of whether or not they are enrolled in day care.

Social Support and Day Care

Appropriate amounts of social support characterized by a "good fit" can influence both marital relations and parenting and children's development in day care (see Belsky, 1984). However, the degree and manner in which social support is associated with day care issues is quite ambiguous. A good number of studies (e.g., Crnic, Greenberg, Ragozin, Robinson, & Basham, 1983; Crockenberg, 1981) clearly suggest links between social support received and marital relations. Most likely, emotional support in the form of affect and interpersonal acceptance, instrumental help, and advice regarding parenting and childcare issues aid the familial system to maintain its adaptive balance which, in turn, may have an "enabling" effect on children's ability to make the transition to and become integrated into the day care peer group.

Potentially, social support can influence day care families' functioning in at least three different but interrelated ways. First, role strain emerging from the inability to effectively combine employment and parenting roles can be kept in check if parents develop and maintain strong social and interpersonal ties with relatives and friends. These individuals could provide the emotional refueling parents need in their tough and demanding multiple roles. Indeed, women benefit from having a social network of confidants who share similar values (Power &

Parke, 1984), and close contacts with others affect parental competence (see Abernathy, 1973; Powell, 1980). Second, emotional support from friends, relatives, and one's spouse can help allay guilt and anxiety that may ensue due to difficulty encountered in finding quality child care, leaving young children to return to work, and combining highly competitive roles that are time consuming. Take for example, a husband who is supportive to his wife: provides positive feedback, shares in childcare tasks, and becomes involved in his child's day care center along with his wife. This degree of support would inevitably have positive influences on mother-child and father-child relationships. Moreover, from a practical standpoint, paternal involvement in childcare related tasks may prevent women from becoming overburdened at home, while simultaneously placing the father in a position where he becomes more accessible to his child in the early process of socialization. Third, information from day care staff on children's performance in daycare and on parenting in general can help to develop continuity and consistency in socialization practices. The benefits here are obvious. Consistency and continuity in regulating children's behaviors would make children's transition from one environment to the other easier and parents' and caregivers' jobs less stressful.

Parents' Job Satisfaction/Status and Day Care

Although it is uncertain as to how husbands' and wives' job satisfaction and status affect their children's social and cognitive development in day care, we know that employment/unemployment affects parenting. The impact of economic loss on parent-child relationship has received thorough treatment in several recent reviews (e.g., McLoyd, 1989). Fathers who experienced heavy financial loss were irritable, tense, and explosive; these tendencies predisposed the men to becoming more punitive and inconsistent in their discipline. Needless to say, these types of parental strategies were associated with temper tantrums, irritability, and negativism in young children (Elder, 1979; Elder, Liker, & Cross, 1984; Elder, Nguyen, & Caspi, 1985). This is a particularly relevant issue in the 1990s given the massive economic problems facing families and children in all sectors of North American society. The severity of economic hardship can have severe implications for children's lives at home and could have spillover effects on children's behaviors in day care.

Other recent reviews on the effects of maternal employment (e.g., Hoffman, 1989); childcare and children's development (Belsky, 1990), parental employment and family life (Menaghan & Parcel, 1990) suggest links between employment patterns, job stability and satisfaction, work-family conflict and individual and family well-being. For the most part, jobs that provide opportunities for growth and self-direction would promote personal well-being, which should lead to a more positive orientation in the home. Unfortunately, most women are not in stable careers and a good number work outside of the home because they must. The economic problems in the 1990s will place an undue burden on families to achieve economic stability and to find adequate low cost child care for their children. It is highly unlikely that families who are economically strapped will be able to shield their children from the stresses associated with a lesser degree of job satisfaction and lower income.

Parent-Child Relationships and Children's Peer Relationships

Based on our discussion earlier, a prevailing assumption in the child development literature is that conflict-ridden familial relationships would have negative consequences for children's peer group participation, while more harmonious family relationships should foster the development of instrumental competencies that allow children to function in various social milieus. This view is substantiated by studies of the parent-child relationships of children sociometrically determined as popular or unpopular. Fathers of high-status boys provide more reinforcements, discourage aggressive behaviors, and use little punishment or deprivation of privileges (Wider & Rau, 1962); while rejected and isolated children appear to have patriarchal dominant family structures, with parents reporting low self-confidence, low preference for young children, infrequent use of praise, lack of promotion of independence, unreasonable expectations of children's behaviors, poor parenting skills, and negative reactions to the common intrusiveness of children (Perry, Jensen, & Adams, 1985). Related work has shown links between attachment security and peer group popularity (Easterbrooks & Lamb, 1979; Lieberman, 1977).

Perhaps the most compelling findings of concordance between the peer and parent-child systems come from a handful of studies that have attempted to delineate continuity in social relationships between parent-child interactions and peer group popularity and children's play. Mothers who were more positive and less disagreeable during parent-child interactions had children who were viewed as more popular in their classrooms (Putallaz, 1987), and observations of parental instructional strategies suggest that parents of popular children use more explanations and suggestions than parents of unpopular children (Roopnarine & Adams, 1987).

In the same vein, associations have been established between parental interpersonal behaviors and children's play interactions. Mothers', but not fathers', use of reasoning and guidance, and degree of involvement with children showed significant relationships with children's positive peer group interaction in nursery school that involved positive interchanges and cooperative play. The more reasoning and guidance mothers used, the less likely their children were to direct negative behaviors that involve aggression toward their peers (Roopnarine, 1987). And, in a psychophysiological study (Gottman & Katz, 1989) it was reported that couples who were assessed as angry and underaroused had children who engaged in low levels of play.

In all, these findings clearly demonstrate that there are strong ties between the parent-child and peer socialization systems. The relative importance of the wide range of family interpersonal variables on the development of peer social skills is largely unexplored. In the next few sections, we consider some factors that may influence day care children's peer group behaviors, in particular play.

Family Dynamics and Day Care Children's Peer Group Play

Following the theoretical propositions of Belsky (1984; 1990) and Bronfenbrenner (1986), we embarked upon a series of studies aimed at examining the links between parenting behaviors, marital relations, personal well-being, job satisfaction, social support and children's peer group play and social activities. In our initial work in this domain (Roopnarine, Mounts, & Casto, 1986; Roopnarine & Hempel, 1988), we conducted two surveys to assess parental satisfaction with their children's supplemental care, their perceptions of their own intrapersonal and interpersonal relationships and parent-child activities and children's development. Subsequently, we conducted observations of children's peer group play and assessed parents' interpersonal and intrapersonal functioning. Let us summarize our work starting with the parent perception data.

Survey Data

In a sample of 62 intact Euro-American families from lower- to middle-income backgrounds whose children were enrolled in full-time day care, and a sample of 58 families from almost identical backgrounds but whose children were enrolled in full-time family-based care, we gathered data on parenting skills, marital relationships and children's perceived development in day care (see Roopnarine et al., 1986). The portion of data from this study that are of importance to the current discussion involve the assessments of parent-child relationship, marital relationship, and children's cooperative activities and sharing behavior with peers. For the day care group, there was a positive association between perceptions of mother-child relationship and the emotional quality of husband-wife relationship ($r = .36, p < .05$) and a negative association between perceptions of mother-child relationship and marital conflict ($r = -.39$, $p < .05$). Although the correlations were in the same direction, significant associations were not found for mother-child relationship and marital relationship among families who used home-based care. In addition, neither parent-child relationship nor marital relationship was significantly related to mothers' assessments of children's cooperativeness and sharing behavior.

In another survey study that included 40 Euro-American middle-class families (Roopnarine & Hempel, 1988), we expanded our focus in our attempts to explore the relationship between the family system and daycare children's behaviors. Especially noteworthy in the second survey was the inclusion of measures that assess the emotional quality of the marriage, occupational satisfaction, and social support networks along with parental assessments of children's growth in day care. Mothers', but not fathers', assessments of their interactions with children were significantly associated with mothers' personal well-being ($r = .37$, $p < .01$), job satisfaction ($r = .40$, $p < .01$), and social activities and emotional support from others ($r = .37$, $p < .05$). With parent-child interaction partialled out, there were significant associations between mothers' assessments of marital companionship and their assessments of children's problem-solving skills ($r = .45$, $p < .01$), and between fathers' assessments of marital companionship and their assessments of children's problem-solving skills ($r = .38$, $p < .05$) and language development ($r = .41$, $p < .01$); the marital measures were not linked to assessments of children's social skills with peers, however.

Taken together, these data provide partial support for Belsky's (1984) contention that parent-child relations are embedded within the larger social contexts in which development occurs. Mothers' intrapersonal and interpersonal functioning were associated with their assessments of parent-child activities. Contrary to most of the extant data, the findings obtained from the two surveys failed to show significant links between parents' perceptions of parent-child relations and their perceptions of their children's peer group relations. This latter tendency may be due, in part, to the fact that we were assessing parental perceptions. Parents may not have been fully informed about the day to day social activities of their children in the day care environment and hence were not as "in tune" with their children's social skills. In the study described next, we observed children's peer play interactions in the day care setting to get a better picture of the complexity of their social participation.

Observational Data

Because of the importance accorded marital relationships for children's development (Belsky, 1984), we conducted a study of the marital relations and parenting behaviors in a separate sample of 40 middle-income Euro-American intact families and their 3- to 4-year-old children's peer group play in high quality day care centers. Since the study has been published elsewhere (see Roopnarine, Church, & Levy, 1990), an attempt will be made to provide an overall summary of our assessment techniques and the data. We will attempt to strengthen our presentation by providing a reanalysis of some of the data with an additional measure that was not included in the original report and with a more thorough discussion of children's play.

Mothers and fathers were asked to fill out two marital measures (*Marital Stress, Marital Companionship*) (see Miller & Sollie, 1980; Pearlin, 1975); the *Parent's Report* (Cohen, Dibble, & Grawe, 1977), and a personal well-being scale (see Campbell, Converse, & Rodgers, 1976). The marital measures were used to assess the emotional quality of the marriage and degree of companionability, while the personal well-being measure was employed to assess intrapersonal functioning. The parenting measure was aimed at gathering data on positive and negative parenting styles.

We focused on children's play interactions for several reasons. Play encompasses a good deal of children's activities in day care and should reflect differentiated patterns of cognitive and social growth. Researchers have shown that fairly complex cognitive activities are reflected in children's pretend play (Golomb & Cornelius, 1977; McCune-Nicolich, 1981; Rubin, 1980); that constructive play may be linked to children's problem-solving activity (Forman & Hill, 1980) and children may learn a sense of independence and initiative (Goldman, 1980), while solitary play involves goal-directed activities (Rubin, Maioni, & Hornung, 1976) and cooperative play may ease children into the development of good peer relationships (see Gottman & Parkhurst, 1980).

Different cognitive and social modes of play have been observed separately or in a nested system to examine the value of different toys and activities (Rubin, 1977), playground design (Campbell & Frost, 1985), effects of spatial density (Lidell & Kruger, 1989) and the impact of classroom structure on children's peer group participation (Mounts & Roopnarine, 1987; Shindler, Moely, & Frank, 1987). Interest in the role of play in the development of language, cognitive, and social skills have led to the categorization of play forms in terms of their complexity and adaptive value.

Starting with the work of Parten (1932), the social participation of preschoolers has been classified into unoccupied behavior, solitary play, onlooker behavior, parallel play, associative and cooperative play. Social participation was marked by a preponderance of solitary activity between 2 and 2¹/₂ years, parallel play between 2¹/₂ and 3¹/₂ years, and associative play between 3¹/₂ and 4¹/₂ years. In terms of the cognitive modes of play, Smilansky (1968) influenced by Piaget's (1962) conceptual framework on play, categorized play as functional (simple repetitive muscle movements with or without objects), constructive (manipulating objects to build something), dramatic (pretend activities), and games with rules (acceptance of prearranged rules and the adjustment of these rules). The development of these cognitive play forms appear in an invariant sequence with functional play appearing first and games with rules manifesting itself during concrete operations. Rubin and Maioni (1975) reported that preschoolers engage in significantly more functional and constructive play than in dramatic play or games with rules.

During the decades following Parten's observations, it has been suggested that parallel play may not be a stage of play but may instead be used as a "preparatory" phase for more complex peer group participation (Bakeman & Brownlee, 1980) and that about 50 percent of children's solitary play contained educational goal-directed activities (Moore, Everston, & Brophy, 1974). These findings have led developmental psychologists to question the relative importance of solitary and parallel play. From a complexity standpoint, solitary and cooperative play should be viewed as more mature than parallel play (see Johnson, Christie, & Yawkey, 1987).

By observing day care children's social and cognitive modes of play—solitary, parallel, functional, constructive, interactive, and dramatic—and correlating them with parents' marital relations, personal well-being, and parenting behaviors, we hoped to determine what modes of play are related to different dimensions of parents' interpersonal functioning and parenting styles. Of primary importance were the associations between personal well-being , marital relations and parenting styles and the relationship of both of these to lower and higher forms of social and cognitive modes of play.

Out of the 5 parenting behaviors assessed (use of guilt and anxiety, cold and detached treatment, warmth and child centeredness, respect for autonomy, and consistency) mothers' assessments of marital companionship showed a negative association with cold and detached treatment ($r = -.29, p < .06$) and their assessments of marital stress showed positive associations with guilt and anxiety ($r = .41, p < .01$). Interestingly, personal well-being did not show significant associations with parental behaviors. No significant associations were found between fathers' assessments of their marriage and personal well-being and parenting styles.

We also failed to find significant associations between the parenting variables and children's peer group play for both mothers and fathers. However, mothers' personal well-being was significantly associated with children's participation in dramatic play ($r = .30, p < .05$) and interactive play ($r = .36, p < .01$); mothers' assessments of their marital companionship were positively associated with children's participation in solitary play ($r = .35, p < .05$) and negatively with constructive play ($r = -.31, p < .05$) while their assessments of marital stress were negatively associated with dramatic play ($r = -.29, p < .05$). As was noted in the published report (Roopnarine et al., 1990), two path models confirmed the links between marital relations and children's play suggesting that for mothers only, marriage and personal well-being may have direct implications for children's participation in mature forms of play in the day care classroom.

Why did maternal personal well-being and marital relations, but not parenting, show significant associations with higher forms of children's cognitive and social modes of play? Child development experts (e.g., Gottman & Katz, 1989) have argued that the marriage contains affective qualities that may be powerful enough to influence children's play behaviors directly. With respect to marital stress, it may affect children's ability to regulate their emotional states. That is, in families riddled with conflict, children's affective states may be overwhelmed which, then, may have a negative impact on peer group participation (Gottman & Katz, 1989). By comparison, a healthy personal well-being, and good companionship in marriage would provide children with an atmosphere that is positive and warm. It seems likely that these adult characteristics would have positive consequences on children's social skills and peer group play.

Because our earlier work (Roopnarine, 1987; Roopnarine & Adams, 1987) indicated good associations between parental socialization variables and peer group behaviors, the lack of associations between the two sets of measures in this latter investigation was surprising. As we did not observe parent-child interactions, it is hard to say what our assessments of parental behaviors mean. Holden and Edwards (1989) argue that most parental measures do not consider parents' social-cognitive understanding of instrument items and thus purely perceptual data may be inaccurate. Furthermore, our assessments of parental behavior may be suspect given that we noted dissatisfaction in parental modes of functioning.

Finally, the lack of significant associations between father-child relationships, fathers' marital relationship and personal well-being and children's social activities and play were quite consistent across studies. It is generally held that men still show ancillary involvement in childcare and household tasks regardless of whether their wives work outside of the home or not, and role renegotiations and interpersonal relationships are often viewed within a traditional framework. Thus, fathers' appraisals of their interpersonal relationships may not give a true picture of how they feel and behave and consequently would not be expected to be significantly correlated with children's social skills.

Implications and Summary

Our data begin to address two key issues in the provision of quality care for young children outside of the home. Foremost, the link between parent-child activities and marital relations, and marital relations and children's peer group play point to the importance of interpersonal relationships in the home for children's participation in the peer group. Early childhood educators who are aware of these links may be better able to meet the social and cognitive needs of children in the day care environment by considering both parental and childhood functioning variables in concert. This, then, should enhance intervention efforts or curriculum modification.

Next, delineating the link between parents' interpersonal functioning and children's peer group play in day care provides us with pertinent information on continuity/discontinuity in children's adaptation between the home and day care environments. Thus, data on two adjoining and complementary socialization systems could have implications for caregiver-parent child relations particularly for maintaining similar socialization and cognitive goals for children and for caregiver-child relationships.

It is our hope that the above discussion of the family correlates of daycare children's play behaviors will complement other research in the area that focuses on issues that pertain to quality care but are tied more directly to the day care environment. However, there is an explicit need to examine concordance between the parent-child and day care systems simultaneously, because the degree to which one influences the other could undermine or aid children's participation in their day care peer group and affect family development.

REFERENCES

Abernathy, V. (1973). Social network and response to the maternal role. *International Journal of Sociology of the Family, 3*, 86-92.

Bakeman, R., & Brownlee, J. (1980). The strategic use of parallel play: A sequential analysis. *Child Development, 51*, 873-878.

Baumrind, D. (1967). Child care practices anteceding three patterns of preschool behavior. *Genetic Psychology Monographs, 75*, 43-88.

Baumrind, D. (1971). Current patterns of parental authority. *Developmental Psychology Monographs, 4* (1, Part 2).

Belsky, J. (1984). The determinants of parenting: A process model. *Child Development, 55*, 83-96.

Belsky, J. (1990). Parental and nonparental child care and children's socioemotional development: A decade in review. *Child Development, 52*, 885-903.

Belsky, J., Gilstrap, B., & Rovine, M. (1984). The Pennsylvania Infant and Family Development Project, I: Stability and change in mother-infant and father-infant interaction in a family setting at one, three, and nine months. *Child Development, 55*, 692-705.

Bronfenbrenner, U. (1986). Ecology of the family as a context for human development: Research perspectives. *Developmental Psychology, 22*, 723-742.

Campbell, A., Converse, P., & Rodgers, N. (1976). *The Quality of American Life*. New York: Russell Sage.

Campbell, S. D., & Frost, J. L. (1985). The effects of playground type on the cognitive and social play behaviors of grade two children. In J. L. Frost & S. Sunderlin (Eds.), *When Children Play* (pp. 81-88). Wheaton, MD: Association for Childhood Education International.

Clarke-Stewart, K. A. (1989). Infant day care: Maligned or malignant. *American Psychologist, 44*, 266-273.

Cohen, D. J. Dibble, E., & Grawe, J. M. (1977). Parental style. *Archives of General Psychiatry, 34*, 445-451.

Crnic, K. A., Greenberg, M. T., Ragozin, A. S., Robinson, N. M., & Basham, R. B. (1983). Effects of stress and social support on mothers and premature and full-term infants. *Child Development, 54*, 209-217.

Crockenburg, S. B. (1981). Infant irritability, mother responsiveness, and social support influences on the security of infant-mother attachment. *Child Development, 52*, 857-865.

Easterbrooks, M. A., & Lamb, M. E. (1979). The relationship between quality of infant-mother attachment and infant competence in initial encounters with peers. *Child Development, 50*, 380-387.

Elder, G. (1979). Historical change in life patterns and personality. In P. Baltes & O. Brim (Eds.), *Life Span Development and Behavior* (Vol. 2, pp. 117-159. New York: Academic Press.

Elder, G., Liker, J., & Cross, C. (1984). Parent-child behavior in the Great Depression: Life course and intergenerational influences. In P. Baltes & O. Brim (Eds.), *Life Span Development and Behavior* (Vol. 6, pp. 109-158). Orlando, FL: Academic Press.

Elder, G., Caspi, A., & Nguyen, T. (1986). Resourceful and vulnerable children: Family influence in hard times. In R. K. Silbereisen, K. Eyferth, & G. Rudinger (Eds.), *Development As Action in Context* (pp. 167-186). New York: Springer-Verlag.

Emery, R. (1982). Interparental conflict and the children of discord and divorce. *Psychological Bulletin, 92*, 310-330.

Forman, G., & Hill, F. (1980). *Constructive Play: Applying Piaget in the Preschool.* Monterey, CA: Brooks Cole.

Goldman, J. (1981). Social participation in same-age and mixed-age classrooms. *Child Development, 52*, 644-650.

Golomb, C., & Cornelius, C. (1977). Symbolic play and its cognitive significance. *Developmental Psychology, 13*, 246-252.

Gottman, J. M., & Katz, L. F. (1989). Effects of marital discord on young children's peer interaction and health. *Developmental Psychology, 25*, 373-381.

Gottman, J., & Parkhurst, J. (1980). A developmental theory of friendship and acquaintanceship process. In A. Collins (Ed.), *Minnesota Symposium of Child Psychology* (Vol. 13). Hillsdale, NJ: Erlbaum.

Hartup, W. W. (1979). The two social worlds of childhood. *American Psychologist, 34*, 944-950.

Hoffman, L. (1989). Effects of maternal employment in the two-parent family. *American Psychologist, 44*, 283-292.

Holden, G. W., & Edwards, L. A. (1989). Parental attitudes toward child rearing: Instruments, issues, and implications. *Psychological Bulletin, 106,* 29-58.

Johnson, J., Christie, J., & Yawkey, T. (1987). *Play and Early Childhood Education.* Evanston, IL: Scott-Foresman.

Lamb, M. E., Owen, M. T., & Chase-Lansdale, L. (1979). The father-daughter relationship: Past, present and future. In C. B. Kopp & M. Kirkpatrick (Eds.), *Becoming Female: Perspectives on Development.* New York: Plenum.

Lieberman, A. (1977). Preschooler's competence with a peer: Relation with attachment and peer experience. *Child Development, 48,* 1277-1287.

Liddell, C., & Kruger, P. (1989). Activity and social behavior in a crowded South African township nursery: A follow-up study on the effects of crowding at home. *Merrill-Palmer Quarterly, 35,* 209-226.

McCune-Nicholich, L. (1981). Toward symbolic functioning: Structure and early pretend games and potential parallels with language. *Child Development, 52,* 785-797.

McLoyd, V. C. (1989). Socialization and development in a changing economy: The effects of paternal job and income loss on children. *American Psychologist, 44,* 293-302.

Menaghan, E. G., & Parcel, T. L. (1990). Parental employment and family life: Research in the 1980s. *Journal of Marriage and the Family, 52,* 1079-1098.

Miller, B. C., & Sollie, D. L. (1980). Normal stresses during the transition to parenthood. *Family Relations, 29,* 459-465.

Mondell, S., & Tyler, F. (1981). Parental competence and styles of problem-solving/play behavior with children. *Developmental Psychology, 17,* 73-78.

Moore, N. V., Evertson, C. M., & Brophy, J. E. (1974). Solitary play: Some functional reconsiderations. *Developmental Psychology, 10,* 830-934.

Mounts, N. S., & Roopnarine, J. L. (1987). Social-cognitive play patterns in same-age and mixed-age preschool classrooms. *American Educational Research Journal, 24,* 463-476.

Parten, M. B. (1932). Social participation among preschool children. *Journal of Abnormal and Social Psychology, 27,* 243-269.

Patterson, G. R., DeBaryshe, B. D. & Ramsey, E. (1989). A developmental perspective on antisocial behavior. *American Psychologist, 44,* 329-335.

Pearlin, L. (1975). Status inequality and stress in marriage. *American Sociological Review, 40,* 344-357.

Pederson, F. (1982). Mother, father, and infant as an interactive system. J. Belsky (Ed.), *In the Beginning: Readings on Infancy.* New York: Columbia University Press.

Peery, J. C., Jensen, L., & Adams, G. R. (1985). Relationship between parents attitudes regarding child rearing and the sociometric status of their preschool children. *Journal of Psychology, 119,* 567-574.

Piaget, J. (1962). *Play, dreams and imitation in childhood.* New York: Norton.

Powell, D. R. (1980). Personal social networks as a focus for primary prevention of child maltreatment. *Infant Mental Health Journal, 1,* 232-239.

Power, T., & Parke, R. (1984). Social network factors and the transition to parenthood. *Sex Roles, 10,* 949-972.

Putallaz, M. (1987). Maternal behavior and children's sociometric status. *Child Development, 58,* 324-340.

Roopnarine, J. L. (1987). Social interaction within the peer group: Relationship to perceptions of parenting and to children's interpersonal awareness and problem solving ability. *Journal of Applied Development Psychology, 8,* 351-362.

Roopnarine, J. L., & Adams, G. R. (1987). The interactional teaching patterns of mothers and fathers with their popular, moderately popular, or unpopular children. *Journal of Abnormal Child Psychology, 15,* 125-136.

Roopnarine, J. L., Church, C. C., & Levy, G. D. (1990). Day care children's play behaviors: Relationship to their mothers' and fathers' assessments of their parenting behaviors, marital stress, and marital companionship. *Early Childhood Research Quarterly, 5,* 335-346.

Roopnarine, J. L. & Hempel, L. M. (1988). Day care and family dynamics. *Early Childhood Research Quarterly, 3,* 427-438.

Roopnarine, J. L., Mounts, N. S., & Casto, G. (1986). Mothers' perceptions of their children's supplemental care experience: Correlation with spousal relationship. *American Journal of Orhtopsychiatry, 56,* 581-587.

Rubin, K. H. (1977). The social and cognitive value of preschool toys and activities. *Canadian Journal of Behavioral Science, 9,* 382-385.

Rubin, K. (1980). Fantasy play: its role in the development of social skills and social cognition. In K. Rubin (Ed.) *Children's Play* (pp. 69-85). San Francisco: Jossey-Bass

Rubin, K., & Maioni, T. (1975). Play preference and its relationship to egocentricism, popularity and classification skills in preschoolers. *Merrill-Palmer Quarterly, 21,* 171-179.

Rubin, K., Maioni, T., & Hornung, M. (1976). Free play behavior in middle- and lower-class preschoolers: Parten and Piaget revisited. *Child Development, 47,* 414-419.

Schindler, P. J., Moely, B. E., & Frank, A. L. (1987). Time in day care and social participation of young children. *Developmental Psychology, 23,* 255-261.

Sears, R. R., Maccoby, E. E., & Levin, H. (1957). *Patterns of Child Rearing.* Evanston, IL: Harper & Row.

Smilansky, S. (1968). *The effects of sociodramatic play on disadvantaged preschool children.* New York: Wiley.

Weisman, M. M., & Paykel, E. S. (1974). *The depressed woman: A study of social relations.* Chicago: University of Chicago Press.

Winder, C. L., & Rau, L. (1962). Parental attitudes associated with social deviance in preadolescent boys. *Journal of Abnormal and Social Psychology, 64,* 418-424.

4

Infant Day Care Facilitates Later Social Behavior and School Performance

Tiffany M. Field

One of the ongoing concerns about infant day care relates to reports of later assertiveness, aggressivity, noncompliance and uncooperativeness with peers and adults. These data have been primarily reviewed by Belsky in a few provocative papers (Belsky, 1986; 1987; 1988). In the first of these Belsky (1986) suggested that infants who experienced day care anytime during the first year showed later negative behaviors such as these. For example, he cites a study by Schwartz et al (Schwartz, Strickland & Krolick, 1974) who reported that preschool children who had attended infant day care were more verbally and physically aggressive with their peers and adults, and were less tolerant of frustration and less cooperative with adults. Similarly, he notes that Farber and Egeland (1982) reported less compliance, less persistence in dealing with difficult problems and more negative affect in day care infants even though the effects were not persistent beyond two years. In still a third sample infants who had received day care during their first year showed decreased compliance and temper tantrums (Rubenstein, Howes & Boyle, 1981). Finally, in the Bermuda preschool study maladjustment (a rating of children's anxiety levels by caregivers) was greater in the Bermuda preschoolers who were cared for in family day care homes (McCartney, Scarr, Phillips, Grajeck & Schwartz, 1982). Barton and Schwartz (1981) also noted higher levels of misbehavior and greater social withdrawal in the same population.

In contrast, other studies suggest more positive outcomes for infants experiencing day care during the first year of life (c.f. Phillips, McCartney, Scarr and Howes, 1987, reply to Belsky). In a study by Howes and Stewart (1986), for example, children (and particularly boys) who entered day care as younger infants and experienced very few changes in day care were more likely to engage in higher levels of play with objects. In another center children with extensive experience in day care centers showed a lower incidence of hitting, kicking and pushing than children with less day care experience (Haskins, 1985). Other

The author would like to thank the children and teachers who participated in this study and the research assistants who assisted in collecting data. This research was supported by grants #MH40779 and #MH00331 to Tiffany Field. Requests for reprints should be sent to Tiffany Field, Mailman Center for Child Development, University of Miami Medical School, P.O. Box 016820, Miami, FL 33101.

positive reports include that by Howes and Rubenstein (1985) who noted higher frequencies of touching and laughing in children who entered day care at extremely young ages (between two and 20 months). In addition Schwartz et al (Schwartz, Krolick & Strickland, 1973) noted that children experiencing infant day care showed more positive affect and less anxiety when entering their peer group and had higher social interaction scores than children who entered day care at the preschool age. Thus the negative and the positive data are inconsistent.

In his more recent review, Belsky (1988) more specifically ascribed these negative outcomes to center-based care in the first year. He claimed that based on the Bermuda studies (McCartney et al, 1982; Schwartz, 1983), Scarr (1983) had recently suggested that center-based care in the first year may be the most problematic of the types of day care. Belsky then suggested that empirical support for infants from centers being most at risk comes from a number of investigations linking aggression, noncompliance and maladjustment of children with center-based infant care (Haskins, 1985; McCartney et al, 1982; Rubenstein et al, 1981; Schwartz et al, 1974). Again, however, there are positive data which appear to be inconsistent with those data implicating center-based care as the most risky. For example in at least two studies infants who had received center-based care showed an increased ability to get along with their peers and were not noncompliant and uncooperative with adults (Gunnarson, 1978; McCrae & Herbert-Jackson, 1975). Dismissing those findings, Belsky (1988) cites the studies of Haskins (1985) and Schwartz et al. (1974) as having documented that subjects who displayed heightened aggression in those studies were cared for in high quality, university-affiliated programs.

There are a number of reasons for the inconsistency in this literature. One of the most obvious is that the data are confounded by differences between families who elect to place their children in day care and families who do not (including differences in family stress, single versus two parent caregiving, dual versus single wage earning families, etc). Other confounds are differences in the child's age of entry into care, length of time in care and stability and quality of care. A more acceptable design would be a comparison of infants who received day care and who were denied day care in the same setting, the latter remaining on the waiting list. To alleviate the most serious confound, comparisons could be made between early versus later day care in the same center or in centers of similar quality. Similarly, part-time and full-time care could be assessed in the same or similar quality centers. To address the question of early day care per se, it would seemingly be important to observe quality care inasmuch as nobody would ever advocate nonquality care.

Because reviews of the literature such as those by Belsky are still raising questions about negative outcomes for infants who experienced early day care, and now particularly for infants who experience that care in center-based programs with some implication that even those who experienced quality center-based care were at risk, more studies are needed on the outcomes of children who experienced quality center-based care. The purpose of this chapter is to review studies in which we compared early versus later infant care in groups that started at different times within the same high quality infant care center and comparisons between infants who started part-time care at early ages and those who started at later ages in a family cooperative infant nursery of the same quality as the full-time infant care center. These data have been presented elsewhere (Field et al, 1988). In addition, we will present new data on children who attended that quality day care center and are now in grade school. And, finally, we will present correlational data from a group of 60 preadolescents (in sixth grade) who attended quality center-based day care for different periods of time. Basically, the data from these three studies converge to suggest that children who experience more years of day care are advantaged socially, emotionally and academically.

Study 1

Early Versus Later Infant Care and Part-Time Versus Full-Time Infant Care

In this study (Field et al, 1988) comparisons were made between infants who received early versus later infant care in groups who started at different times within the same high quality infant care center. Comparisons were also made between infants who started part-time care at early ages and those who started at later ages in a different family cooperative infant nursery of the same quality as the full-time infant day care center. The environment and curriculum of both of the centers were designed by the same individuals, the centers were located near each other and they served families from the same middle-class socioeconomic and educational backgrounds. The children in the infant care center attended full-time, while the infants in the family cooperative center attended parent-child classes with their mothers for an hour and a half per week. Children did not begin center care in the family center without a parent until they were two years old. The presence of the mother in part-time versus full-time infant care was clearly confounded in the latter center. Nonetheless, data from both centers were used to address the question of early versus later infant care and part-time versus full-time day care.

Method

Samples and Programs

The sample for the full-time infant day care center was 36 preschool children ranging in age from 25 months to 65 months (M = 44.4 mos.). Seventeen of these children had entered day care during the first six months of infancy and 19 had entered after six months of age. The children who were members of the late entry infant care group had to remain in home care with their mothers because of a long waiting list. The sample for the part-time family center program was 35 preschool children ranging in age from 23 to 68 months (M = 48.3). The programs were similar in philosophy, curriculum, teacher training, teacher-child ratios and organization of the environment. In both settings the development of language, creativity, imaginative play, problem solving and social skills was reinforced through a variety of learning opportunities. Classrooms were divided into learning centers with a large portion of the space devoted to imaginative play and creative activities. Similarly, both centers had highly imaginative playgrounds for fantasy and gross motor play.

Procedures

The children, at the preschool stage, were compared on their reunion behaviors with their parents, their peer interactions, and their teachers' and parents' ratings of their behavior. For an assessment of their reunion behavior we used the Field et al procedure (Field, Gewirtz, Cohen, Garcia, Greenberg & Collins, 1984), which effectively differentiated children with ambivalent versus children with nonambivalent detachment styles. For these observations behaviors were coded on a simple behavior checklist from the time the parent entered the playground until the parent and child left. The parent behaviors included: calls child, moves toward child, smiles, kisses-hugs, and talks to child. The child behaviors included: calls parent, moves toward parent, smiles, reaches to parent, hugs-kisses, talks to parent, continues play, moves away and leads departure. In addition, the child was assigned an attachment rating based on the child's general reunion behavior as (a) anxious-avoidant; (b) securely attached; or (c) anxious-resistant. Peer interactions were assessed during freeplay playground observations. They were coded for those behaviors that had been previously highlighted in the literature including withdrawal behavior, different levels of play, affect and aggression. Behaviors included aimless wandering, watching, solitary, parallel and cooperative play, constructive and fantasy play, smiling-laughing, fussing-crying, gross motor activity, positive and negative verbal interaction, positive and negative physical interaction, interaction directed towards another child or adult and seeking comfort from an adult. Finally, behaviors were rated by the mothers and the head teacher of the children on the Preschool Behavior Rating Scale (Behar and Stringfield, 1974) and the Preschool Behavior Questionnaire (Schwartz, 1974). These scales were used since they had been featured in previous studies on day care/non-day care comparisons.

Results

The results of this study can be summarized as follows: a) The early versus late entry groups did not differ on any of the parent or child reunion behaviors or attachment ratings; b) No differences were noted between the early (less than 6 months) versus later (greater than 6 months) entry children or the full time versus part-time children on any of the teacher ratings. However, when the total samples of full-time versus part-time day care were compared the ratings on aggression and assertiveness were higher for children in the full-time program. No differences emerged, in contrast, on the parent ratings. c) On the peer interaction data, no differences emerged between the early versus the late entry children on any of the play behaviors. However subtle differences were noted between the early entry full-time versus the early entry part-time samples. The part-time sample engaged in significantly more watching, solitary play and teacher comfort-seeking behavior and in less cooperative play and positive affect behavior (smiling/laughing) than did their full-time peers (See Table 4.1). Similarly, when the total full-time and part-time samples were compared, the less experienced part-time children showed more watching, solitary play and teacher comfort-seeking behavior along with less cooperative play and less positive affect.

Table 4.1   Mean Proportion of Time That Play Behaviors Occurred in Full-time and Part-time Day care Samples with Early (≤6 months) and Late (> 6 months) Entries to Day care (*p < .001 for adjacent groups). Interobserver Reliabilities are in Parentheses.

Play behaviors	FULL-TIME		PART-TIME		F.T. total[2]		P.T. total[2]
	Early	Late	Early	Late			
Wandering (.78)	7.3	5.9	8.8	7.2	5.8		8.4
Watching (.79)	17.0[1]	15.8	40.4[1]	38.1	15.4	*	39.8
Solitary play (.84)	23.1[1]	16.8	46.7[1]	23.8	15.6	*	34.6
Parallel play (.85)	14.0	12.9	14.6	13.7	12.7		14.8
Cooperative play (.94)	30.1[1]	40.7	10.3[1]	28.5	41.2	*	17.7
Constructive play (.85)	26.2	34.5	15.6	27.6	32.7		22.0
Fantasy play (.89)	12.4	17.9	8.9	18.8	18.2		13.0
Smiling/laughing (.90)	7.9[1]	11.8	3.2[1]	6.4	10.8	*	4.6
Fussing/crying (.87)	.8	.6	.7	.4	1.2		1.0
Gross motor activ. (.89)	35.8	26.2	38.9	26.0	30.7		29.7
Pos. verbal inter. (81)	17.9	25.3	22.4	32.8	27.5		24.0
Neg. verbal inter. (.89)	1.9	1.9	1.0	1.5	2.0		1.2
Pos. phys. inter. (.82)	1.2	.8	1.0	1.8	1.0		1.6
Neg. phys. inter. (.83)	.9	.6	.9	1.6	.8		1.4
Inter. child (.92)	28.2	32.1	15.9	38.8	33.2		24.3
Inter. adult (.96)	5.5	5.4	6.1	5.2	5.5		5.4
Teacher com. seek (.80)	1.1[1]	.3	2.7[1]	2.0	.5	*	2.4

NOTE.   [1]DIFFERENCES BETWEEN EARLY FULL-TIME AND EARLY PART-TIME GROUPS AT P < .001.
[2]ADJUSTED CALL MEANS RESULTING FROM ANCOVA ON CURRENT AGE.

Discussion

These data suggest that children who receive quality center-based care as infants are not at risk, as Belsky has suggested (Belsky, 1988). To the contrary, early and later entry infants showed no differences on attachment (reunion) behavior and sociability. In fact, children with more day care experience appeared to be more advantaged, namely they were more socially interactive. Children with greater day care experience showed less watching, solitary play and teacher comfort-seeking behavior as well as more cooperative play and positive affect. They also spent more time interacting with their peers and had more frequent positive verbal interactions. Although the teachers' ratings of them as being more assertive—aggressive could be construed as a negative finding, the more objective playground observation data yielded a very low incidence of observed aggression (both verbal and physical) and identical amounts of aggression in the full- and part-time children.

As Field et al pointed out there were some limitations of this study as follows: a) the assessments were made at only one point in time rather than over several periods; b) the age of the child entry and length of time in the part-time program limited between-group comparisons in that sample; and c) six months may have been an inappropriate cut-off between early and late entry groups given the possibility that children who are placed in infant care at the height of attachment formation (between six and 18 months) may be more disrupted by early entry than infants placed at either an earlier or later age. Finally, the children in this study were only preschool age, suggesting the need for a longer term follow-up, for example at the grade school period. For that reason follow-up data were collected on the same sample at grade school age and are presented in Study 2.

Study 2

Grade School Follow-Up Data on Children Who Attended Full-Time Day Care in a Quality Center-Based Infant Nursery

This questionnaire study was designed to assess the parents' perceptions and the child's perceptions of the grade school stage in children who had been cared for in our nursery program. Questionnaires were used, as opposed to live observations, because the children were currently attending several different schools in distant locations. Since much of the negative infant day care outcome literature is based on parent and teacher questionnaires, and because there was no reason to expect variability in adequacy of parents' reports in this homogeneously, well-educated sample of mothers, we considered the questionnaire format adequate.

Sample and Programs

The sample was comprised of 28 children ranging in age from five to eight years (M = 6.8 years). The children, on average, were in second grade (range = kindergarten through fourth grade). On average the children had started infant day care at 10.9 months and had spent a mean of 3.1 years in this nursery school.

Infant/toddler programs. Since the environment is always an important aspect of the quality of day care, a description will be given here. The infant nursery, which serves 16 infants, provided free-play stimulation in a large room (14m x 16m) which separated (by a folding door) sleep and play areas. The play area (7m x 8m) was completely carpeted in a soft crawlable carpet and featured a multilevel structure with a sunken waterbed, slopes, stairs for crawling and climbing practice and "busy board" manipulable objects installed in the walls of the structure. The second large structure featured a mirror slide and a tunnel with a sunroof. Outdoor eating and play areas were entered from the classroom by a wall of sliding glass doors. The teacher-child ratio was 1:4. The toddler nursery, which served 16 toddlers (age 15 months to 24 months) provided free play and a preschool readiness curriculum. This room (9m x 6m) featured a number of learning center-play areas separated by shelving containing the objects for those areas. Included were a block area, doll area, and puzzle-art area on the first level and an elevated level that included a circular staircase leading to a reading loft and a catwalk terminating in a slide and landing pad. This room also featured an outdoor play area entered by a sliding glass wall. The teacher-child ratio was 1:5.

Procedures

A list of 40 children who had graduated from this school in the last few years were sent a packet of questionnaires. The parents were given a demographic questionnaire, the internalizer-externalizer scale (Buck, 1977) to rate their own introverted-extraverted behavior, and the Behavior Rating Scale (Santrock & Warshak, 1979) for rating their child's behavior. The demographic questionnaire included a number of background questions on the child (age, years in school, whether the child was in the gifted program, specific honors the child had received, specific extracurricular activities the child participated in and the number of friends the child had).

The Buck internalizer-externalizer scale essentially taps introversion-extraversion and was given to determine whether this factor had any relationship to children's ongoing performance and whether the parent ratings are similar to the children's ratings. This 20-item scale is rated on a 5-point Likert type rating from "not at all characteristic" to "always characteristic." Examples of items, "I am warm and friendly to others," "I am shy," and "I have many friends." The

Behavior Rating Scale (Santrock & Warshak, 1979) is a 33-item questionnaire which is scored on a 5-point scale (not typical to very typical). This rating scale is summarized by four factors including peer relations, work-study habits, emotional well-being, and adult-child relations. Parents were also asked to rate the children using a Likert-type rating scale on attractiveness, assertiveness, aggressiveness, popularity and leadership characteristics.

In the same questionnaire package the child was asked to complete the Piers-Harris Children's Self Concept Scale (Piers & Harris, 1969) and to draw a self-portrait with a set of magic markers. The Piers-Harris Children's Self Concept Scale is entitled "what I am like" and is comprised of 80 bipolar yes-no items such as "I am a happy person," "It is hard for me to make friends," "I get worried when we have tests in school," and "I have good ideas." The children's version of the Buck (1977) internalizer-externalizer scale was also given to the children to assess their extraversion-introversion. The self-portraits the children were asked to draw were coded subsequently for a number of features including use of dull colors, use of single color, missing body parts, displaced-distorted body parts, small size of drawing and unhappy face. High scores on self-drawings have been correlated with depressed mood state in previous studies on childhood stress (Field & Reite, 1984).

Results

Because the primary question for this follow-up study was the relationship between the amount of time spent in infant day care and later social-emotional-behavioral outcomes, a correlation model was used for analysis of data. The means and correlation coefficients are given in Table 4.2. As can be seen in Table 4.2, more than half of this group of 28 children had been assigned to the gifted programs in the public school system. In addition the children averaged 1.5 honors (SD = 1.5), 2.2 extracurricular activities (SD = 1.2) and 4 friends (SD = 1.7). Also as can be seen in Table 4.2, a number of significant relations emerged in the correlation analysis. Amount of time spent in infant care was positively related to the number of extracurricular activities (r = .40) and the number of friends (r = .48). Relations between parents' ratings on the child behavior rating scale and amount of time in day care included positive relations between amount of time in day care and emotional well-being (r = .31), leadership (r = .40), popularity (r = .47), attractiveness (r = .34), assertiveness (r = .34) and a negative relation to aggressiveness (r = -.57). The only relation found for the children's data was a negative relation between their drawing ratings and the amount of time they spent in the school (r = -.80), suggesting that the greater amount of time spent in infant care the less depressed the child was as evidenced by characteristics of the self-portraits. Low ratings on these drawings have also been associated with positive self-esteem in previous studies.

Table 4.2   Means and Correlation Coefficients for Those Variables

Significantly Correlated with Time Spent in University

Day Care Program (N = 28, p < .05).

BACKGROUND VARIABLES	MEAN	S.D.	CORRELATION COEFFICIENT
Age	6.8	2.5	—
Years in day care program	3.1	1.4	—
Current grade in school	2.1	2.3	—
# children in gifted	19		—
# honors	1.5	1.5	—
# extracurricular activities	2.2	1.2	.40
# friends	4.0	1.7	.48
CHILD VARIABLES			
Self-drawing	1.9	1.3	-.80
Piers-Harris self-esteem	65.1	4.8	—
Internalizer/Externalizer	83.5	7.1	—
PARENT RATINGS			
Internalizer/externalizer	26.1	7.0	—
CHILD BEHAVIORS			
Peer relations	4.1	.5	—
Work study	4.1	.7	—
Emotional well-being	4.4	.5	.38
Adult/child relations	3.9	.4	—
Attractiveness	4.7	.5	.39
Assertiveness	4.4	.8	.39
Aggressivity	3.4	1.0	−.57
Popularity	4.3	.8	.47
Leadership	4.2	1.0	.40

Discussion

Judging from the children's self-portraits those with more infant care appeared to be less depressed and have higher self esteem. By parent report those children with more infant care were also more involved with friends and extracurricular activities and were judged more attractive and popular. This is perhaps not surprising because these children have had more extensive experience with other children which could be expected to lead to greater social skills and popularity. The positive relations between amount of infant care and assertiveness and leadership abilities are probably related to each other. The positive relation with assertiveness and the highly negative relation with aggressiveness suggests that these two dimensions are very separate in the minds of these parents. Although Belsky (1986) has claimed that preschoolers who attended infant day care show "heightened aggressiveness, noncompliance and withdrawal," this study, much like our previous study on preschoolers, suggests that there is a positive relationship to assertiveness but a negative relationship to aggressiveness. Finally, the positive relation noted between emotional well-being and years in infant care probably reflects a similar relation noted between the child's self-esteem (his self-portrait) and years of infant care.

These data, like the data from study 1, suggest no undesirable outcomes for grade school age children who started day care at an early age of 10 months. Instead, they once again suggest that children with a greater quantity of infant care are showing more social interaction in the form of friends and popularity, greater assertiveness (but not aggressiveness), and greater emotional well-being. It is, of course, conceivable that mothers who place their children in infant care earlier simply have a more positive, socially-oriented mindset about their children. In this regard it is interesting that in this correlation analysis the mother's extraversion score on the Buck (1977) externalizing-internalizing scale was correlated positively with all the positive child traits and negatively with all the child negative traits. Extraverted mothers may tend to enter their children in infant care at an earlier date just as they ensure that their children are entered into the gifted program, participate in extracurricular activities, have lots of friends around them and then positively rate their children on qualities such as emotional well-being, attractiveness, popularity and leadership skills.

Because both Study 1 and Study 2 were based on South Florida's model infant care programs, the question arises as to whether these data generalize to other quality day care programs. In addition, the children of Study 2 were on average only two years older than the children of Study 1, suggesting the importance of follow-up data from an even older age group. Study 3 was conducted to explore the effects of day care on preadolescents who had received varying amounts of day care in a variety of day care centers.

Study 3

Relations Between Amount of Infant Care and Sixth Grade Performance

In this study the question of day care was very peripheral to the central purpose of studying preadolescent friend pairs versus acquaintance pairs. The study was conducted in a school attended by children from middle SES, highly educated, multi-ethnic parents who happened to have sent their children to day care primarily because the parents were dual career families. For this study peer interactions were videotaped, the teachers rated the children's behavior, and the child's final grades were obtained from the school principal.

Method

Sample

The sample was recruited from the two sixth grade classes at a University laboratory elementary school. Fifty-six children constituted the final, fairly heterogeneous ethnic sample (Caucasian, Black, and Hispanic). The children came from middle socioeconomic status, highly educated parents and averaged 11.5 years of age at the time of the study.

Procedures

Following a series of sociogram procedures completed by the children and their teachers, children were assigned to best friend dyads to be videotaped during face-to-face interactions. The children were asked to have a conversation about anything they desired. Following the interaction the children were given the Piers-Harris Self-Concept Scale (Piers and Harris, 1969) to determine whether close friends were more similar than acquaintances on the level of their self-confidence. This scale as has been previously noted, is labeled "What I am like" and is comprised of 80 bipolar yes-no items such as "I get worried when we have tests in school", "It is hard for me to make friends", "I am a happy person", and "I have good ideas". The teachers were given the same behavior rating scale that had been given to the parents in Study 2 (Santrock and Warshak, 1979). This is, once again, a 33-item questionnaire which is scored on a 5-point scale (not typical to very typical). This rating scale is summarized by four factors including peer relations, work/study habits, emotional well-being and adult/child relations. The teachers were also asked to rate the children using a Likert-type rating scale on attractiveness, assertiveness, aggressiveness, popularity and leadership attributes. The videotapes of the children's 10-minute face-to-face conversations were coded for affect, vocalization, activity level, physical affection and playfulness. These were rated on a 5-point Likert-type scale.

Results

Once again, because all of these children attended infant day care (in relatively high quality centers), the question was how the amount of infant care was related to child outcomes. Thus, once again, a correlation model was used.

As can be seen in Table 4.3, a number of interesting relations emerged. Of the interaction behavior ratings, physical affection was significantly related to years in day care (r = .19) Extraversion in the child, as rated by the child, was also positively related to years in day care (r = .20). On the teacher behavior rating scale the following ratings were positively related to years of day care: a) emotional well-being (r = .32); b) attractiveness (r = .39); and c) assertiveness (r = .20). In the area of academics, assignment to the gifted program was positively related to years in day care (r = .29) and of the three final sixth-grade grades (reading, writing and math), the math grade was significantly related to years in day care (r = .38).

Table 4.3   Correlation Coefficients of Variables Significantly Correlated with Time Spent in Day Care Center Programs (N = 56, p < .05)

VARIABLES	CORRELATION COEFfiCIENT
Physical affection toward peers	.19
Extraversion (self-rating)	.20
Teacher ratings	
• emotional well-being	.32
• attractiveness	.39
• assertiveness	.20
Academic performance	
• gifted program	.29
• final math grade	.38

Discussion

Once again, children with more infant day care were rated as more attractive and assertive by adult figures in their lives, in this case teachers (in Study 2, mothers). And, once again, assertiveness is clearly distinguished from aggressiveness by the teachers (assertiveness was related –.88 to aggressiveness in the teachers' ratings). Assertiveness could have been mistaken for aggressiveness in some of the previous studies reporting that negative outcome for infant day care. It is interesting that the mothers of Study 2 whose children received more infant care rated their children's emotional well-being, attractiveness and assertiveness higher, and similarly, the teachers of Study 3 rated these three qualities as higher for those children who had experienced more infant day care. While the mothers in Study 2 certainly knew their children had received considerable infant care, the teachers in Study 3 had no knowledge of the amount of infant day care their sixth graders had experienced.

That the high quantity infant day care children rated themselves as more extraverted suggests that they view themselves that way. This quality is perhaps not inconsistent with the teachers having rated them as more assertive. Physical affection during interactions which included everything from rough house play to hugging, holding hands and touching other body parts was particularly highly rated amongst children who had more infant day care. This is perhaps not surprising inasmuch as these children have had more experience with their peers including physical affection and touch behaviors. These physical behaviors could have been construed as greater aggressiveness in previous negative outcome studies. While typically having different affects associated with them, physical rough and tumble play can be interpreted as aggressivity by those who are concerned about physical harm but fail to read the children's affective cues.

Finally, the surprising data were those pertaining to academics. Significant relations were noted between being assigned to the gifted program and years in infant care and final math grades and years in infant care. Although being assigned to the gifted program was not directly related to final math grades, a positive relation was noted between being in the gifted program and the math SAT scores ($r = .25$). Since so little is known about the unique properties of gifted children, it is difficult to speculate about the relation between assignments to gifted programs and years of infant day care. It is conceivable that one criterion for early placement in day care is the parents' sense of the child's giftedness, with the notion being that the child could adapt to day care more easily and might derive more preschool-oriented curriculum from a model day care program. Higher math grades may also relate to more experience in "school-like" settings where the three R's (and their flash cards) are present even in the earliest day care environments.

However these findings are interpreted, they certainly do not suggest that the child with more infant care is disadvantaged. It appears from these studies combined that the child is not only advantaged at the preschool period but is advantaged during the early grade school years and the final grade school years by having experienced more infant day care. These positive findings do not appear to be limited to socialization skills, but extend to the child's apparent emotional well-being and even to the child's academic performance and status. Since assertiveness type characteristics are repeatedly emerging in these studies as being related to quantity of infant care, it would appear that assertiveness is one of the qualities most affected, whether that is interpreted in a positive or a negative fashion. Although assertiveness has been negatively interpreted in previous day care outcome studies, in this study assertiveness was not only negatively related to aggressiveness ($-.88$), but positively related to emotional well-being ($r = .66$), popularity ($r = .34$), leadership ($r = .55$), physical affection ($r = .34$), and then to academic performance ($r = .42$ for reading grades, $r = .46$ for writing grades, $r = .28$ for spelling grades, $r = .41$ for the reading SAT score and $r = .29$ for the SAT math score). From this set of correlations, it would appear that assertiveness is not a quality that is bothersome to the children's peers (i.e., they are more popular), or to the teachers (i.e., they rate them more positively on behavior rating scales and the children receive better grades).

The children all attended different infant day care programs, albeit they were quality programs. Thus, the findings from Study 2 on the sample of children who attended the same infant day care program are no longer limited to that specific infant day care program. The generalizability of the results is also suggested by the heterogeneous sample of this study. Certainly, the results of these studies combined imply the opposite from the suggestion made by Belsky (1988). Center-based infant day care did not lead to negative outcomes in this case; they led to very positive outcomes. Being from middle SES, highly educated parents, there is no question but that these children attended high quality day care programs. This makes the observation of Belsky (1988) on heightened aggression in the Haskins (1985) and Schwartz et al (1974) studies where children were cared for in high quality, university-affiliated programs appear very bizarre. The data, however, are consistent with those of Phillips et al (1987) who noted that children who had experienced more high quality day care were more social. As Phillips et al (1976) suggested, quality day care may prove to be the most critical variable for optimal outcomes. Certainly the optimal study remains to be conducted, namely a large, frequent observation longitudinal study of children attending a high quality day care center. Only when we provide the best day care that we can provide will we know whether day care per se can have positive effects.

REFERENCES

Barton, M., & Schwartz, J. (1981, August). *Day care in the middle class: Effects in elementary school.* Paper presented at the American Psychological Association's annual convention, Los Angeles.

Behar, L., & Stringfield, S. A. (1974). A behavior rating scale for the preschool child. *Developmental Psychology, 10,* 601-610.

Belsky, J. (1986). Infant daycare: A cause for concern? *Zero to three, 6,* 1-7.

Belsky, J. (1987, June 22). The child-care dilemma. *Time Magazine,* p. 63.

Belsky, J. (1988). The "Effect" of infant day care reconsidered. *Early Childhood Research Quarterly, 3,* 227-234.

Buck, R. (1977). Nonverbal communication of affect in preschool children. Relationships with personality and skin conductance. *Journal of Personality and Social Psychology, 35,* 235-236.

Farber, E. A., & Egeland, B. (1982). Developmental consequences of out-of-home care for infants in a low income population. In E. Zigler & E. Gordon (Eds.), *Day care* (pp. 102-125). Boston: Auburn.

Field, T., Masi, W., Goldstein, S., Perry, S., & Parl, S. (1988). Infant daycare facilitates preschool social behavior. *Early Childhood Research Quarterly.*

Field, T., Gewirtz, J. L., Cohen, D., Garcia, R., Greenburg, R., & Collins, K. (1984). Leave-takings and reunions of infants, toddlers, preschoolers and their parents. *Child Development, 55,* 628-635.

Field, T., & Reite, M. (1984). Children's responses to separation from mother during the birth of another child. *Child Development, 55,* 1308-1316.

Gunnarson, L. (1978). Children in day care and family care in Sweden: A follow-up. Bulletin No. 21, Department of Educational Research, University of Gothenburg.

Haskins, R. (1985). Public school aggression among children with varying day-care experience. *Child Development, 56,* 689-703.

Howes, C., & Rubenstein, J. (1985). Determinants of toddlers' experience in day care: Age of entry and quality of setting. *Child Care Quarterly, 14,* 140-151.

Howes, C., & Stewart, P. (1986). *Child's play with adults, peers and toys.* Unpublished manuscript, University of California, Los Angeles.

McCartney, K., Scarr, S., Phillips, D., Grajek, S., & Schwarz, J. C. (1982). Environmental differences among day care centers and their effects on children's development. In E. Zigler & E. Gordon (Eds.), *Day care: Scientific and social policy issues.* Boston: Auburn.

McCrae, J. W., & Herbert-Jackson, E. (1975). Are behavior effects of infant day care programs specific? *Developmental Psychology, 12,* 269-270.

Phillips, D., McCartney, K., Scarr, S., & Howes, C. (1987). Selective review of infant daycare research: A cause for concern! *Zero to Three, 7,* 18-21.

Piers, E. V., & Harris, D. B. (1969). *The Piers-Harris Children's Self Concept Scale.* Nashville: Counselor Recordings and Tests.

Rubenstein, J., Howes, C., & Boyle, P. (1981). A two year follow-up of infants in community-based day care. *Journal of Child Psychology and Psychiatry, 8,* 1-11.

Santrock, J., & Warshak, R. (1979). Father custody and social development in boys and girls. *Journal of Social Issues, 35*, 112-125.

Scarr, S. (1983). *Child care.* A paper presented as a Science and Public Policy Seminar, Washington, D.C.

Schwartz, P. (1983). Length of day-care attendance and attachment behavior in eighteen-month-old infants. *Child Development, 54*, 1073-1078.

Schwarz, J. C., Krolick, G., & Strickland, R. G. (1973). Effects of early day care experience on adjustment to a new environment. *American Journal of Orthopsychiatry, 43*, 340-348.

Schwarz, J. C., Strickland, R. G., & Krolick, G. (1974). Infant day care: Behavioral effects at preschool age. *Developmental Psychology, 10*, 502-506.

5

The Relationship of Child-Care Quality and Play to Social Behavior in the Kindergarten

Ellen Vineberg Jacobs and Donna Romano White

The purpose of this chapter is to report on two longitudinal studies. The rationale for these studies was to assess the idea that *quality* of preschool child-care and type of preschool play experiences affect children's social behavior and school adjustment. It was considered important to take a longitudinal perspective and to focus on the transition of the child from a full-day child-care setting to the elementary school classroom. In the first study, quality of preschool group child-care settings was assessed for 36 four year olds. One year later, these children were evaluated by their kindergarten teachers and were compared to 32 home-reared children on ratings of interest-participation and cooperation-compliance. In the second study, play patterns, categorized as solitary, parallel, prosocial and negative, of 28 four year old children were observed in their child-care settings and were correlated with kindergarten teachers' ratings of interest-participation and cooperation-compliance.

Study 1: Child-Care Quality and Kindergarten Behavior

Kindergarten teachers report differences in the social behavior of day-care and home-reared children. In a study by Baillargeon & Betsalel-Presser (1988), teachers observed that "day-care" children have difficulty respecting classroom rules, are aggressive and have a tendency to form cliques. Rather than attributing these behaviors to child-care attendance per se, the kindergarten teachers in this study suggested that these behaviors might be related to the quality of the child-care setting children attended.

This suggestion is consistent with the findings of a number of research studies investigating the relationship between quality of child-care and children's

This research was supported by a grant from the Fonds Pour la Formation de Chercheurs et l'Aide à la Recherche, (FCAR), Ministry of Education, Province of Quebec.

We extend our gratitude to Evelyn Schliecker, Esther Spector, Joan Spindler, Jancy Watkins and Ronen Nathan for their participation in the data collection. We wish to thank Geoffery Selig for his guidance and expert advice during the analysis of the data.

social competence. Researchers reported that children who attended high quality child-care centers were rated as more confident in their social interactions, more cooperative, considerate, and sociable, and less dependent than children in low quality centers (Howes & Olenick, 1986; McCartney, Scarr, Phillips, Grajek, & Schwarz, 1982; Vandell & Powers, 1983). These results suggest that children from high and low quality centers may bring very different social skills to the kindergarten.

Although there are few longitudinal studies reported in the literature, some support is found for the idea that quality of preschool child-care might affect the transition to kindergarten. Vandell, Henderson & Wilson (1988) reported that children from better quality centers who were retested at eight years of age had more friendly interactions with peers, were rated as more socially competent and happier, and received fewer "shy" nominations from peers. Positive interaction with adults at four years of age was positively related to ratings of empathy, social competence and peer acceptance at eight years. Unoccupied behavior at four years was negatively related to ratings of empathy, conflict negotiation and social competence at eight years.

The study by Vandell et al. (1988) provides the only published longitudinal study to date in which some measure of child-care quality was used. In longitudinal studies which did not measure quality, Haskins (1985) found that children enrolled in a cognitively oriented child-care program beginning at infancy were more aggressive in kindergarten than other groups of center-care children. Gunnarsson (1978) compared five year olds who had been reared in group care since age one with those reared at home and found that center-care children displayed more adult-child cooperative behavior in centers, more peer conflict at home, and no differences in compliance with adult authority.

Several conclusions can be drawn from these studies. First, more longitudinal data examining the relationship of child-care quality and behavior in the elementary school is clearly warranted. Second, comparison of children from high and low quality child-care environments to home-reared children might provide important insights about the transition to kindergarten from different child-care environments. The present study was designed with both of these considerations in mind. Specifically, it was hypothesized that children from high quality group child-care settings would be rated as more interested in kindergarten activities than children from low quality settings. It was also hypothesized that children from low quality settings would be rated as more defiant and less cooperative than children from high quality groups. Comparisons of children in high and low quality group settings with home-reared children were explored, although no specific hypotheses were formulated.

With these goals in mind, it is noted that research on the effects of child-care quality is plagued by methodological challenges. It was considered important to select a measure of child-care quality with reasonable psychometric properties that is widely used and would provide continuity with other research. The Harms & Clifford (1980) Early Childhood Environmental Rating Scale was selected as meeting these criteria. Second, in order to ensure that child-care quality was a stable, salient influence on the children, only children who had been in full-time care for a minimum of one year were included in the study. Third, language comprehension and socioeconomic status (SES) were measured and used as control variables. Finally, the Social Competence Scale, developed by Kohn, Parnes and Rosman (1976), was selected as a measure of the behaviors shown by previous research to be important for good adjustment to kindergarten. This scale allows one to describe social behavior along two dimensions: interest-participation versus apathy-withdrawal and cooperation-compliance versus anger-defiance.

Method

Subjects

Sixty children had previously participated in an earlier research study on the effects of quality of care and socioeconomic status on vocabulary development (Schliecker, White, & Jacobs, 1989). All of the 60 subjects met the following criteria: they had been enrolled in the same child-care center for more than 35 hours per week for at least one year prior to the center ratings; they were attending child-care on a full-time basis at the time of the study; they understood and spoke English; they were eligible to attend kindergarten in the next academic year; and their parents had provided written consent for their participation.

Of the original 60 children, it was possible to follow 36 who were attending English kindergartens. The loss of 24 subjects was due to a variety of causes. Some of the families enrolled their children in French or French Immersion kindergartens. In order not to confound the effects of learning a new language with those of child-care experiences, these children were eliminated from the study. Job transfers to other cities or relocation within the city without leaving a forwarding address also prevented a number of children from participating.

An additional group of 32 children attending the same kindergarten classrooms was included in the study. These children were selected on the basis of the following criteria: they had never been enrolled in group child-care on either a full- or part-time basis; they understood and spoke English; and their parents provided written consent for their participation in the study.

Proportions of boys and girls were similar in all three types of child-care: low quality care, high quality care, and the home-reared, no child-care group. In each group, the proportion of girls:boys was approximately 60 percent:40 percent.

Measures

ECERS. The Early Childhood Environmental Rating Scale (ECERS) (Harms & Clifford, 1980) was used to evaluate the quality of the child-care and kindergarten environments. The ECERS is composed of 37 items divided into seven subscales: personal care routines, furnishings and displays for children, language-reasoning experiences, fine and gross motor activities, creative activities, social development and adult needs. Each item within the subscales is scored within a seven point range with one designated as inadequate, three as minimal, five as good and seven as excellent. Full descriptions are provided for each of the odd-numbered markers on the scale and these serve as guidelines in the assignment of ratings. An overall environmental rating is obtained through the addition of the subscale scores. Thus, the highest possible score is 259, the lowest score is 37, and the mean score is 148. Harms & Clifford (1980) report reasonable validity, good inter-rater rank order reliability, and good internal consistency for this scale.

The ECERS was also used to rate the kindergarten environments. Two of the seven subscales, greeting and departure and adult needs, were eliminated from consideration because they did not differentiate among kindergarten classrooms. The highest possible score on the adjusted version of the ECERS is 161, the lowest score is 23, and the mean score is 92.

Receptive language. The vocabulary of each subject was measured by the child's performance on the Peabody Picture Vocabulary Test-Revised, Form M (PPVT-R) (Dunn & Dunn, 1981). This is a norm-referenced, individually administered test of receptive language. PPVT-R scores have good split-half reliability coefficients for young children (Dunn & Dunn, 1981) and have been related to measures of intelligence such as the Wechsler Preschool and Primary Scale, the Stanford Binet, and the McCarthy Scale of Children's Abilities (Sattler, 1988).

Socioeconomic status. The socioeconomic status (SES) of each child's family was measured via the Home Prestige Scale developed by Nock & Rossi (1979). It is based on research findings which indicate that the characteristics of family members combine in different ways in social stratification depending on the family constellation. Thus, on this scale, family SES is composed of marital status; age, education, and occupational prestige of the parents; and the number of minor children in the home. The occupational prestige determination is the product of a method developed by Seigel (1971 cited in Gottfried, 1985) for use in sociological research. The Home Prestige Scale is highly correlated with other SES measures such as the Hollingshead Four Factor Index (Mueller & Parcel, 1981).

Social competence. The social competence rating of each child was obtained through the use of the Social Competence Scale (Kohn, Parnes, & Rosman, 1976). It is a 64-item, 5 point Likert-type scale composed of two bipolar factors. Factor one is entitled interest-participation versus apathy-withdrawal and addresses the general topic of utilization of opportunity in the classroom. For example, eagerness to try new things, enthusiasm about work or play, and withdrawal from peer contact are items included in this factor. Factor two is entitled cooperation-compliance versus anger-defiance and addresses the general topic of conformity to rules, regulations and routines of the classroom. Examples of items from this factor include willingness to carry out reasonable teacher suggestions, active defiance of teacher rules, and compliance with specific rules such as putting things away.

Procedure

Centers. Ten child-care centers in the Montreal area were selected for this study based upon a list of licensed centers published by the Québec Office des Services de Garde à l'Enfance. Only those centers which operated primarily in English were selected. Center ratings represented a broad range of quality, and centers were divided into two groups, high and low quality. As can be seen from Table 5.1, high quality was defined as ECERS ratings between 202 and 239 and low quality was defined as ratings between 93 and 119. Two centers with intermediate scores of 166 and 130 were not included in the study.

Table 5.1   Harms and Clifford

Early Childhood Environment Rating Scale Scores

DAY-CARE TYPE	SCORE	MEAN	S.D.	RANGE
Low Quality		107.9	9.95	26
02	119			
06	102			
07	93			
08	102			
High Quality		226.7	12.11	37
01	239			
04	202			
09	230			
10	213			

Kindergartens. Subjects were enrolled in 20 kindergartens. Ratings of these classrooms on the adjusted ECERS ranged from 104 to 157. As all of these ratings were above the mean, and as the range of ratings was relatively small, kindergartens were treated as a homogeneous group of good quality classrooms.

Families of children who had participated in a previous child-care study were contacted by phone and the follow-up procedures were described. For those subjects who agreed, a signed letter of consent was obtained. Consent letters were then presented to the schools in which the children were enrolled. Arrangements for individual testing, observation and rating of the kindergarten classroom, teacher completion of the rating scales, and solicitation of control subjects for the no-day-care group were made. All of the schools contacted agreed to participate and all of the teachers completed the ratings for target children in the study and for the no-day-care subjects. Children were given the PPVT-R in individual test sessions. SES information was collected through telephone calls to the parents. Classroom ratings were made over a period of several observation sessions.

Results

The correlations between interest ratings, compliance ratings, PPVT-R scores and SES scores for the 68 subjects in this study are presented in Table 5.2. As can be seen from these data, interest and compliance ratings of the teachers are moderately correlated with one another. Given these correlations, a multivariate analysis of variance was selected as the statistical procedure for analysis of the data.

Table 5.2   *Correlations between Interest Ratings, Compliance Ratings PPVT-R Scores and SES.*

	INTEREST	COMPLIANCE	SES
Compliance	.32*		
SES	.17	.15	
PPVT-R	.28*	.34*	.31*

*p < .05

As can be seen in Table 5.2, vocabulary scores of the children are related to both interest and compliance ratings of the teachers and to the family's socioeconomic status. This pattern of correlations raises the issue of whether PPVT-R scores and SES should be controlled by using them as covariates in the analysis. Though it would be of interest to know if child-care status makes an independent contribution to teacher ratings, it is possible to argue that statistically controlling for SES and vocabulary in these analyses is artificial and might be misleading. What teachers are actually asked to rate is a child in whom SES, intelligence or vocabulary skills, and child-care experience are combined and inseparable. It is possible to argue that the analysis of choice is one which allows us to examine teacher ratings with the effects of all three variables, SES, vocabulary scores, and type of child-care, reflected (and confounded) in the type of child-care grouping.

For these reasons, a one-way between groups multivariate analysis was performed on interest and compliance ratings, without covariates. These results indicate that there is an overall effect of type of care on teacher ratings (Wilks Lambda = .78, $F(4,128) = 4.33$, $p = .003$). Further analysis of the univariate effects indicates that teachers ratings of interest-participation rate significantly different for the three types of child-care ($F (2,65) = 4.37$, $p = .017$).

Examination of the mean interest ratings presented in Table 5.3 indicates that children in either high or low quality day care were rated as more interested in classroom activities than home reared children. Children in high versus low quality group environments did not differ from one another on interest ratings by their teachers. Joint Bonferroni 95 percent confidence intervals support visual inspection of the means and indicate that children who did not attend child-care differ significantly from those who attended high quality care ($t = 2.78$, $p = .007$), while children in high versus low quality care did not differ from one another ($t = .67$, $p = .50$).

Table 5.3 *Mean and Standard Deviations for Interest and Participation as a Function of Type of Child–Care*

	MEAN	STANDARD DEVIATION
Interest		
Low quality	53.77	14.59
High quality	57.68	15.51
No group care	43.66	19.64
Compliance		
Low quality	−21.41	15.52
High quality	−14.53	17.04
No group care	−13.00	10.42

Further examination of the univariate analyses indicates that teacher ratings of compliance-defiance did not differentiate children in various types of child-care, though the test approaches significance ($F(2,65) = 2.12$, $p = .128$). Examination of the means in Table 5.3 indicate that children in low quality care

are rated as less cooperative and more defiant than children in high quality child-care or home care, though this trend is only marginally significant and must be interpreted with caution.

Finally, it seemed reasonable to explore whether controlling for SES and PPVT-R scored would change these findings. A one-way between groups multivariate analysis was performed on interest and compliance with vocabulary and socioeconomic status as covariates. Examination of the multivariate and univariate F tests and of the adjusted means revealed the same pattern of results as performing the analysis without covariates. As expected, there was a significant joint effect of the covariates on both interest ($F(2,63)$ = 3.93, $p < .05$) and compliance ($F(2,63)$ = 3.26, $p < .05$). Vocabulary and SES accounted for about 11 percent of the variance in interest ratings and 9 percent of the variance in compliance ratings. As can be seen in Table 5.4, children in highly rated centers came from families with higher SES ratings than either children from centers with low ratings or children who had not attended day care. Children in high quality centers also had the highest PPVT-R scores.

Table 5.4   *PPVT–R and SES Scores for Children as a Type of Child Care*

	PPVT–R	SES
Low Quality Group Setting	96.9 (12.6)	56.6 (6.8)
High Quality Group Setting	115.7 (12.2)	70.0 (11.0)
No Group Day-care	109.8 (13.7)	56.7 (8.3)

Discussion

The first hypothesis of this study was not supported. It was predicted that children from high quality centers would be rated by their kindergarten teachers as more interested than children from low quality centers. Instead, children who attended either high or low quality child-care centers were rated as more interested than home-reared children. Greater interest and less withdrawal seems to be related to attending group child-care regardless of the environmental quality of the center, and regardless of the fact that children in low quality care also have lower vocabulary scores and come from homes with lower SES levels than children in high quality care.

It seems that children who have prior extensive group experience (such as full-time child-care for two years) might be more attuned to the communal nature of functioning within a large group setting. Child-care center experience seems to be characterized by group involvement. Almost all functioning within the center appears to be conducted on a group basis; this includes instruction, general activities, meals, sleeping arrangements and play time. An experienced day-care child's reaction to the group setting of the kindergarten may be one of a readiness to participate without first having to take the time to adjust to being part of a group. Day care children have also had the opportunity to be in social situations with adults other than their own parents. These factors might well give the kindergarten teacher the impression that these children show more interest and participation than non-day-care children. Experienced day-care children have learned how to function in their group setting—interest and participation leads to involvement in a group activity, whereas apathy or withdrawal may result in being left out of the activity and not being part of the mainstream. Therefore, rather than standing back and waiting to see what will happen, the day-care children dive into the activity and get involved.

Familiarity with the activity being presented might also have been a positive factor. The children who had attended group care may have participated in activities similar to those being presented by the kindergarten teacher and may be more confident of their ability to perform the required task. Rather than fearing that repetition bores children, these results seem more consistent with the idea that familiarity enhances participation.

These data offer only minimal support for our second hypothesis that children from low quality settings are rated as less compliant and more defiant than children from either high quality group care or home care. In spite of the marginal significance of the result, the widespread belief that aggression is related to child-care attendance makes it necessary to examine the finding. One possible explanation of this finding is that low quality day care does shape aggressive, noncompliant behavior in children. However, the mean cooperation-defiance rating for children in the low quality centers in this study is roughly within normal limits. The average teacher rating of children from low quality centers was –21: the range of scores possible on the compliance-defiance scale is –109 to +7. The children are seen as somewhat less compliant than children from high quality centers or home environments, but are not seen as extremely defiant. Thus, another explanation of the differences in teacher ratings is suggested. One of the distinguishing features of the low quality day care centers in this study was the restrictive nature of the environment. There were many controls in place which limited the children's freedom in play situations and supported more teacher directed activities. The kindergarten settings, on the other hand, offered a great deal of freedom particularly during the play period. The relative freedom of kindergarten play periods compared to a highly structured day care may have been difficult for some children to interpret. Perhaps they simply had not learned the rules of conduct appropriate to an unstructured group situation and their behavior was then seen by teachers as somewhat defiant.

Study 2: Play Patterns in Group Child-Care and Kindergarten Behavior

Studies of kindergarten teachers reports (Baillargeon & Betsalel-Press, 1988) and the first study reported in this chapter offer some support for the notion that children from low quality day care are perceived as less compliant and more aggressive than children from high quality child-care or children who have no group child-care experience. Studies of the effect of day care quality upon children's play patterns in the preschool aged group lend further support to the idea that low quality care might facilitate negative play and peer interactions. Although not all studies have found play differences as a function of quality (Bjorkman, Poteat, & Snow, 1986), White, Jacobs, & Schliecker (1988) found that play patterns of four year old children in group day care were related to environmental quality ratings using the ECERS (Harms & Clifford, 1980). Even when socioeconomic status and verbal ability were controlled, children in low quality settings were found to engage in more negative play and interactions than children in settings with excellent environmental quality ratings. Holloway and Reichhart-Erickson (1988) found that absorption in solitary play was related to several indicators of high quality child-care. These investigators did not find a relationship between low quality care and negative play patterns, but pointed out that the low frequency of negative play or interactions in their study did not allow an adequate test of this hypothesis.

In summary, some research does offer support for the suggestion that preschool play patterns are related to environmental differences in day care settings. On the other hand, there have been very few studies which attempt to investigate the relationship of play patterns in group child-care settings with kindergarten or elementary school classroom behavior or social interactions. The current preliminary study attempted to relate observed patterns such as solitary play, parallel activity, prosocial interactions and play, and negative interactions and play in four year olds attending group day care settings to kindergarten teachers' ratings of interest-withdrawal and cooperation-defiance.

Method

Subjects

Twenty-eight of 60 children who had participated in an observation of play study (White et al, 1988) were located and agreed to participate in the current research. A fairly small proportion of the 60 children participated in the follow-up study as many of the children had been placed in French kindergartens. Because it was felt that learning a new language might affect children's response to kindergarten as well as teacher ratings, only those children who were currently in kindergartens where they spoke English were included in the study. The 28 children in this study were fairly representative of the original sample with respect to SES level, language ability, and type of play exhibited in the day care observation (See Table 5.5). The original sample included 30 boys and 30 girls: the longitudinal sample included 13 boys and 15 girls.

Table 5.5   *Comparison of Longitudinal Sample*

and Original Play Sample

	LONGITUDINAL SAMPLE	ORIGINAL SAMPLE
Number of Subjects	28	60
SES	60.6	61.0
PPVT-R	98.0	98.0
Negative play/interaction	2.75	2.72
Solitary play	3.79	3.96
Parallel activity	8.43	6.07
Prosocial play/interaction	4.86	4.58

Measures

Three measures used in Study 1 were also used in this study: the Peabody Picture Vocabulary Test—Revised (Dunn & Dunn, 1981) was used to measure receptive vocabulary; the Nock & Rossi (1979) formula was used to calculate SES based upon parents educational levels, occupations, and family structure; and the Social Competence Scale (Kohn, Parnes & Rosman, 1976) was used to obtain teacher ratings of interest-participation (versus apathy-withdrawal) and compliance-cooperation (versus defiance/anger).

An observational coding scheme was devised in order to tabulate the frequency of play and social interactions. Nineteen four-digit codes were defined in order to structure the observations. The first digit of the code represented the context of the situation, i.e., solitary, parallel, or interactive. The second digit noted if the child was engaged in a play, social interaction, or unoccupied-onlooker behavior. The tone of the observed behavior (positive, negative/aggressive, or inappropriate) was noted in the third digit of the code, and the mode, either verbal or non-verbal was recorded in the fourth digit.

Procedure

Children in the original study were drawn from eight day care centers. Each of these urban centers was licensed by the Québec Office des Services de Garde à l'Enfance and operated primarily in English. All of the children were four years of age at the time of entry into the study; all spoke English; all had been in the same day care center for at least one year on a full time (>35 hours per week) basis; and all had written permission from their parents to participate in the study. The PPVT-R was administered by a female researcher who visited the day care and saw the children individually. This same researcher telephoned each child's parents to obtain the information needed to calculate socioeconomic status.

Observational data describing play were collected by two additional female observers who were blind to the children's vocabulary scores and SES ratings. Approximately 10 percent of the observations in each center were collected simultaneously, but independently by both observers in order to establish reliability.

Fifty observations were recorded for each child over a two to three week period: 35 observations were made during free play situations and 15 observations during structured situations such as story time, television watching, or snack. The division of observations was intended to reflect the relative time allotted for various activities in the centers.

Prior to actual data collection, each observer visited a center several times until it was apparent that the children were relatively immune to her presence. If queried, the observers told the children they were there to "look at your school." Observers avoided interacting with the children and moved freely about the room, although they attempted to remain on the periphery as much as possible.

The order of observation was randomly determined prior to each visit to a center. The child was observed for a 10-second period during which the context, tone, and mode of behavior were noted and subsequently recorded by hand on a checklist. If the nature of the behavior changed within the 10-second interval, timing was stopped and the clock reset for an additional period. After four unproductive attempts, a situation was considered uncodable and observation of the next target began.

Children's parents were contacted in the following year and asked to consent to having the child's kindergarten teacher rate her or his current social behaviors. All of the children who could be located and who were currently in an English kindergarten agreed to participate. Kindergarten teachers were then asked to complete the Social Competence Scale.

Results

Reliability

In the White et al's (1988) original study, 50 observations on each of 30 children or 1,500 sample observations were obtained. Ten percent (150) observations were independently coded by two observers. Percent agreement was calculated on these joint observations using the formula: number of agreements divided by number of agreements plus number of disagreements times 100. The percentage agreement obtained was 92.6 percent, indicating reliable use of the coding system.

Reduction and Description of Observational Codes

Due to the low frequency of some of the 19 originally derived categories and to the small sample size and preliminary nature of this study, four combined codes were derived for the analyses. These codes include: solitary play; parallel activity; prosocial interaction-play and negative interaction-play. Solitary play was positive and usually nonverbal pretend play such as playing with blocks or fantasy play with dolls, trucks or other toys. Parallel activity was originally intended to reflect play, but in most instances observed in this study, it was teacher directed. For example, the teacher might direct children to choose a toy and sit down at a table with other children and "play quietly." Therefore, parallel activity refers to instances when children were involved in the same (or very similar) activities as peers, but were instructed not to interact with one another. Prosocial play-interaction included all instances of cooperative play as well as positive interactions. Both verbal and non-verbal prosocial play-interactions were included in this category. Instances of prosocial play included cooperative games, pretend activities, or joint block building. Examples of prosocial activity included help giving, smiling, hugging, shared laughter, compliments, and praise. Negative play-interaction was defined as play or interactions that were aggressive or antisocial. This category included kicking, hitting, shoving, fighting, derisive laughter, *intense* (uncontrolled) rough and tumble play, and teasing.

Table 5.6 Correlations Between Interest and Cooperations
Ratings and Play Categories

| | TEACHER RATINGS | |
	Interest	Cooperation
SES	.26	.41**
PPVT-R	.19	.16
Solitary play	.11	.09
Negative play/interaction	−.35*	−.17
Parallel activity	−.25	−.08
Prosocial play/interaction	.29	.07

$*p = .033$
$**p = .014$

Correlations

Due to the small number of subjects in the study, only simple correlational analyses were conducted to examine the relationship between early predictors (such as type of play, vocabulary level and SES) and kindergarten teacher ratings of social behavior. As can be seen from Table 5.6, teacher ratings of the child's interest-participation versus withdrawal-apathy is predicted only by negative play/interactions. A greater number of negative play behaviors in the day-care is related to less interest and participation (or more withdrawal) in the kindergarten classroom. Teacher ratings of the child's cooperation-compliance versus anger/defiance is not significantly related to any part of the play categories, but is significantly related to the child's socioeconomic status.

Discussion

While these results should be interpreted cautiously as they may reflect an oversimplification due to the multivariate relationship among the variables, they do lend some support to the importance of both the home environment and child care experience as predictors of social behavior. Moreover, the importance of negative interactions and play, even when such behavior is of relatively low frequency, is underlined by these results.

It is difficult to interpret the finding that greater negative play experiences are related to low interest-high withdrawal. In this study, the negative code was assigned whenever the target child was engaged in a negative or aggressive interaction. The child could either have instigated the aggression or been the target of an aggressive act. Our findings are consistent with the idea that the child may have been involved in, though not necessarily an instigator of, negative play and may have learned to withdraw from group or social activities in the classroom. Kindergarten teachers rate these children as somewhat more withdrawn and less interested than those with fewer negative experiences.

An interpretation with more serious repercussions is that negative interactions which involve aggressive encounters or other antisocial behaviors may be related to rejection by peers. Children who are rejected by their peers are at risk for the development of long-term, serious psychopathology (Cowen, Pederson, Babigan, Izzo, & Trost, 1973). Such an interpretation is consistent with the idea that child-care experience, particularly low quality experience, is related to more aggressive behavior and less compliance in the kindergarten classroom, but was not supported by the present study. Instead, less compliance and greater defiance, while unrelated to negative play experiences, was moderately correlated with socioeconomic status.

Conclusions

Given the interesting results of these studies, we would urge that more longitudinal research be conducted to explore the relationship of quality child-care experiences, types of care, play and interactions patterns, and subsequent social behavior. Continued attention needs to be paid to methodological problems such as increasing sample size so that sex differences can be analyzed. A large sample is also required to counteract the loss of subjects which inevitably occurs in longitudinal studies. It would be ideal if one could draw upon a subject pool which included children from high and low socioeconomic backgrounds who attend both high and low quality child-care centers. However, it seems that high SES children in North America rarely attend low quality centers. In view of this reality, we would urge investigators to continue to measure both SES and intelligence or language ability and to examine the multivariate effects of these variables in addition to child-care quality, type of care, and play patterns. It also seems reasonable to continue to compare center and home care groups, as well as to further differentiate and define quality of home environments. Future studies should rely on multiple measures of child behavior in the kindergarten and elementary school classrooms. The use of teacher ratings provides good insights, but direct observation of social behaviors in the classroom can provide the rich information required to elaborate the relationship between home, group child-care, peer relations, play, and subsequent social behavior. Finally, children should be followed beyond the kindergarten level.

In spite of methodological shortcomings, the results of the two studies reported here support the longitudinal relationship between group child-care experiences and social behavior in the elementary school. Furthermore, the results of the first study provide support for the idea that child-care experience, in either high or low quality day care environments, may actually benefit children in terms of preparing them for group participation. It is important to note that the low quality centers in this study were actually in Harms & Clifford's minimal (26-50 percent) range rather than inadequate (0-25 percent) range: none of the children in this study received inadequate group care. It seems that center care reflecting minimal to excellent environmental ratings is related to good interest-participation ratings in the kindergarten.

This research also reiterates the idea that the relationship between home environments, child-care quality, play experiences, and later social behavior is a complex one. Reducing this relationship to the statement that "day care children are aggressive" is probably far too simplistic (Baillargeon & Betsalel-Presser, 1988). Instead, many factors including socioeconomic status, environmental quality of group child-care, negative play and interaction in the group child-care and the quality of the kindergarten setting all contribute to whether children will display aggressive responses, will withdraw from group activities, and/or will be accepted or rejected by their peers. As all of the children in this study attended high quality kindergarten classes, some effects of negative experiences or poor quality care may have been ameliorated. From a purely speculative point of view, it is disturbing to consider what might befall a child who attends a low quality child-care center followed by a low quality kindergarten experience.

Given the complex nature of these variables, it would be interesting to create a model which could predict the social skill development of day care children. Such a model would include the quality of the child-care center attended plus the home background both of which would be considered as influential in the development of children's play styles and these in turn would predict the social competence of the child. As well, parents influence play styles through their encouragement of turn taking, pretense, and mutual involvement. They influence the development of social skills though modeling, reinforcement, and induction. The caregivers in the child-care centers influence play styles through reinforcement, modeling, instruction, and facilitation and support. There is also a reciprocal relationship between play styles and social skills. Play facilitates the development of rule comprehension, problem solving, negotiation, cooperation, and perspective taking. The possession of these skills make the child a better play partner, thereby encouraging and facilitating more complex, more prosocial, and less aggressive play.

REFERENCES

Baillargeon, M., & Betsalel-Presser, R. (1988). Effects de la garderie sur le comportement social et l'adaption de l'enfant: Perception des enseignantes de la maternelle. *Canadian Journal of Research in Early Childhood Education, 2,* 91-98.

Bjorkman, S., Poteat, G. M., & Snow, C. W. (1986). Environmental ratings and children's social behavior: Implications for the assessment of day care quality. *American Journal of Orthopsychiatry, 56,* 271-277.

Cowen, E. L., Pederson, A., Babigan, H., Isso, L. D., & Trost, M. A. (1973). Long-term follow-up of early detected vulnerable children. *Journal of Consulting and Clinical Psychology, 41,* 438-446.

Dunn, L. M., & Dunn, L. M. (1981). *Peabody Picture Vocabulary Test— Revised,* Circle Pines, MN: American Guidance Service.

Gottfried, A. W. (1985). Measures of socioeconomic status in child development research: Data and recommendations. *Merril-Palmer Quarterly, 31,* 85-92.

Gunnarsson, L. (1978). Children in day care and family care in Sweden: A follow-up. *Bulletin No 21,* Department of Educational Research, University of Gothernburg, Sweden.

Harms, T., & Clifford, R. M. (1980). *Early Childhood Environment Rating Scale.* New York: Teachers College Press.

Harms, T., & Clifford, R. M. (1983). Assessing preschool environments with the Early Childhood Environment Rating Scale. *Studies in Educational Evaluation, 8,* 261-269.

Haskins, R. (1985). Public school aggression among children with varying day-care experience. *Child Development, 56,* 689-705.

Holloway, S. D., & Reichhart-Erickson, M. (1988). The relationship of day care quality to children's free play behavior and social problem-solving skills. *Early Childhood Research Quarterly, 3,* 39-53.

Howes, C., & Olenick, M. (1986). Child care and family influences on toddlers' compliance. *Child Development, 57,* 202-216.

Kohn, M., Parnes, B., & Rosman, B. L. A test and scoring Manual for the Kohn Problem Checklist and Kohn Social Competence Scale (Revised edition), Unpublished manuscript. The William Alanson White Institute of Psychiatry, Psychoanalysis, & Psychology. New York City, NY.

McCartney, K., Scarr, S., Phillips, D., Grajek, S., & Schwarz, J. C. (1982). Environmental differences among day care centers and their effects on children's development. In E. F. Ziegler & E. W. Grodon (Eds.), *Day care, scientific and social policy issues.* Boston: Auburn House.

Mueller, C. W., & Parcel, T. L. (1981). Measures of socioeconomic status: Alternatives and recommendations. *Child Development, 52,* 13-30.

Nock, S. L., & Rossi, P. H. (1979). Household typs and social standing. *Social Forces, 57,* 1325-1345.

Sattler, J. M. (1988). *Assessment of Children* (3rd ed.), San Diego: J. M. Stattler.

Schliecker, E., White, D. R., & Jacobs, E. (1989). Predicting preschool language comprehension from SES, family structure, and day care quality. *Research Bulletins, 7,* No. 002. Montreal: Center for Research in Human Development.

Vandell, D. L., Henderson, V. K., & Wilson, K. S. (1988). A longitudinal study of children with day-care experiences of varying quality. *Child Development, 59,* 1286-1292.

Vandell, D. L., & Powers, C. P. (1983). Day-care quality and children's free play activities. *American Journal of Orthopsychiatry, 53,* 493-500.

White, D. R., Jacobs, E., & Schliecker, E. (1988). Relationship of day-care environmental quality and children's social behavior. *Canadian Psychology, 29,* Abstract #668.

6

Dramatic Play in Day Care: What Happens When Doctors, Cooks, Bakers, Pirates and Pharmacists Invade the Classroom?

Nina Howe, Lora Moller, and Bette Chambers

The notion that play serves as a facilitator for young children's socialization and early development has been a central feature of the traditional nursery school curriculum (Clarke-Stewart & Fein, 1983; Read, 1971). In recent years, early childhood education curriculum experts have called for the implementation of dramatic or pretend play centers in settings such as day care which are designed for preschool-aged children (e.g., Hendrick, 1988). Opportunities to engage in dramatic play are seen as promoting children's social, cognitive, social-cognitive, and language abilities. With increasing numbers of children spending many hours in day care, questions and issues concerning the curriculum are of central importance to educators. However, there has been little empirical work conducted on how the design of dramatic play centers affects children's play behaviors. Instead, there appears to be an assumption that the availability of a housekeeping area will provide sufficient impetus for stimulating pretend play. In the present study, both traditional housekeeping and novel dramatic play centers were employed in a day care setting to compare the effects of theme, novelty, and duration of the centers on children's social and cognitive play.

Pretend Play and Development

Pretend play is one aspect of preschoolers' play that has been intensely studied (see Rubin, Fein & Vandenberg, 1983 for a review) under various labels such as dramatic, fantasy, imaginative, make-believe or sociodramatic play (Fein, 1982). Nevertheless, central to all these terms is that during pretend play the child engages in role playing, defined by Curry and Arnaud (1974) as instances when "the child transforms himself in pretend play to be a person or object other than himself, as indicated by his verbal and/or motoric enactment of his perception of that role" (p. 274).

We would like to thank the director, teachers and children at the Concordia University Day Care Center who participated in the project, Cristina Santos for collecting the data, and William M. Bukowski for critical comments on the manuscript. This project was funded by an Internal Research Grant, Concordia University to the first author.

Many researchers have argued that pretend has a crucial role in promoting development in the social and cognitive domains (Rubin et al., 1983); the belief is that children's ability to decenter or consider many aspects of a situation or another a point of view simultaneously with their own is the mechanism facilitating the link between pretend play and cognitive, social, social-cognitive, and language development. In fact, a number of studies report positive associations between engaging in pretend play and classification and spatial perspective-taking (Rubin & Maioni, 1975), creativity (Dansky, 1980), social competence, popularity, and role-taking (Connolly & Doyle, 1984; Rubin & Maioni, 1975). Following Smilansky's (1968) seminal study which demonstrated that training significantly improved disadvantaged Israeli children's ability to engage in dramatic play, training in pretend play has been reported to be positively associated with language development, group cooperation, creativity, and perspective-taking skills (see McLoyd, 1982; Rubin et al., 1983 for critical reviews). Based on this line of research, curriculum experts advocate including opportunities for young children to engage in pretend play and in day care centers, dramatic play centers are designed for this purpose.

Developmental and Gender Influences on Dramatic Play

Developmental and gender differences are apparent in pretend play. Two-year-olds can engage in brief bouts of pretend play, while four-year-olds can produce extended, sophisticated episodes of such play (e.g., Fein, 1981; Nicholich, 1977; Sachs, Goldman, & Chaille, 1984). Conflicting findings regarding sex differences in pretend play have been reported; some find girls engage in more dramatic play than boys (Woodward, 1984), while others report the reverse (Rubin, Maioni, & Hornung, 1976; Silver & Ramsey, 1983). The kinds of themes children typically enact also follow a developmental sequence (Garvey, 1976). Children begin by acting out familiar domestic scenes (e.g., dinnertime, caring for baby), and then become involved in rescue situations (e.g., the baby is sick, the dog dies). Finally, children enact themes involving a sudden threat, such as a monster popping out of the cupboard. At the same time, boys are fascinated with heroic or superhero themes (Kostelnik, Whiren, & Stein, 1986), while girls are more likely to focus on domestic themes (Cramer & Hogan, 1975; Pulaski, 1973).

Ecological Factors and Play

The influence of ecological factors in the day care setting on patterns of preschooler's play has received only limited attention in the literature, nevertheless, children's play behavior is affected by the type and quantity of materials available (Christie & Johnsen, 1987). Although preschool children are increasingly able to use less concrete and less realistic props in their pretend (Elder & Pederson, 1978; Fein, 1975; Golumb, 1977), even five-year-olds appear to be dependent on props to stimulate their pretend play. Certain materials (e.g., dress-up clothes, vehicles) and those which are of moderate as opposed to high or low degrees of realism are more likely to produce both inventive and sociodramatic play (McLoyd, 1983; Pulaksi, 1973; Rubin, 1977a, 1977b). A review of the literature revealed no studies examining how the environment within the dramatic play center might influence children's play.

Dramatic Play and the Curriculum

Current early childhood education texts promote the view that dramatic play centers should be an integral part of the day care environment (e.g., Beatty, 1984; Spodek, Saracho, & Davis, 1987). Nevertheless, few research-based guidelines are provided about how to implement dramatic play centers effectively. For example, students are advised to change props and equipment frequently in order to provide new stimuli and challenges for children (Hendrick, 1988), but no indication is given about how often this should be done. In addition, as children mature and their repertoire of experiences expands, they can presumably engage in role-appropriate play in a wider variety of simulated settings, but few guidelines exist about what constitutes a developmentally appropriate setting. While young children might feel more comfortable with the familiar housekeeping corner, older children might be challenged by novel settings (e.g., post office), provided that they have been given parallel enriching experiences (Day, 1988). Nevertheless, there is no information about the age at which children play in housekeeping versus novel centers or if they play in a similar or different manner in these centers. In regard to props, Hendrick (1988) suggests that realistic props which are simple, concrete, and durable can enhance pretend play, especially for younger children. Furthermore, it is likely that children will explore the props before using them in pretend play. Nevertheless, a number of questions remain unanswered, for example: (a) how many props are appropriate, (b) how the degree of realism or structure influences play, and (c) when do children go beyond the simple exploration of materials and begin to engage in pretend play in a novel setting?

Given the limitations of the above advice, we turned to the research literature, but our search indicated only a few investigations of how manipulations of the play environment (e.g., kinds of themes, quality of centers, type and numbers of materials) influenced children's behavior. In an early study, Crabtree (cited in Stokes, 1975) compared the degree of structure in two types of dramatic centers on children's thinking. Unstructured dramatic play centers characterized by general themes, moderately realistic toys and minimal teacher direction were more successful than highly structured, teacher-directed centers with specific themes and highly realistic toys in facilitating higher levels of divergent and complex thinking.

Some authors (e.g., Paley, 1973; Woodard, 1984) have suggested that the typical dramatic play center, the housekeeping corner, is more appealing to girls than boys and consequently, attracts more females. Paley (1973) removed the doll corner from her kindergarten class and in an anecdotal report observed that domestic scenes appeared in other areas of the classroom, with girls predominantly acting out mother-baby situations. In a more rigorous study, Levy, Schaefer and Phels (1986) found that exposure to novel dramatic play centers (hospital, circus, grocery store) and the traditional housekeeping corner significantly improved preschool boys' scores on a measure of receptive vocabulary. The authors argued that females had high participation rates in housekeeping centers prior to the implementation of the novel centers, thus, producing a ceiling effect. Unfortunately, no measures of the level or quality of the children's pretend play were included.

In one of few reports examining ways to facilitate dramatic play in the classroom, Woodard's (1984) early childhood education students designed and implemented novel dramatic play centers (e.g., unisex hair salon, ice cream shop, airport). Students also provided relevant experiences for each theme such as field trips, invited guests, books, filmstrips, puppet shows, and flannelboard presentations. Woodard stated that the children engaged in more dramatic play, over time, became more proficient players and gained an understanding of the different roles associated with various themes. Unfortunately, these observations were not based on objectively collected data.

The lack of properly designed studies to investigate how the introduction of novel dramatic centers affects the quality and frequency of children's social and cognitive play is apparent. Moreover, both traditional housekeeping and novel centers may vary in terms of quality, developmentally appropriate themes, appeal, numbers and types of materials; most of these issues remain unexplored.

The Present Study

Given these issues, the present study was designed to examine the impact of novel dramatic play centers on the social and cognitive play of preschool children in a day-care center. Five novel centers were designed and implemented by first-year students in a teacher training program. Children's play was observed in the housekeeping center before, immediately after, and one month after the implementation of the novel centers and also during the first and last day of each novel center. We hypothesized that during the novel centers children would engage in more social (i.e., group) and cognitive (i.e., pretend) play than in the traditional housekeeping centers. Moreover, children would be more likely to engage in exploratory behaviors on day one ⁻and pretend on day three of each novel center. Finally, children were predicted to engage in higher levels of social and cognitive play in more familiar versus less familiar centers.

Method

Subjects

The 45 children (ages 2 1/2 to 5) enrolled in the university day-care center participated in the project. Eighteen students (16 female, 2 male) in the introductory practicum in the Specialization in Early Childhood Education program (teacher training for kindergarten to grade three) at Concordia University designed the novel centers, however two students (1 female, 1 male) withdrew from the course before the project was completed.

Procedure

During the morning free-play period (from 8:15-9:30 A.M.), all children were in one large room containing activity centers typically found in high quality early childhood settings (e.g., books, construction toys, art). The dramatic play center, approximately 3 meters by 3 meters, was normally set up as a housekeeping center and equipped with standard items such as a stove, fridge, table, chairs, a couch, dolls, crib, dishes, pots, pans and dress-up clothes.

Students were assigned to five groups (3-4 students each) and designed the following centers: (1) a *hospital* center containing a doctor's office with appropriate medical equipment (e.g., stethoscopes, bandages) and a reception area with desk, telephone, typewriter; (2) a *bakery* counter with cash register and baked goods for purchase and also a preparation table with baking items (e.g., rolling pins, playdough, recipes); (3) a *pharmacy* with a computer, playdough pills, weigh scales, cash register and drug store items (e.g., shampoo, kleenex); (4) a *pirate ship* (a wooden rocking boat) with a beach and footsteps leading to a treasure chest containing gold and jewels; (5) a *pizzeria* with a table for making playdough pizza, an eating area for customers and a delivery truck placed outside the center. Theme-related dress-up clothes were provided for each center. Each group set up their own center for three days in the area reserved for the housekeeping center.

The social and cognitive play of the children was observed in the dramatic play center during four time periods: (1) two days during the week prior to the novel centers; (2) days one and three of each of the five novel centers; (3) two days during the week immediately following the novel centers; and (4) two days during the week one month after the novel centers. Observations were conducted during the last half hour of free play, a time when the majority of the children had arrived in the day care. Four children were allowed in the center at one time and for the observations, one child was randomly selected as child #1 and observed for 10 seconds; this procedure was followed until all four children were observed and then the order was repeated. When a new child entered the center, he/she was inserted into the order and observed next.

Measures

Rubin's Pretend Observation Scale (Rubin, 1985; Rubin & Mills, 1988) was employed to record the children's play; this instrument nests Smilanky's (1968) cognitive play categories (functional, constructive, dramatic play, games-with-rules) within Parten's (1932) social participation categories (solitary, parallel, group). Definitions are reported in Table 6.1. In this system, it is possible to examine levels of social play (e.g., solitary vs. group) within a cognitive category such as dramatic play. Additionally, the scale includes the following non-play categories: onlooker, unoccupied, transitional, rough-and-tumble behavior, and peer conversations. Two additional non-play categories (wandering and conversations with teachers) were added. Inter-rater reliability was conducted before and during the implementation of the novel centers and an overall Kappa coefficient of .79 was achieved.

Table 6.1   Definitions of Play and Non-Play Behaviors

BEHAVIOR	DEFINITION
Solitary	Child engages in an activity entirely alone or with back to others.
Parallel	Child engages in an activity beside but not with others.
Group	Child engages in activity with other(s), in which a goal or purpose is shared by all members.
Functional	Child experiences sensory stimulation through simple, repetitive muscular movements.
Constructive	Child creates or constructs something.
Dramatic	Child dramatizes life situations or brings life to an inanimate object.
Games-with-rules	Child engages in competitive game-type activity following pre-established rules and limits.

Table 6.1   Definitions of Play and Non-Play Behaviors (continued)

BEHAVIOR	DEFINITION
Exploratory	Child seeks sensory information.
Unoccupied	Child exhibits behavior with lack of goal or focus.
Onlooker	Child watches the behaviors and activities of other children.
Transition	Child moves from one activity to another or prepares for, sets out, or tidies up an activity.
Conversation	Child actively listens or communicates verbally with (a) peers, (b) teachers.
Aggression	Child expresses displeasure, anger, disapproval through physical means.
Rough-and-Tumble	Child is engaged in playful physical activity.
Wandering	Child aimlessly meanders about the center.

Results

The results are presented in the following order: (a) the influence of dramatic play centers on children's overall social and cognitive play and then within the novel centers, (b) the impact of theme familiarity, and (c) play on day one versus day three of the novel centers.

Play and Non-Play Behaviors

Reported first are the types of play observed within the combined novel centers, second the types of play observed in specific centers and third, findings regarding levels of social play within the novel centers.

The first purpose of our study was to determine whether novel dramatic play settings influenced the social and cognitive play of preschool-aged children. First, the results indicated that novel dramatic play centers elicited different types of social play in the children frequenting these centers (see Table 6.2). An examination of the means indicate that the centers facilitated more parallel and group play than solitary play. Overall, as might be expected, dramatic play was the most frequent type of cognitive play. The other categories of cognitive play were either observed infrequently (functional, constructive, exploratory) or not at all (games-with-rules). Non-play behaviors constituted little of the time spent in the centers.

Table 6.2   Mean Frequencies and Standard Deviations of

Play and Non-Play Behaviors

TYPE OF PLAY	CENTER THEMES							
	H1	Hos	Pir	Bak	Pha	Piz	H2	H3
Solitary								
M	.10	.10	.07	.07	.04	.27	.04	.07
SD	.30	.30	.26	.26	.20	.45	.19	.25
Parallel								
M	.25	.23	.22	.45	.34	.26	.27	.38
SD	.44	.42	.41	.50	.48	.44	.44	.49
Group								
M	.27	.27	.26	.12	.20	.16	.31	.14
SD	.44	.44	.44	.33	.41	.37	.47	.35
Functional								
M	.04	.00	.03	.03	.03	.04	.01	.04
SD	.20	.00	.18	.16	.17	.20	.11	.21
Constructive								
M	.02	.06	.02	.06	.08	.06	.03	.03
SD	.15	.24	.15	.23	.28	.24	.16	.17
Exploratory								
M	.02	.03	.03	.02	.05	.03	.03	.03
SD	.15	.18	.18	.13	.22	.17	.18	.17
Dramatic								
M	.53	.50	.46	.55	.42	.56	.55	.48
SD	.50	.50	.50	.50	.50	.50	.50	.50
Games								
M	.00	.00	.00	.00	.00	.00	.00	.00
SD	.00	.00	.00	.00	.00	.00	.00	.00
Transitional								
M	.05	.05	.02	.07	.09	.05	.05	.05
SD	.21	.22	.13	.25	.29	.22	.22	.22
Unoccupied								
M	.02	.05	.03	.03	.02	.03	.05	.07
SD	.15	.22	.18	.16	.14	.17	.22	.25
Onlooker								
M	.12	.16	.18	.11	.09	.07	.07	.12
SD	.33	.37	.38	.31	.29	.26	.25	.32
Peer Conversation								
M	.09	.05	.08	.07	.09	.08	.14	.07
SD	.29	.22	.27	.26	.29	.27	.35	.26

Howe, Moller, and Chambers

Table 6.2   Mean Frequencies and Standard Deviations of
Play and Non-Play Behaviors (continued)

TYPE OF PLAY	CENTER THEMES							
	H1	Hos	Pir	Bak	Pha	Piz	H2	H3
Teacher Conversation								
M	.07	.08	.10	.06	.09	.04	.05	.08
SD	.25	.27	.31	.23	.29	.20	.21	.27
Rough & Tumble								
M	.01	.01	.04	.02	.00	.04	.01	.00
SD	.11	.09	.20	.13	.00	.20	.08	.00
Wandering								
M	.02	.01	.02	.01	.03	.01	.01	.03
SD	.13	.09	.15	.09	.17	.10	.11	.17

H1 = Housekeeping Pre-Intervention
H2 = Housekeeping Post-Intervention
H3 = Housekeeping One-Month Follow-Up
Hos = Hospital
Pir = Pirates
Bak = Bakery
Pha = Pharmaceutical Counter
Piz = Pizzeria

NOTE: THESE FREQUENCIES ARE BASED ON A TOTAL OF 1020 OBSERVATIONS

Second, to investigate the influence of the novel dramatic play set-ups, we conducted a series of one-way analyses of variance (ANOVAs) to examine differences in the various types of (a) social play, (b) cognitive play and, (c) non-play behaviors within each center.[1] Regarding social play, there was significantly more solitary play in the pizzeria than in all the other arrangements ($F(7,1012) = 7.33, p < .001$). Children engaged in more parallel play in the bakery than in the traditional housekeeping (before and immediately following the novel centers), hospital, pirate, and pizzeria centers ($F(7,1012) = 4.02, p < .001$). Significantly more group play was observed in the immediate follow-up housekeeping center than in the bakery or the one month follow-up ($F(7,1012) = 3.81, p < .001$). In terms of cognitive play, no significant differences in the levels of cognitive activity were observed across the centers; dramatic play was consistently the most common type of cognitive play. Finally, for non-play categories, significantly more rough-and-tumble behavior was observed in the pirate and the pizzeria centers than in the remaining arrangements ($F(7,1012) = 2.09, p < .04$).[1]

Third, the types of social-dramatic play within each of the centers was investigated. A 3 (solitary, parallel, and group social play) by 8 (pre-, post-, follow-up housekeeping and five novel centers) ANOVA using frequency of dramatic play as the dependent variable was conducted. There was a significant main effect for social play ($F(2,597) = 38.68, p < .001$: solitary $M = .58$, parallel $M = .83$, group $M = .94$) and the social play by center interaction ($F(14,597) = 6.05, p < .001$) suggesting that group dramatic play was observed most frequently in the restaurant, bakery, hospital, and the pre- and post-intervention housekeeping centers. Post-hoc analyses further indicated that the lowest amount of dramatic play was also solitary play which was observed in the pharmacy, hospital, pirate and pre-intervention housekeeping center.

Theme Familiarity and Play

To address the question of the extent to which the novelty of center themes influenced the children's play, centers were grouped by degree of familiarity (high versus low). The bakery, pizzeria, and the traditional housekeeping centers were classified as highly familiar, because these were settings that children often encounter in their daily lives. The hospital, pharmacy, and pirate ship set-ups were designated as novel (or less familiar), because children were less likely to have contact with these situations. The hypothesis that more dramatic play would be displayed in the familiar centers was supported ($t(713) = 2.25, p < .03$: $M = .54, .46$), however, the findings for the social play categories were not as predicted. More solitary play was observed in familiar than novel centers ($t(715) = 2.90, p < .004$: $M = .14, .07$).

Day One Versus Day Three of the Novel Centers

To determine the effects of time on children's play, t-tests were conducted to compare the frequencies of the different types of play on the first and third days of each novel center. Contrary to our hypothesis, children engaged in more parallel play ($t(830) = 2.88, p < .004$: $M = .35, .26$) and dramatic play ($t(830) = 2.78, p < .006$: $M = .55, .45$) on the first than the last day the centers were present. In contrast, on the third day, more functional play ($t(525) = -3.53, p < .001$: $M = .01, .05$) and onlooker behavior ($t(776) = -2.63$), $p < .009$: $M = .09, .15$) was observed. No differences were found for exploratory play on day 1 versus 3 ($t(832) = .66$, n.s.: M = .04, .03), thus our hypothesis was not supported.

Discussion

The present study addressed issues concerned with the influence of the physical environment of dramatic play centers on children's play in a day care setting. Specifically, we focused on the impact of familiar versus novel centers on children's social and cognitive play.

In both the standard housekeeping and novel centers, children were primarily observed engaging in dramatic play, as opposed to other types of cognitive play (functional, constructive, exploratory, games-with-rules) or non-play behavior. Thus, the presence of such centers appeared to facilitate the goal of encouraging children to engage in pretend play, supporting both the research literature (e.g., Smilansky, 1968) and the advice of curriculum experts (Day, 1988; Hendrick, 1988).

In addition, the presence of the centers appeared to facilitate more parallel and group than solitary play, which is in line with the literature suggesting that the goal of such centers is to facilitate group interaction (Rubin et al., 1983). However, when the patterns of social play were investigated, some interesting findings emerged for the specific centers. The pizzeria center appeared to encourage more solitary play than all other centers. Anecdotal descriptions of the set-up indicated that the delivery truck was very popular and only allowed for a single driver, thus, facilitating solitary rather than interactive social play. Higher frequencies of parallel play were observed in the bakery than the traditional housekeeping, hospital, pirate and pizzeria centers. One again, this finding can be explained by the design of the center; the bakery preparation table included playdough and related baking items (e.g., rolling pins, muffin tins) placed in a row. Thus, the children spent the majority of their time standing next to one another making playdough delicacies, rather than engaging in group interactions. Group play was observed most frequently in the post-intervention housekeeping center. We speculate that the degree of familiarity in terms of setting and roles facilitated group play, after having been stimulated by the presence of the novel centers. Finally, the finding that the pirate and pizzeria centers produced the most rough-and-tumble play may also be related to the physical environment. Although, the pirate center did not contain any weapons, the children may have associated the search-for-treasure theme with more rambunctious behavior. The pizza delivery truck was designed so that the children could climb into the back and be hidden from view, a feature which appeared to excite the children. Additionally, at the time of our study, Ninja turtles were very popular and the presence of a center which focused on the turtle's favorite food (pizza) may have contributed to the children's behavior. In conclusion, the physical arrangements of the individual centers and the materials used appeared to facilitate specific types of social play in the individual centers, a finding also reported by Rubin (1977b) and Christie and Johnsen (1987).

A closer examination of the relation between engaging in dramatic play and social play revealed that when children engaged in pretend activities, they did so most frequently in groups. Furthermore, the specific center had an impact on the levels of social-dramatic play. The most group dramatic play was observed in the pizzeria, bakery, hospital and pre-and post-intervention housekeeping centers;

with the exception of the hospital, these centers had been rated as being high in familiarity. Whereas, in the pharmacy, hospital, pirate and housekeeping centers, low frequencies of solitary pretend play were observed. Thus, we conclude that some kinds of centers were more successful in facilitating group dramatic play than others. The previous discussion about the role of the physical environment on the levels of children's social play indicates that similar effects were present when social and dramatic play were jointly considered. Clearly, when designing dramatic centers, the environment should be structured so that the children are more likely to engage in group interactions than in parallel or solitary play. Thus, creating centers with one truck driver or playdough to manipulate in a parallel manner may reduce opportunities for group dramatic play.

When differences in play on day 1 and day 3 were examined, more parallel and dramatic play was observed on the first than on the third day of the centers; additionally, there was more functional play and onlooker behavior on the third than the first day. No differences were observed for exploratory play on day one versus day three. These findings suggest that the impact of the specific centers on the more sophisticated categories of play (dramatic and parallel) was greatest on day one. By day three, the children may have been losing interest in the centers and engaged in simpler or less mature behaviors (functional play and onlooker behavior). These findings were contrary to our hypothesis that children would initially engage in exploratory behaviors on day one and then show increased levels of dramatic play on day three. Children did not appear to spend a long time exploring the centers, rather clearly they understood that the purpose of the centers was to engage in pretend play and did so immediately. These findings have implications for the establishment of dramatic play centers in day care settings and suggest that the novelty of the centers wears off quickly; therefore, one should vary the centers frequently. Although this finding supports Hendrick's (1988) advice regarding frequent changes of centers, information is still lacking about the ideal length of time novel centers should be present in the classroom. Alternatively, the rapid decrease in interest may reflect the fact that the student teachers who set up the centers were present only on day one of the center. Two other groups of interns supervised the centers on days two and three and may not have provided that same degree of supervision and commitment to facilitating dramatic play as the day one interns. The adult's role and presence in stimulating dramatic play over a period of time, is a question that demands further research.

In order to investigate the influence of theme familiarity on children's play, we grouped the centers into two groups (low and high). More dramatic play was observed in the familiar centers than the novel ones, suggesting that for children to engage in pretend play in novel settings, additional information about the roles is required, a finding supported by others (Smilansky, 1968; Woodard, 1984). As Lawton (1988) argues, the notion of integrated curriculum planning may be important, that is, using a specific theme (e.g., hospital) across all areas of programing such as music, art, science, circle-time activities and dramatic play centers. In this way, the connections between different content areas are strengthened and clarified for the children, instead of being presented as isolated bits of information. By providing extra experiences and information (e.g., stories, films, field trips), the teacher enables children to build a foundation of knowledge about how the world functions from which they can create pretend roles. Unfortunately, in our experience, many day care staff neglect the dramatic play center by failing to add new materials to the housekeeping center or by not introducing novel centers. Thus, we recommend that greater attention be paid to the dramatic play center in the day care.

Implications for Teaching

The findings of the present study have implications for early childhood educators working in day care. In programs where teachers define one program goal as that of stimulating pretend play, then dramatic play centers should be established for the children in such classrooms. Based on the present study, we offer the following guidelines: (a) centers should be changed relatively frequently, (b) more familiar as opposed to less familiar themes appear to facilitate pretend play at least when few preparatory experiences (e.g., books, films, visits) are provided, (c) a thematic approach to introducing less familiar centers should be used by integrating the theme across all aspects of the curriculum, and (d) careful attention should be paid to the design of the physical setting in order to stimulate group as well as solitary or parallel dramatic play. Specifically, equipment and materials should be designed which require the interaction of two or more children to be used effectively (e.g., a truck with two steering wheels). For early childhood educators, the ease of setting up and repeating dramatic play centers can be facilitated by collecting theme-related materials in prop boxes (Bender, 1971).

Directions for Future Research and Practice

While teacher-training programs based on principles of child development typically educate student teachers about the value of play for young children, only general information is usually provided about what types of play are appropriate for developing various abilities. Clear, specific, easy-to-implement guidelines are not readily available for educators to apply when establishing creative, educational dramatic centers. This research provides some initial empirical direction for curriculum designers and early childhood educators looking for recommendations regarding the creation of stimulating dramatic play centers in the day care. This preliminary study marks the beginning of a more thorough investigation into the influence of dramatic play centers on children's development. Many research questions remain unanswered; for example, which type of themes are most appropriate for young children? Do boys and girls of different ages play in different thematic centers (e.g., familiar versus unfamiliar)? Do boys and girls engage in the same or different patterns of social and cognitive play in different kinds of centers? How frequently should centers be changed? What is the role of the teacher in facilitating dramatic play and group interaction in these centers? In conclusion, we are addressing some of these questions in work currently underway and are planning future projects which will continue the investigation of the ecological influences on children's play.

REFERENCES

Beatty, J. J. (1984). *Skills for preschool teachers.* Columbus, OH: Charles E. Merrill.

Bender, J. (1971). Have you ever thought of a prop box? *Young Children, 26,* 164-169.

Christie, J. F., & Johnsen, E. P. (1987). Preschool Play. In J. H. Block & N. R. King (Eds.), *School Play: A Source Book.* New York: Garland.

Clarke-Stewart, A., & Fein, G. (1983). Early childhood programs. In P. H. Mussen (Ed.), *Handbook of child psychology, Vol. II,* (pp. 917-1000). New York: Wiley.

Connolly, J., & Doyle, A. B. (1984). Relation of social fantasy play to social competence in preschoolers. *Developmental Psychology, 20,* 797-806.

Cramer, P., & Hogan, K. A. (1975). Sex differences in verbal and play fantasy. *Developmental Psychology, 11,* 145-154.

Curry, N. E., & Arnaud, S. H. (1974). Cognitive implications in children's spontaneous role play. *Theory into Practice, 13,* 273-277.

Dansky, J. L. (1980). Make-believe: A mediator of the relationship between play and associative fluency. *Child Development, 51,* 576-579.

Day, B. (1988). *Early childhood education: Creative learning activities.* New York: MacMillan.

Elder, J., & Pederson, D. (1978). Preschool children's use of objects in symbolic play. *Child Development, 49,* 500-504.

Fein, G. G. (1975). A transformational analysis of pretending. *Developmental Psychology, 11*, 291-296.

Fein, G. G. (1981). Pretend play: An integrative review. *Child Development, 52*, 1095-1118.

Fein, G. (1982). Pretend play: New perspectives. In J. F. Brown (Ed.), *Curriculum planning for young children.* Washington, DC: NAEYC.

Garvey, C. (1976). Some properties of social play. In J. S. Bruner, A. Jolly, & K. Sylva (Eds.), *Play: Its role in development and evolution* (pp. 570-583). New York: Basic Books.

Golomb, C. (1977). Symbolic play: The role of substitutions in pretense and puzzle games. *British Journal of Educational Psychology, 47*, 175-186.

Hendrick, J. (1988). *The whole child: New trends in early education.* Toronto: Mosby.

Kostelnik, M. J., Whiren, A. P., & Stein, L. C. (1986). Living with He-Man. *Young Children, 41*, 3-9.

Lawton, J. T. *(1988). Introduction to child care and early childhood education.* Glenview, IL: Scott, Foresman and Co.

Levy, A., Schaefer, L., & Phelps, P. C. (1986). Increasing preschool effectiveness: Enhancing the language abilities of 3- and 4-year-old children through planned sociodramatic play. *Early Childhood Research Quarterly, 1*, 133-140.

McLoyd, V. C. (1982). Social class differences in sociodramatic play: A critical review. *Developmental Review, 2*, 1-30.

Moller, L. C., & Rubin, K. H. (1987). *Gender and grade differences in children's play.* Paper presented at the Society for Research in Child Development, Baltimore, MD.

Nicolich, L. (1977). Beyond sensori-motor intelligence: Assessment of symbolic maturity through analysis of pretend play. *Merrill-Palmer Quarterly, 23*, 89-99.

Paley, V. (1973). Is the doll corner a sexist institution? *School Review, 81*, 569-576.

Parten, M. (1932). Social participation among preschool children. *Journal of Abnormal Psychology, 27*, 243-269.

Pulaski, M. A. (1973). Toys and imaginative play. In J. L. Singer (Ed.), *The child's world of make-believe.* New York: Academic Press.

Read, K. (1971). *The nursery school.* Philadelphia: Saunders.

Rubin, K. H. (1977a). Play behaviors of young children. *Young Children, 32,* 16-24.

Rubin, K. H. (1977b). The social and cognitive value of preschool toys and activities. *Canadian Journal of Behavioural Science, 9,* 382-385.

Rubin, K. H. (1985). Socially withdrawn children: An "at risk" population? In B. H. Schneider, K. H. Rubin, & J. E. Ledingham (Eds.), *Children's peer relationships: Issues in assessment and intervention.* New York: Springer-Verlag.

Rubin, K. H., Fein, G. G., & Vandenburg, B. (1983). Play. In P. H. Mussen (Ed.), *Handbook of Child Psychology, Vol. IV,* (pp. 694-775). New York: Wiley.

Rubin, K. H., & Maioni, T. L. (1975). Play preference and its relationship to egocentrism, popularity, and classification skills in preschoolers. *Merrill-Palmer Quarterly, 21,* 171-179.

Rubin, K. H., Maioni, T. L., & Hornung, M. (1976). Free play behaviors in middle and lower class preschoolers: Parten and Piaget revisted. *Child Development, 47,* 414-419.

Rubin, K. H., & Mills, R. (1988). The many faces of social isolation in childhood. *Journal of Clinical and Consulting Psychology, 56,* 916-924.

Sachs, J., Goldman, J., & Chaille, C. (1984). Planning in pretend play: Using language to coordinate narrative development. In A. D. Pellegrini & T. D. Yawkey (Eds.), *The development of oral and written language* (pp. 119-128). Norwood, NJ: Ablex.

Silver, P. G., & Ramsey, P. G. (1983). Participant observation: Broadening points of view. *Early Childhood Development and Care, 10,* 147-156.

Smilansky, S. (1968). *The effects of sociodramatic play on disadvantaged preschool children.* New York: Wiley.

Spodek, B., Saracho, O. N., & Davis, M. D. (1987). *Foundations of Early Childhood Education.* Englewood Cliffs, NJ: Prentice-Hall.

Stokes, A. (1975). Applying research to play in the preschool classroom. *Childhood Education, 51,* 232-237.

Woodard, C. Y. (1984). Guidelines for facilitating sociodramatic play. *Childhood Education, 60*, 172-177.

NOTE

1. Previous research has demonstrated differences in social and cognitive play to be a function of age and sex (Moller and Rubin, 1987); therefore, the ANOVAs were repeated controlling for age and sex. These results were identical to the original analyses with the exception that no significant differences were found in the amount of rough-and-tumble behavior exhibited by children across the various centers.

7

Play, Story-song, and Eating Times in Child Care: Caregiver Responses to Toddlers and Threes

Donna S. Wittmer and Alice S. Honig

Caregivers, including parents and teachers, react differentially to children's behaviors depending on children's gender, age, or activity setting. Social learning theory proposes that those behaviors that are responded to will increase in frequency and rate, while those behaviors that are ignored will decrease. Child development professionals need to discover what child behaviors adults respond to more frequently than others, and how the type of teacher technique varies according to child gender, age, and activity setting. Helping caregivers achieve their goals of increasing prosocial play and learning among preschoolers depends on professionals' awareness of the nuances of adult-child interactions and their outcomes.

Caregiver Techniques and Child Gender

Some researchers suggest that caregivers react differently when boys and girls exhibit the same behavior (Dunn & Morgan, 1987). In 15 preschool classes, boys received more attention than girls for aggressive behaviors. When behaving appropriately, boys were more likely than girls to receive nurturant and instructional attention (Serbin, O'Leary, Kent, & Tonick, 1973). Teachers of toddlers attended far more to boys' assertive behaviors than to girls' (Fagot, Hagan, Leinbach, & Kronsberg, 1985).

Caregiver techniques also vary depending on gender of child. In the Serbin study, boys received higher rates of instructions (directions and conversations) and of praise and hugs. Teachers have initiated and used more verbal interactions to catch and hold the attention of preschool boys compared with girls (Cherry, 1975), and have given more verbal stimulation to facilitate boys' cognitive development (Weitzman, Birns, & Friend, 1985). However, in another study caregivers gave more instructional and social contacts to preschool girls and more disciplinary responses to boys (Appleford and Ryan, 1977). Thus, research provides conflicting evidence regarding positive adult input as a function of child gender, but consistent evidence that boys receive more attention for negative behaviors.

119

Caregiver Techniques and Age of Child

Caregivers may be reacting to different child behaviors at different ages because children are behaving differently at those ages. Play becomes more complex with increasing preschool age (Pellegrini, 1985). Also, two-year-olds may be expected to be involved in more negative behaviors than three-year-olds because they are struggling toward autonomy (Erikson 1963). Caregivers may then find themselves responding to more negative behaviors with twos than with threes. Caregivers may also respond to more distress behavior among twos than threes because (1) twos exhibit more distressful needy behavior and (2) caregivers see twos as younger and thus more vulnerable and in need of being taken care of by adults. Threes, on the other hand, may make more cognitive demands of caregivers, as they take more initiatives (Erikson 1963) and as their language capabilities expand. With their disadvantaged mothers, children initiated significantly more interactions at 30 months than at 12, 18, and 24 months (McGlaughlin, Empson, Morrissey & Sever, 1980). This increase in bids may be due to the fact that by 30 months the children were often initiating their *own* play activities as opposed to the mothers' more active role in facilitating child play at earlier ages. Mothers' responses became more positive as the child reached 30 months of age. Teaching and the provision of intellectual interactions increased significantly from 24 to 30 months. Parents used more control techniques with one-and-a-half-year-olds than with children one and two years older (McLaughlin, 1983).

In a high-quality university run child-care center, the proportion of informational inputs from adults decreased as the age of the children increased from one to four years. However, there was a rise with increasing age in the use of adult inquiries (Honig, Caldwell, & Tannenbaum, 1970). Two-year-olds in a nursery setting in Britain were involved in fewer total contacts with staff (20 percent of observations) than were the three and four-year-olds (47 percent of observations) (Ferri, 1981). Age of child, then, does seem to exert an influence on the quantity and quality of techniques caregivers direct toward young children.

Caregiver Techniques and Activity Setting

Caregivers behave differently with young children depending on the activity setting in which the interaction takes place. Children self-select into particular play activities, such as art and dramatic play, according to age and gender, and qualitative differences in play are found in particular settings (Pellegrini & Perlmutter, 1989). For example, highly trained caregivers of toddlers in child care exhibited far fewer positive social-emotional behaviors at lunch time. While negative social-emotional input ranged from 4 percent of teacher repertoire in the mornings to 11 percent of teacher repertoire in the afternoons, negative social-emotional behaviors represented about 20 percent of the teacher behaviors at lunch time (Honig & Lally, 1988).

Caregiver Techniques and Child's Prior Behavior

Child effects on caregivers cannot be dismissed as a minor influence on caregivers' behavior. Martin, Maccoby, Baran, & Jacklin (1981) concluded that for children 18 months-of-age the effects of child negative behavior on mother negative behavior seemed large compared to all other contingencies.

Research Questions

Questions asked in this study are the following:

What were children in child care doing when teachers interacted with them?

Are there gender, age, and setting differences in child behavior occurring prior to a teacher's attempt to interact with a child?

What techniques do teachers use when interacting with children?

Do teacher techniques differ according to child gender, age, activity setting, and behavior?

This paper explores activities of two- and three-year-olds and the responses of their teachers in order to identify immediate contingencies and effects of caregivers on children and children on caregivers. We also attempted, as Lytton (1980) has suggested, to "analyze the mechanisms by which social behavior patterns arise and are maintained and eliminated, and show how behavioral changes are a function of interactional-contextual factors" (p. 11).

Methodology

To analyze the specific interactions occurring in child care, fine grained observational studies focusing on microanalytic chains of adult-child interactions are needed. Direct observation of events as they naturally occur allows one to draw conclusions about relationships between persons that are occurring in a particular setting, as well as the influence of the setting on the behavior. "Direct observations of interchanges preserve the powerful effects of setting, the influence of the ongoing acts of the other person, and variations in immediate bodily states, as well as the child's unique and enduring contributions to relationship" (Cairns, 1979, p. 202).

Subjects

Children included in this study were 50 males and 50 females from low-income families attending ten child care centers in a moderately sized urban area. Of the 100 subjects, 25 males and 25 females were two-year-olds, 24-30 months, (mean age 27 months). The other 25 males and 25 females were three-year-olds, 36-42 months, (mean age 39 months). Of the two-year-old boys, 16 were black and 9 white, and of the two-year-old girls 14 were black and 11 white. There were 17 black three-year-old boys and eight white and 15 black three-year-old girls and 10 white. Thus, the two-year-old population was comprised of 30 black and 20 white children and the three-year-old population of 32 black and 18 white children. Twenty-one two-year-old boys and nineteen two-year-old girls had one parent in the home, while 21 three-year-old boys and 19 three-year-old girls lived with mother in a single-parent family.

Subjects were observed in ten child-care centers. Thus, the total sample of children in the appropriate age ranges was observed. Selection of children across centers minimizes the possibility that caregiver-child behaviors will be idiosyncratic to caregiver or child functioning or activity setting in any one particular child care center and increases the external validity of research findings.

The ten child-care centers had populations ranging from 30-100 children. The majority of two-year-old children attended age-segregated classrooms with children ranging in age from 18 months to three-years-of-age. Only one center included the two-year-olds with the three-and four-year-olds. Nine of the centers enrolling three-year-olds maintained age-segregated classrooms, typically including three-and four-year-olds together.

The average size of the age-segregated classes was 12 children while the age-mixed classes ranged from 30-40 children. The age-mixed classes had access to several rooms offering activity choices for play. The average ratio of adults to children was three or four children to one teacher regardless of whether the classrooms were age-mixed or age-segregated. Classrooms typically had a head teacher and two assistants.

The majority of the caregivers did not have professional degrees in early education or child development. Approximately half the teachers were black and half were white.

Measures

The observational system used was APPROACH (A Procedure for Patterning Responses of Adults and Children) (Caldwell & Honig, 1971). APPROACH provides a microanalytic record of continuous sequential chains of behaviors in natural settings relative to a designated central figure.

The behavioral record for each child is obtained by stationing an observer near the subject to be observed and having the observer whisper every five seconds into a tape recorder every unit of behavior emitted by the subject and every response directed toward the subject or emitted within his or her social range (Honig, Caldwell & Tannenbaum, 1970).

Four graduate students carried out the observations. Observer reliability above 85 percent for each behavioral category was obtained. Reliability was computed by determining the (number of agreements) divided by the (number of agreements plus the number of disagreements) for each behavioral category (subject, behavioral predicates, object of behavioral predicates, and supplementary information). The recorders did not know the purpose of the data gathering. The caregivers were told only that certain children in their classrooms were being observed, but were not told specifically who was being observed nor for what purpose. They were not alerted to the fact that their behavior was also being observed as they interacted with the central figure.

Alison Clarke-Stewart (1979) has stated that "generalizations from naturalistic observations are challenged by the extreme variability between children's natural settings." To counteract the problem of differences in settings and to study potential influences of these differences, toddlers and threes were observed in five different settings which are typically found in group child care.

1. Story/song (listen to teachers reading stories, sing songs, play rhythm games, listen to records, etc.—in a structured teacher-led activity)

2. Creative (paint, glue, play in sand, dramatic movement/dance/play, etc.)

3. Eating (wait for food, attempt to obtain food for self and others, eat food).

4. Fine Motor (play with beads, pegs, small animals, small blocks, small wooden or plastic people; cut, stencil, etc.)

5. Gross Motor (climb, jump, play with large blocks, swim, ride toys, etc.)

Each child was observed four times for four minutes in each of five typical child care settings during morning hours for a total observed time of 80 minutes per child. No more than two observations per child were carried out for a particular setting on any given day and no more than five observations per child were recorded on any one day.

Thus a minimum time to observe a child was four mornings, although the average number of days to complete the observations on any one child was nine days. The average time span for observing a child was 60 days. A child was not observed if the child had begun the program within the past two weeks or if the child had been ill and had just returned to the child care center. Children in a classroom were not observed if more than one of the permanent staff were absent for the day.

Coding System

The method used to code caregiver-child interactions was a modification of Bronson's (1974) coding system. This system permitted reliable categorization of a child's behavior occurring prior to a caregiver's attempt to interact with the child and a caregiver's subsequent behavior. Each case of a caregiver interacting or attempting to interact with the target child was analyzed. These cases included events when a target child approached a caregiver and initiated the interaction *when* the caregiver responded to the child's bid. If the caregiver did not respond to the child, then the child's behavior did not become a part of the analysis. Attempts on the part of the caregiver to interact with the target child and the child's behavior occurring prior to the caregiver's attempt to interact are reported in this paper.

Child Behavior Prior to Teacher Bid

Each child behavior occurring prior to a caregiver interaction was coded into one or a combination of the following four categories.

1. Actively Involved in Play with Objects or People: Includes child "actively involved," "involved with food," "positively engaged with peers," "expressing happiness," "caregiving," and "complying," alone or in combination with each other.

2. Expressed Need: Includes "making bid to caregiver" and child "expressing distress or displaying need."

3. Nonengaged: Child stands around, waits, wanders, does not attend to activity in which child is to be engaged.

4. Negatively involved: Includes child "misbehaving," non-complying," "Negatively engaged with peers," alone, or in combination with each other, and/or in conjunction with "nonengaged" or "expressing need."

The behaviors of the children were coded independent of the technique a caregiver used following the behavior. Reliability was established with one graduate student in Child and Family Studies and one professor of Child

Development (ASH). Intercoder reliability was $r = .89$ with the student and $r = .90$ with the professor. Reliability was determined by dividing (agreements) by (agreements plus disagreements). These child behaviors prior to an adult bid were then ordered from more positive to less positive by three independent coders. Reliability was 100 percent.

Caregiver Bids to Children

A bid is defined as a caregiver attempt to interact with a child in order to give the child an opportunity to respond. Caregiver bids were coded according to latent content analysis. "Context, role relations, gestures, and psycholinguistic features, reactions of listener and sender, etc." (Schachter, 1976) were taken into consideration. Thus, caregiver A's technique, "What are you doing?" in a kind voice was coded as "questioning" while caregiver B's bid, "Who do you think you are?" (although in an interrogative form) said in an angry voice, was coded as negatively controlling. Reliability was established with a graduate student ($r = .88$) and a professor (ASH) ($r = .92$). Each caregiver bid to a child was coded into one and only one of the following six categories.

1. Ego Boosting: Includes caregiver "positively reinforcing," alone or in conjunction with a "teaching," "facilitating" and/or "directing to learning activity" and/or "questioning" technique. Encouraging the child positively was the *primary* purpose of the adult bid.

2. Teaching/Facilitating: Includes caregiver "informing," "facilitating," and/or "directing to learning activity."

3. Questioning: Includes questioning technique, alone, or in conjunction with "informing," "facilitating," and/or "directing to learning activity."

4. Combining (Positive) and (Negative and/or Commanding Techniques): Includes caregiver "informing," "facilitating," "directing to a learning activity" and/or "questioning" with "commanding" and/or "negatively reinforcing," "inhibiting/forbidding," and/or "restricting."

5. Commanding: Includes giving orders, suggestions, and requests that a child behave in a certain manner (does not include directing a child to a learning activity).

6. Negatively Controlling: Includes teacher "negatively reinforcing," "inhibiting/forbidding" and/or "restricting," alone, in combination, or in conjunction with "commanding."

The caregiver bids were rank ordered from more positive to less positive by three independent coders. Reliability was 100 percent. ANOVAS were used to analyze major effects of sex, age and interactions of sex/age.

Results

A total of 8308 attempts were made by teachers to communicate with 100 2- and 3-year-old boys and girls in 8000 minutes or 133.33 hours of observation in ten typical day care settings. An average of 83 caregiver-child interactions or attempted caregiver-child interactions occurred for each child within 80 minutes of observation. Each child had the opportunity to respond to an average of 16 caregiver bids during each of five settings. Thus, caregivers attempted to communicate with each child, on the average, once a minute.

Child Behavior Prior to a Teacher Bid

Approximately 55 percent (4502) of the child behaviors occurring prior to a caregiver bid were "active involvement" (see Table 7.1).

Table 7.1   Frequency and Percentage of

Child Behavior Prior to Teacher Bid

CHILD PRIOR BEHAVIOR	FREQUENCY	PERCENTAGE
Active Involvement	4502	54.19%
Expressing Need	1721	20.72%
Nonengagement	479	5.77%
Negatively Involved	1606	19.33%

Child prior behaviors that "expressed need" comprised 20.7 percent of the child behavior occurring prior to teacher bids. Another 20 percent of child prior behaviors were "negative" behaviors including noncompliance, misbehavior, or negative peer interaction. Only 5.8 percent of the child behaviors were "nonengagement" at the time of a teacher bid.

Gender and Age Differences in Child Behavior Prior to a Teacher Bid

Two-year-old boys were involved in significantly more interactions with caregivers than were two-year-old girls (boys 2180, girls 1847). No such differences were found for threes (see Table 7.2).

Table 7.2 Child Prior Behavior: Sex Differences

PRIOR BEHAVIOR	NUMBER	MEAN	SD*	%*	M%*
(Twos and Threes)					
Actively Involved					
Female	2353	47.06	23.77	59.30%	58.57%
Male	2149	42.98	20.10	49.52%	48.70%
Expressing Need					
Female	802	16.04	12.84	20.21%	19.88%
Male	919	18.38	9.49	21.18%	21.41%
Nonengagement					
Female	219	4.38	4.04	5.52%	5.68%
Male	260	5.20	3.72	5.99%	6.67%
Negatively Involved					
Female	594	11.88	8.05	14.97%	15.87%
Male	1012	20.24	11.80	23.52%	23.23%
Total					
Female	3968	79.36	30.87		
Male	4340	86.80	31.19		
(Two–year–olds)					
Actively Involved					
Female	1127	45.08	21.60	61.02%	59.92%
Male	979	39.16	18.77	44.91%	44.01%
Expressing Need					
Female	307	12.28	5.71	16.62%	17.54%
Male	422	16.88	6.91	20.47%	19.36%
Engagement					
Female	140	5.60	3.91	7.58%	7.85%
Male	153	6.12	3.80	7.02%	7.48%
Negatively Involved					
Female	273	10.92	9.46	14.78%	14.70%
Male	626	25.04	13.43	28.72%	28.04%
Total					
Female	1847	73.88	26.34		
Male	2180	87.20	32.05		
(Three–year–olds)					
Actively Involved					
Female	1226	49.04	26.05	57.80%	54.17%
Male	1170	46.80	21.03	54.17%	53.39%
Expressing Need					
Female	495	19.80	16.64	23.34%	22.21%
Male	497	19.88	11.47	23.01%	22.35%

Table 7.2   Child Prior Behavior: Sex Differences (continued)

PRIOR BEHAVIOR	NUMBER	MEAN	SD*	%*	M%*
Nonengagement					
Female	79	3.16	3.87	3.73%	3.52%
Male	107	4.28	3.47	4.95%	5.83%
Negatively Involved					
Female	321	12.84	6.40	15.13%	17.05%
Male	386	15.44	7.46	17.87%	18.43%
Total					
Female	2121	84.84	34.48		
Male	2160	86.40	30.95		

*SD = STANDARD DEVIATION   % = PERCENT THAT CHILD PRIOR BEHAVIOR REPRESENTS OF ALL CHILD PRIOR BEHAVIOR FOR THAT AGE   M% = MEAN PERCENT.

Caregivers directed 4027 bids toward twos while directing 4281 toward threes. This difference was not significant. Neither was there a difference in number of interactions between two-year-olds and three-year-olds when females and males were analyzed separately. There was a main effect of gender of child for proportion of "active involvement" ($F = 15.21$ $p = .000$) and a gender X age interaction effect ($F = 5.69$ $p = .019$) (see Table 7.3). Two-year-old girls' active involvement represented a higher percentage of their behavior prior to a teacher interaction than for any other gender or age group. Two-year-old girls' active involvement represented almost 60 percent of their behavior prior to a teacher interaction while two-year-old boys' active involvement represented 44 percent. Three-year-old children were "expressing need" (asking questions or asking for help or attention) significantly more than twos (see Table 7.3).

Table 7.3   Child Prior Behavior: ANOVAS for Sex and Age of Child

SOURCE	DEPENDENT VARIABLE	F	p
Sex (a)	Percent—Active Involvement	15.21	.000
Sex/Age (a d)	Percent—Active Involvement	5.69	.019
Age (d)	Number—Expressing Need	8.08	.005
Age (c)	Number—Nonengagement	8.08	.005
Age (c)	Percent—Nonengagement	8.84	.004
Sex (b)	Number—Negatively Inv.	19.06	.000
Age (c)	Number—Negatively Inv.	4.02	.048
Sex/Age (b c)	Number—Negatively Inv.	9.05	.003

Table 7.3   Child Prior Behavior: ANOVAS for Sex and Age of Child (continued)

SOURCE	DEPENDENT VARIABLE	F	p
Sex (b)	Percent—Negatively Inv.	14.30	.000
Age (c)	Percent—Negatively Inv.	3.47	.065
Sex/Age (b c)	Percent—Negatively Inv.	9.07	.000

A = GIRLS HIGHER   B = BOYS HIGHER   C = TWOS HIGHER   D = THREES HIGHER

Analysis of the number of "nonengagement" behaviors prior to teacher bids revealed a main effect for age ($p = .005$), but not gender of child (see Table 7.3). An ANOVA on percentage score for nonengagement behaviors prior to teacher bid also revealed a main effect of age ($p = .004$). Twos were nonengaged in play more often than threes when teachers approached them.

A significant gender X age interaction as well as a main effect of sex occurred for numbers of "negatively involved" child behaviors (See Table 7.3). For percentage of "negatively involved" prior behaviors there was a significant main effect of gender and a significant gender X age interaction. Two-year-old boys exhibited higher numbers (626) and percentages (28 percent) of "negatively involved" behaviors prior to a caregivers' bid than any other gender X age group considered in this study. Two-year-old males exhibited a mean of 25.04 negative behaviors prior to teacher bid, while three-year-old males exhibited a mean of 15.44. The number of two-year-old males' negative behaviors occurring prior to a teacher bid exceeded that of any other group (see Table 7.4):

two-year-old boys:	626
three-year-old boys:	386
three-year-old girls:	321
two-year-old girls:	273

Table 7.4   Child Prior Behavior: Age Differences

PRIOR BEHAVIOR	NUMBER	MEAN	SD*	%*	M%*
(Males and Females)					
Actively Involved					
Twos	2106	42.12	20.25	52.30	51.96
Threes	2396	47.92	23.46	55.97	55.30
Expressing Need					
Twos	729	14.58	6.69	18.10%	19.00%
Threes	992	19.84	14.14	23.17%	22.28%

Table 7.4   Child Prior Behavior: Age Differences (continued)

PRIOR BEHAVIOR	NUMBER	MEAN	SD*	%*	M%*
Nonengagement					
Twos	293	5.86	3.82	7.28%	7.66%
Threes	186	3.72	3.68	4.35%	4.67%
Negatively Involved					
Twos	899	17.98	13.53	22.32%	21.37%
Threes	707	14.14	7.00	16.51%	17.74%
(Females)					
Actively Involved					
Twos	1127	45.08	21.60	61.02%	59.92%
Threes	1226	49.04	26.05	57.80%	57.22%
Expressing Need					
Twos	307	12.28	5.71	16.62%	17.54%
Threes	495	19.80	16.64	23.34%	22.21%
Nonengagement					
Twos	140	5.60	3.91	7.58%	7.85%
Threes	79	3.16	3.87	3.73%	3.52%
Negatively Involved					
Twos	273	10.92	9.46	14.78%	14.70%
Threes	321	12.84	6.40	15.13%	17.05%
(Males)					
Actively Involved					
Twos	979	39.16	18.77	44.91%	44.01%
Threes	1170	46.80	21.03	54.17%	53.39%
Expressing Need					
Twos	422	16.88	6.91	19.36%	20.47%
Threes	497	19.88	11.47	23.01%	22.35%
Nonengagement					
Twos	153	6.12	3.80	7.02%	7.48%
Threes	107	4.28	3.47	4.95%	5.83%
Negatively Involved					
Twos	626	25.04	13.43	28.71%	28.04%
Threes	386	15.44	7.46	17.87%	18.43%

*SD = STANDARD DEVIATION   % = PERCENT THAT PRIOR BEHAVIOR
 REPRESENTS OF ALL PRIOR BEHAVIORS FOR THAT AGE GROUP
 M% = MEAN PERCENT.

Setting Differences in Child Behavior Prior to Teacher Bid

The largest number of interactions (2157) between caregivers and children occurred in story-song setting. Almost 26 percent of all attempted caregiver interactions with children occurred in this setting which was always a teacher-led activity with children participating in groups (see Table 7.5).

Table 7.5   Teacher-Child Interactions Within Settings: Frequencies and Percentages

SETTING	FREQUENCY	PERCENTAGE
Story/Song	2157	25.96%
Creative	1728	20.80%
Eating	1405	16.91%
Fine-Motor	1767	21.27%
Gross-Motor	1251	15.06%

Approximately one-fifth of the teacher interactions occurred in creative setting and one-fifth in fine-motor setting. These settings were quite similar in that teachers usually led a group activity and children were allowed to play with certain teacher-chosen materials. The major difference was that fine-motor materials typically had a final correct result that children worked toward such as putting together a puzzle or copying templates. In creative activity more "open materials" were available that allowed children to concentrate on process rather than product.

Almost 17 percent (1405) of the teacher interactions with children occurred during eating. The fewest adult interactions with children occurred in gross-motor activity setting.

Story/song setting had 1474 "active involvements" while gross-motor setting had 539 (see Table 7.6). Within story-song setting, then, almost three times as many positive child behaviors of "active involvement" occurred just before a caregiver bid than in gross motor setting. On the other hand, in story-song and creative settings, equal numbers of "negatively involved" child behaviors occurred prior to a teacher bid (655) when compared with fine-motor and gross-motor activities (653). The fewest "nonengagement" prior behaviors (47) occurred in gross-motor setting where most children were generally allowed to play and explore the environment freely and the most (145) in story-song where children were usually required to sit in a group and listen to an adult read a story.

"Expressing need" occurred the most (419) in fine-motor and the least in story-song (195). A high number (403) of "expressing need" behaviors also occurred in eating setting.

Table 7.6 *Child Prior Behaviors Within Settings:*

Frequencies and Percentages

| | CHILD PRIOR BEHAVIOR | | | |
Setting	AI*	EN*	NE*	NI*
Story/Song				
Number	1474	195	145	343
Percentage**	68.34%	9.04%	6.72%	15.90%
Creative				
Number	975	366	75	312
Percentage	56.42%	21.18%	4.34%	18.06%
Eating				
Number	579	403	125	298
Percentage	41.21%	28.68%	8.90%	21.21%
Fine-Motor				
Number	935	419	87	326
Percentage	52.91%	23.71%	4.92%	18.45%
Gross-Motor				
Number	539	338	47	327
Percentage	43.09%	27.02%	3.76%	26.14%

* AI = ACTIVE INVOLVEMENT   EN = EXPRESSING NEED   N = NONENGAGEMENT
  NI = NEGATIVELY INVOLVED
** PERCENTAGE THAT NUMBER REPRESENTS OF ALL CHILD PRIOR BEHAVIOR IN
   THAT PARTICULAR SETTING

Teacher Bids to Children

The majority of caregiver bids were teaching bids (3830, 46.10 percent) (see Table 7.7). Questions to children comprised 23.6 percent of teacher repertoire while ego boosts were 7.5 percent. Encouragingly, then, 77.2 percent of teacher bids to children were positive in nature.

Almost 17 percent of teacher bids involved "negatively controlling" or "commanding" children. Another 6 percent of teacher bids were "combining positive and negative" techniques. Thus, almost one-fourth of teacher bids to twos and threes included a negative technique or a command.

Gender and Age of Child and Caregiver Bid

An ANOVA analyzing the effects of gender and age of child on percentage of adult "ego boosting" revealed a trend for a main effect of child age ($F = 3.55$, $p = .062$) (see Table 7.8), with twos receiving a higher percentage than threes (see Table 7.9).

Table 7.7   *Frequency and Percentage of Teacher Bids to Children*

TEACHER BIDS	FREQUENCY	PERCENTAGE
Ego Boosting	619	7.45%
Teaching	3830	46.10%
Questioning	1962	23.61%
Combining	503	6.05%
Commanding	770	9.27%
Negatively Controlling	624	7.51%

Table 7.8   *Teacher Bids: ANOVAS for Sex and Age of Child*

SOURCE	DEPENDENT VARIABLE	F	p
Age (c)	Percent—Ego Boosting	3.55	.062
Age (d)	Number—Questioning	7.67	.007
Sex (a)	Percent—Questioning	6.05	.016
Age (d)	Percent—Questioning	6.01	.016
Sex (b)	Number—Combining	7.76	.006
Age (c)	Number—Combining	3.30	.072
Sex/Age (bc)	Number—Combining	5.75	.018
Sex (b)	Percent—Combining	5.64	.020
Age (c)	Percent—Combining	4.47	.076
Sex/Age (bc)	Percent—Combining	3.22	.076
Sex (b)	Number—Negatively Con.	8.60	.004
Sex (b)	Percent—Negatively Con.	8.60	.004

A = GIRLS HIGHER   B = BOYS HIGHER   C = TWOS HIGHER   D = THREES HIGHER

"Teaching" bids represented almost 45 percent of the teacher bids children received whether they were two or three, male or female (see Tables 7.9 and 7.10).

An ANOVA revealed a main effect of age ($p = .007$) for number of questions (see table 8), and both a main effect of gender ($p = .016$) and age ($F = 6.01$, $p = .016$) for percentage of questions. Three-year-olds received more caregiver questions than two-year-olds (1129 versus 833) (see Table 7.9). Three-year-old girls received the highest number of questions (601). Almost 30 percent of the bids they received from teachers were questions. Two-year-old boys received almost 200 fewer questions than did three-year-old girls.

A higher percentage of questions was directed at females than at males (see Table 7.10). Questions represented almost 26 percent of the interactions between teachers and girls while questions comprised approximately 20 percent of boys' interactions with teachers.

Table 7.9   Teacher Bids to Children: Age Differences

TEACHER BID	NUMBER	MEAN	SD*	%*	M%*
(Males and Females)					
Ego Boosting					
Twos	326	6.52	4.82	8.10%	8.02%
Threes	293	5.86	4.90	6.84%	6.34%
Teaching					
Twos	1853	37.06	16.19	46.01%	45.83%
Threes	1977	39.54	18.01	46.18%	45.73%
Questioning					
Twos	833	16.66	7.13	20.69%	21.38%
Threes	1129	22.58	13.25	26.37%	25.92%
Combining					
Twos	289	5.78	5.20	7.18%	6.77%
Threes	214	4.28	3.33	5.00%	5.00%
Commanding					
Twos	388	7.76	4.93	9.63%	9.71%
Threes	382	7.64	4.15	8.92%	9.78%
Negatively Controlling					
Twos	338	6.76	5.54	8.39%	8.29%
Threes	286	5.72	4.51	6.69%	7.22%
(Females)					
Ego Boosting					
Twos	142	5.68	5.60	7.69%	7.08%
Threes	143	5.72	4.96	6.74%	6.17%
Teaching					
Twos	874	34.96	14.97	47.32%	46.83%
Threes	970	38.80	19.60	45.73%	45.00%
Questioning					
Twos	430	17.20	7.69	23.28%	23.75%
Threes	601	24.04	14.59	28.33%	28.11%
Combining					
Twos	91	3.64	2.23	4.93%	5.03%
Threes	103	4.12	3.11	4.86%	4.76%
Commanding					
Twos	193	7.72	5.35	10.45%	10.64%
Threes	180	7.20	4.04	8.49%	9.67%
Negatively Controlling					
Twos	117	4.68	4.77	6.33%	6.68%
Threes	124	4.96	3.39	5.85%	6.29%

Table 7.9   Teacher Bids to Children: Age Differences (continued)

TEACHER BID	NUMBER	MEAN	SD*	%*	M%*
(Males)					
Ego Boosting					
Twos	184	7.36	3.84	8.44%	8.95%
Threes	150	6.00	4.92	6.95%	6.50%
Teaching					
Twos	979	39.16	17.37	44.91%	44.82%
Threes	1007	40.28	16.64	46.62%	46.47%
Questioning					
Twos	403	16.12	6.63	18.49%	19.02%
Threes	528	21.12	11.87	24.44%	23.73%
Combining					
Twos	198	7.92	6.38	9.08%	8.52%
Threes	111	4.44	3.58	5.14%	5.24%
Commanding					
Twos	195	7.80	4.56	8.94%	8.78%
Threes	202	8.08	4.29	9.35%	9.89%
Negatively Controlling					
Twos	221	8.84	5.55	10.14%	9.91%
Threes	162	6.48	5.37	7.50%	8.15%

*SD = STANDARD DEVIATION   % = PERCENTAGE THAT TYPE OF TEACHER BID REPRESENTS OF ALL TEACHER BIDS FOR THAT SEX/AGE GROUP   M% = MEAN PERCENT.

A main effect for number of caregiver "combination" techniques was found for gender of child ($p = .006$) (see Table 7.8) as well as a significant sex X age interaction ($p = .018$). A main effect for percentage of "combination" techniques was found ($p < .02$) as well as an interaction effect of gender and age ($p = .076$). Two-year-old boys were receiving, by far, higher numbers and percentages of "combination" bids from teachers. ($M = 4.44$). For two-year-old boys "combination" bids comprised almost 10 percent of the bids they received from teachers. In contrast, "combined positive and negative" bids were about 5 percent of the bids three-year-old boys received.

Caregivers gave about the same number of commands to two- and three-year-olds. For both twos and threes "commanding" comprised approximately 10 percent of the bids teachers directed toward boys and girls (see Table 7.9).

A significant main effect of gender of child was found for number of adult "negative controlling" bids ($p = .004$) (see Table 7.8). There was no interactive child gender X age effect for number or percentage of adult negative interactions. Boys, in both age groups (twos—221, threes—162) were receiving high num-

Table 7.10   *Teacher Bids to Children: Sex Differences*

TEACHER BID	NUMBER	MEAN	SD*	%*	M%*
(Twos and Threes)					
Ego Boosting					
Female	285	5.70	5.23	7.18%	6.63%
Male	334	6.68	4.42	7.70%	7.72%
Teaching					
Female	1844	36.88	17.37	46.47%	45.91%
Male	1986	39.72	16.85	45.76%	45.65%
Questioning					
Female	1031	20.62	12.05	25.98%	25.93%
Male	931	18.62	9.84	21.45%	21.38%
Combining					
Female	194	3.88	2.69	4.89%	4.89%
Male	309	6.18	5.41	7.12%	6.88%
Commanding					
Female	373	7.46	4.70	9.40%	10.15%
Male	397	7.94	4.39	9.15%	9.33%
Negatively Controlling					
Female	241	4.82	4.09	6.08%	6.48%
Male	383	7.66	5.54	8.82%	9.03%
(Twos)					
Ego Boosting					
Female	142	5.68	5.60	7.69%	7.08%
Male	184	7.36	3.84	8.44%	8.95%
Teaching					
Female	874	34.96	14.97	47.32%	46.83%
Male	979	39.16	17.38	44.91%	44.82%
Questioning					
Female	430	17.20	7.69	23.28%	23.75%
Male	403	16.12	6.63	18.49%	19.01%
Combining					
Female	91	3.64	2.23	4.93%	5.03%
Male	198	7.92	6.38	9.08%	8.52%
Commanding					
Female	193	7.72	5.36	10.45%	10.60%
Male	195	7.80	4.56	8.95%	8.78%

Table 7.10   Teacher Bids to Children: Sex Differences (continued)

TEACHER BID	NUMBER	MEAN	SD*	%*	M%*
Negatively Controlling					
Female	117	4.68	4.77	6.34%	6.68%
Male	221	8.84	5.55	10.14%	9.91%
(Threes)					
Ego Boosting					
Female	143	5.72	4.96	6.74%	6.17%
Male	150	6.00	4.92	6.94%	6.50%
Teaching					
Female	970	38.80	19.60	45.73%	45.00%
Male	1007	40.28	16.64	46.62%	46.47%
Questioning					
Female	601	24.04	14.59	28.34%	28.11%
Male	528	21.12	11.87	23.73%	24.44%
Combining					
Female	103	4.12	3.11	4.86%	4.76%
Male	111	4.44	3.58	5.14%	5.24%
Commanding					
Female	180	7.20	4.04	8.49%	9.67%
Male	202	8.08	4.29	9.35%	9.89%
Negatively Controlling					
Female	124	4.96	3.39	5.85%	6.29%
Male	162	6.48	5.37	7.50%	8.16%

*SD = STANDARD DEVIATION   % = PERCENTAGE THAT TYPE OF TEACHER BID REPRESENTS OF ALL TEACHER BIDS FOR THAT SEX/AGE GROUP   M% = MEAN PERCENT

bers of "negatively controlling" teacher bids in comparison to girls (twos—117, threes—124) (see Table 7.9).

Setting of Child and Caregiver Bid to Child

The highest number of "ego boosting" (170) teacher bids occurred in fine-motor setting while the lowest number (90) occurred in eating (see Table 7.11). Children received 1013 "teaching" bids in story/song setting compared to 564 in eating and 561 in gross-motor. "Teaching" bids in story-song and creative settings represent over 20 percent of all teacher bids made to children. By far the highest number of adult questions occurred in story-song setting. Children received 680 questions or almost 35 percent of all questions while they were in story-song setting. Over 20 percent of all teacher questions were asked in fine-motor setting.

Table 7.11   Teacher Bids Within Settings: Frequencies and Percentages

| | SETTING | | | | |
Teacher Bid	S/S*	C*	E*	FM*	GM*
Ego Boosting					
Number	106	153	90	170	100
Percentage**	4.91%	8.85%	6.41%	9.62%	7.99%
Teaching					
Number	1013	881	564	811	561
Percentage	46.96%	50.98%	40.14%	45.90%	44.84%
Questioning					
Number	680	323	309	452	198
Percentage	31.53%	18.69%	21.99%	25.58%	15.83%
Combining					
Number	76	115	110	110	92
Percentage	3.52%	6.66%	7.83%	6.23%	7.35%
Commanding					
Number	177	128	186	118	161
Percentage	3.21%	7.41%	13.24%	6.68%	12.87%
Negatively Controlling					
Number	105	128	146	106	139
Percentage	4.87%	7.41%	10.39%	6.00%	11.11%

 * S/S = STORY/SONG C = CREATIVE E = EATING FM = FINE MOTOR
   GM = GROSS MOTOR
**PERCENTAGE THAT NUMBER REPRESENTS OF ALL TEACHER BIDS IN THAT
   SETTING

"Commanding" occurred frequently in story-song (177), eating (186) and in gross motor (161). "Negatively controlling" bids were represented quite evenly over the five settings with the highest higher number (146) occurring in eating and the lowest number (105) occurring in story-song. The highest percents of commanding and negatively controlling teacher bids, however, occurred in eating and gross motor setting. These two settings are the least structured in terms of teacher planning and perhaps are the most home-like activity settings.

Teacher Bid and Child Behavior Occurring Prior to Teacher Bid

Note the striking change in the number of each type of adult technique in conjunction with a change in the child behavior *prior* to teacher bid (see Table 7.12). For example, caregivers gave 457 ego-boosts to children actively at play or engaged appropriately, but only 9 ego-boosts when children behaved negatively and only 3 ego-boosts when children were nonengaged. Conversely, adult negative controls were used 1 percent of the time in interactions with toddlers and three who were playing appropriately, but in almost 30 percent of the interactions following children's negative interactions.

Table 7.12   Teacher Bids Following Child Prior Behavior: Frequencies and Percentages

	CHILD PRIOR BEHAVIOR			
Teacher Bid	AI*	EN*	NE*	NI*
Ego Boosting				
Number	457	150	3	9
Percentage**	10.15%	8.72%	.63%	.56%
Teaching				
Number	2353	928	200	349
Percentage	52.27%	53.02%	41.75%	21.73%
Questioning				
Number	1350	357	94	161
Percentage	29.99%	20.74%	19.62%	10.02%
Combining				
Number	91	138	25	249
Percentage	2.02%	8.02%	5.22%	15.50%
Commanding				
Number	204	74	123	369
Percentage	4.53%	4.30%	25.68%	22.98%
Negatively Controlling				
Number	47	74	34	469
Percentage	1.04%	4.30%	7.10%	29.20%

* AI = ACTIVE INVOLVEMENT   EN = EXPRESSING NEED
  NW = NONENGAGEMENT   NI = NEGATIVELY INVOLVED
** PERCENTAGE THAT NUMBER REPRESENTS OF ALL TEACHER
   TECHNIQUES USED FOLLOWING THAT CHILD PRIOR BEHAVIOR

    Analysis of the percentage of positive caregiver techniques in response
to each type of child prior behavior revealed a 60 percent difference in teacher
use of positive techniques following children's active involvement
(92.41 percent) compared to their negative involvement (32.31 percent) (see
Figure 7.1).

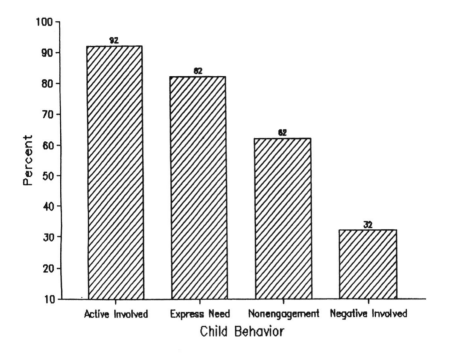

Figure 7.1   Positive Teacher Bid (Following Child Prior Behavior)

    When children were actively involved with toys, food, or peer play, or
were complying with a previous adult bid, then teachers almost always used an
"ego boosting," "teaching," or "questioning" bid. When children were misbehaving, negatively involved with peers, or in the act of noncomplying to a
previous adult bid then only one-third of caregivers' bids were positive teaching
techniques.
    About one-fifth of teacher bids following a negative child prior behavior
were teaching bids. Another 10 percent involved questioning (see Table 7.12).
Negative child behaviors were followed by a high percentage of negative teacher
bids. Almost 70 percent of teacher bids following child negative behavior
included a command and/or negative teacher bid (see Figure 7.2).

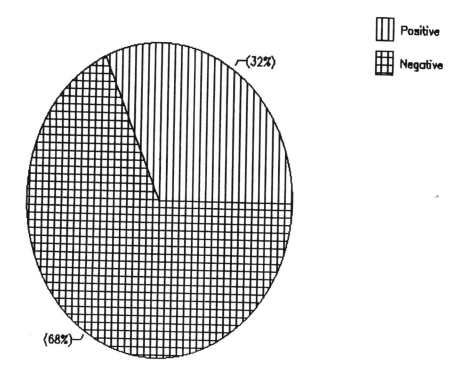

Figure 7.2   Teacher Bid (Following Negative/Nonengaged Child Behaviors)

Discussion

How caregivers respond to children's play and activities has been found in this child-care study to vary with child age and gender and also the setting in which the child was engaged. As well, *the importance of the child's behavior just prior to the adult's bid to the child has been shown to be highly significant in determining the kind of response the teacher gives to the child.* A fine-grained microanalytic technique, APPROACH, made it possible to tease out the interactions of child age, gender, setting, and prior behavior that influence different kinds of adult-child transactions.

Of note in this research is that caregivers were in rather frequent contact with children during the child-care activities, since they communicated with the children on the average of once per minute. Another gratifying finding is that teachers did not interact with the children only when the children expressed need, wandered aimlessly, or were engaged in negative behaviors or peer interactions. In more than half of the episodes when an adult interacted, the children had been involved positively in play or in an appropriate peer activity. Only about one out of twenty caregiver bids was in response to a child's nonengagement.

Gender and age effects as contributing factors to differences in type of teacher interactions were complex. Teachers interacted with toddlers and threes with equal numbers of teacher bids, but significant differences in number of teacher bids to children were found between two-year-old boys and girls. Teachers interacted with boys more frequently. However, a significantly higher proportion of adult bids were given to toddler girls who were actively at play with peers and materials compared with the proportion of such positive caregiver behaviors to any other gender X age group. Nonengaged behaviors of toddlers were more frequent prior to a teacher bid compared with threes. In general, toddler boys' interactions seemed to confirm the reputation of the "terrible twos." Over one-quarter of the time when adults interacted with them they were engaged in negative behaviors, compared with only 15 percent for the three-year-old boys. Toddler boys exhibited the highest rates of negative behavior prior to an interaction with a caregiver compared to all other age/gender groups. Their rates were more than twice that of threes and more than twice that of toddler girls.

These data suggest that teachers will need to be particularly sensitive to the emotional difficulties that male toddlers in child care may exhibit. A teacher who works with two-year-old boys needs to realize that their misbehavior may "entrap" the adult to react to high numbers and percentages of negative child behaviors (fighting, jumping on chairs, running, etc.). Otherwise caregivers may find themselves responding in a *reactive* negative or impatient manner. Such inappropriate teacher responses could exacerbate rather than help the emotional and social development of toddler males, particularly those from more vulnerable home situations (Sroufe, 1985; Wittmer & Honig, 1988). Thus, promoting teacher awareness of *what child behaviors are receiving what kind of adult attention* should be an important part of teacher training.

These data provide some very positive findings concerning the techniques that teachers use in interacting with toddlers and threes. Nearly one-half of teacher interactions were *teaching* interactions. Yet, almost one-fifth of teacher bids did involve negative controls or commands to children, and another 6 percent of bids combined both a positive and a negative technique (often a command to stop an inappropriate behavior coupled with an explanation).

Positive regard and validation of young children have been shown to boost children's self-esteem and increase the prosocial climate of preschool classrooms. In this study, adults proved sensitive to the emotional vulnerability of toddlers, in that they provided more ego-boosts to toddlers than to threes, particularly to male twos. Since problems of separation anxiety and difficulties with dependency and autonomy strivings are more acute for toddlers, this attunement of teachers was gratifying.

Teachers also proved sensitive to the difference in cognitive ability between toddlers and threes. Threes received almost three hundred more adult questions than twos. Our data confirm earlier findings that caregivers are sensitive to age changes in cognitive capacity of preschoolers and provide more verbal challenges to threes compared with twos. Perhaps threes are more intellectually able to capture adult attention for cognitive interchanges, since threes in this study asked for help or attention significantly more than twos did.

In the child-care centers, teaching techniques were distributed about equally to boys and girls, but girls received significantly more questions (over one-quarter of their interactions with teachers) compared with boys (about one-fifth of their interactions with teachers). These data do not support previous findings of increased teacher verbal attentiveness to males.

Toddler males received significantly more combination and negative teacher bids than did any other gender/age group. Approximately one-third of the teacher interactions with a toddler boy involved a combination, commanding, or negative technique. In general, caregivers gave more negatively controlling bids to boys (383) compared with girls (241) regardless of child age. Thus, prior findings that young boys are vulnerable to more negative interactions with caregivers are supported by this research.

These data suggest that caregivers need to self-monitor. Tendencies to "favor" one-gender child over another whether with positive interactions, questions, *or* negative techniques may be difficult interaction styles to recognize in oneself and to attempt to redress any imbalance.

Child behaviors prior to a caregiver bid had a striking impact on the kind of interactions that a teacher offered. When children were playing well with peers or materials, then over 90 percent of teacher bids were positive. Following a negative child involvement with peer or materials, less than one-third of adult responses were positive. Child negative behaviors particularly seemed to call forth a "knee-jerk" negative reaction from caregivers. True, almost one-fifth of teacher responses were informative, and another 10 percent involved inquiries. Yet almost 70 percent of caregiver bids following children's negative behaviors included negative bids or commands. Adults can be easily "hooked" into responding to children's inappropriate behaviors with inappropriate behaviors of their own. These data suggest that teacher training programs need to help caregivers hone their skills at attempting creative solutions to inappropriate child behaviors. Trainers need to encourage those discipline techniques that are more likely to shape positive peer interactions and positive play behaviors with materials. Adults who understand the goals of children's misbehaviors, and who understand the need for preschoolers to learn *prerequisite* skills can better assist children to develop the social, motoric and language skills necessary to enrich their play behaviors and to decrease negative behaviors. Patience, prosocial abilities, and dexterity are slowly built as perceptive adults provide thoughtful feedback and discipline that is intentionally and positively designed to help children develop well.

Child-care settings made a difference in the probability of particular kinds of interchanges between children and adults. More than one-quarter of all adult interactions with toddlers and threes were during story-song time, which is a teacher-led, teacher-dominated group activity. Teaching bids were twice as likely to occur in the teacher-organized story-song setting as during eating. Indeed, questions were also more frequent in story-song setting. Teacher interactions were more frequent during two other teacher-sponsored play times: creative and fine-motor activities. About one-fifth of caregiver interactions occurred during each of these activities. The fewest caregiver attempts to interact with children occurred during the freest play time: gross motor activity. Caregivers may need help in learning to capitalize more on gross motor activity as a time to engage in language and positive interactions with toddlers and threes. During story-song, almost three times as many positive child actions occurred just before an adult bid compared with gross motor play time. Caregivers may want to sensitize themselves to throw in more encouraging comments during freeplay time when children are galloping about a playground. Unfortunately, child-care research has noted that during such times, teachers may be more likely to take time to talk to other adults or rest, rather than engage in positive language interactions with children. Tizard (1981) advises that teachers become aware of the extent that young children's conversations and language exchanges are influenced by the situational constraints of group care.

Setting had a marked influence on the rate at which teacher techniques were utilized. The highest number of ego-boosts (170) was given by adults when children were working with fine motor toys, such as pegboards and puzzles, and the least number (90) was given while toddlers and threes were eating. Such encouragements are vital to children's well-being. If children's behavioral motivations can be improved by encouragements (Dinkmeyer & Dreikurs, 1963) then adults may want to try more creative ways to use ego boosts during a *variety* of play experiences both inside the classroom and on the playground.

Two activities in which young children "expressed need" most just prior to an adult's interaction were "fine motor" and "eating" activities. The high levels of dexterity and coordination required of children in these activities make it more likely that they will experience frustrations with utensils or with difficult puzzle pieces. As a result, children are more likely to behave in what some adults will term "messy" or "naughty" ways. Too great an adult reliance on critical comments or commands during such episodes may subtly shape children's preferences to engage in large muscle play with peers, where fewer demands are placed on them. Children may then avoid striving for excellence in fine motor coordinations and in more challenging fine-muscle activities requiring perseverance and patience.

These data again emphasize the importance of caregiver training to help adults understand how their behavior may be changing according to the activity setting in which the child is engaged.

Conclusions

A microanalytic observation technique, APPROACH, has been used to observe the details of child-adult transactions among 100 two-and three-year-old boys and girls in ten child-care centers that serve primarily children from low-income families. The data reveal complex patterns of influence. Teachers' bids to the children were affected by child age, gender, behavior and situational variables. Overwhelmingly, children's positive play interactions were responded to by positive teacher interactions. Negative involvements with peers and toys were much less likely to receive thoughtful teaching techniques or ego boosting responses that would encourage the children to learn to make more appropriate positive peer and play choices. Two-year-old boys were involved in significantly more negative interactions with caregivers than any other gender or age group.

The data suggest that teacher training programs need to concentrate on specific teaching techniques that can help caregivers curb impulsive reactive responses. Teachers may find it useful to *try more self-reflective techniques prior to responding in play situations* to ensure that their responses will be specifically tailored to enhance and encourage more positive child play skills and learning. The sophisticated metacognitive work that is involved in positive shaping of adult-child interactions in a variety of play situations may require more sophisticated child development training of child-care personnel.

REFERENCES

Appleford, B., & Ryan, T. (1977). An examination social processes in a preschool. *The Journal Of Early Childhood Education, 2* (1), 1-9.

Bronson, W. C. (1974). Mother-toddler interaction: A perspective on studying the development of competence. *Merrill-Palmer Quarterly, 20,* 275-301.

Cairns, R. (Ed.). (1979). *The analysis of social interactions: methods, issues, and illustrations.* Hillsdale, NJ: Lawrence Erlbaum Associates.

Caldwell, B., & Honig, A. S. (1971). APPROACH—A Procedure for Patterning the Responses of Adults and Children. *JSAS Catalog of Selected Documents in Psychology, 1,* 1. (Ms. No. 2).

Cherry, L. (1975). The preschool teacher-child dyad: sex differences in verbal interactions. *Child Development, 46,* 532-536.

Clarke-Stewart, A. (1979). An observation and experiment: complementary strategies for studying day care and social development. In S. Kilmer (Ed.), *Advances in early education and day care.* Greenwich, CT: JAI Press, Inc.

Dinkmeyer, D., & Dreikurs, R. (1963). *Encouraging children to learn.* Englewood Cliffs, NJ: Prentice-Hall.

Dunn, S., & Morgan, V. (1987). Nursery and infant school play patterns: sex-related differences. *British Educational Research Journal, 13*, 271-281.

Erikson, E. (1963). *Childhood and society* (2nd Edition). New York: W. W. Norton.

Fagot, B., Hagan, R., Leinbach, M., & Kronsberg, S. (1985) Differential reactions to assertive and communicative acts of toddler boys and girls. *Child Development, 56*, 1499-1505.

Ferri, E. (1981). The two-year-old in the nursery. *Early Child Development and Care, 7*, 303-316.

Honig, A., Caldwell, B., & Tannenbaum, J. (1970). Patterns of information processing used by and for young children in a nursery school setting. *Child Development, 41*, 1045-1065.

Honig, A. S., & Lally, J. R. (1988). Behavior profiles of experienced teachers of infants and toddlers. In A. S. Honig (Ed.), Optimizing early child care and education (Special Issue). *Early Child Development and Care, 33*, 181-199.

Lytton, H. (1980). *Parent-child interactions.* New York: Plenum Press.

McGlaughlin, B. (1983). Child compliance to parental control techniques. *Developmental Psychology, 19*, 667-673.

McGlaughlin, B., Empson, J., Morrissey, M., & Sever, J. (1980). Early child development and the home environment: consistencies at and between four preschool stages. *International Journal of Behavioral Development, 3*, 299-311.

Martin, J., Maccoby, E., Baran, K., & Jacklin, C. (1981). Sequential analysis of mother-child interaction at 18 months: A comparison of micro-analytic methods. *Developmental Psychology.*

Pellegrini, A. (1985). Social-cognitive aspects of children's play: the effects of age, sex, and activity centers. *Journal of Applied Developmental Psychology, 6*, 129-140.

Pelligrini, A. D., & Perlmutter, J. (1989). Classroom contextual effects on children's play. *Developmental Psychology, 25*, 289-296.

Schachter, F. F. (1976). Everyday caretaker talk to toddlers vs. threes and fours. *Journal of Child Language, 3*, 221-245.

Serbin, L. A., O'Leary, K. D., & Kent, R. N., & Tonick, I. J. (1973). A comparison of teacher responses to the preacademic and problem behavior of boys and girls. *Child Development, 44,* 796-804.

Sroufe, L. A. (1985). Infant-caregiver attachment and patterns of adaptation in preschool: The roots of maladaptation and competence. In M. Permutter (Eds.), *Minnesota Symposium on Child Psychology, 16,* 41-81. Hillsdale, NJ: Erlbaum.

Tizard, B. (1981). Language at home and at school. In C. Cazden (Ed.), *Language in early childhood education.* Washington, DC: N.A.E.Y.C.

Weitzman, N., Birns, B., & Friend, R. (1985). Traditional and nontraditional mothers' communications with their daughters and sons. *Child Development, 56,* 894-898.

Wittmer, D. S., & Honig, A. S. (1988). Teacher re-creation of negative interactions with toddlers. In A. S. Honig (Eds.), Optimizing early child care and education (Special Issue). *Early Child Development and Care, 33,* 77-88.

8

The Play Behaviors of Special Needs Children in Integrated and Non-Integrated Child-Care Settings

Eliana Tobias

Introduction

In the past, early childhood special education has been concerned with compensatory and remedial instruction in order to enrich, compensate or circumvent the child's deficiencies. Programs for special needs preschool children have focused on the children's disabilities and the activities designed to help children gain needed skills in their areas of weaknesses. Early childhood classrooms have been geared towards a structured program where teachers translate children's needs into learning objectives.

Play, however, has received little attention in this literature. Recently, programs for young children with special needs have also focused on enhancing opportunities for peer contact where play is seen as a medium for developing cognitive, social and communication skills for these children. This chapter will explore the play of children with special needs and its relationship to the physical and social composition of the early childhood environment. It will look at the effects of handicapping conditions on play, the types of environments where special needs children are served and the relationship between the quality of the environments and play.

Previous Studies of Special Needs Children in Child Care Settings

What are the effects of handicapping conditions on play behavior? The same developmental sequences observed in the play behavior of normal children are present for special needs children although various types of handicapping conditions affect some qualitative aspects of play (Rogers, 1988). Researchers who have studied cognitive aspects of exceptional children's play using a Piagetian model have reported that sensorimotor and symbolic play develops in the same sequence than in regular children but show delay in their acquisition. The child's disability affects the spontaneity and creativity of play, the attention span and interest and ability for exploration. (Clune, Paolella, and Foley, 1979; Hill and McCune-Nicolich, 1981; Krakow and Kopp, 1983).

Researchers have studied the value of social integration between handicapped and non-handicapped children, in order to understand to what extent contact between these preschoolers takes place (Guralnick, 1981). These studies report that interactions do occur between both groups of children, however the rate of interaction seems to increase when the environment is manipulated (Appoloni and Cooke, 1975; Bricker, 1978; Burstein, 1986; Guralnick, 1978; Pol, Crow, Rider, Offner, 1985). The research has also shown that carefully planned strategies and structure are of great importance for successful integration. (Allen, 1981; Cooke, Ruskus, Apolloni, Peck, 1981; Fenrick, Pearson and Pepelnjak, 1984; Fredericks, Baldwin, Grove, Moore, Riggs, Lyons, 1978; Karnes and Lee, 1978; Kohl and Beckman, 1984). These researchers suggest that physical arrangement, classroom organization, learning through imitation, peer-tutoring, interdisciplinary programming, and program structure are the factors which contribute towards social interaction. Tawney (1981) emphasized the importance of teacher training in order to bring about social change and acceptance of the handicapped child into the regular classroom.

Studies of the relationships between teacher presence in the classroom and children's social integration have yielded mixed results. Field (1980), Novak, Olley, Kearney (1980), and White (1980) have all reported that the teacher's presence appeared to inhibit the play activity of special needs children. However, Jenkins, Speltz, Odom (1985), Peterson (1982) and Rogers, Warren, Ruggles, Peterson, and Cooper (1981), have argued that simply bringing together handicapped and non-handicapped children in the same classroom does not facilitate the social interaction of these children. Their data suggest that teachers need to encourage communication in classrooms and playgrounds and plan for the involvement of children.

There have also been conflicting reports on spontaneous play among handicapped and non-handicapped children in mainstreamed environments. Peterson and Haralick (1977) studied play among five non-handicapped and eight handicapped children. The non-handicapped children chose other non-handicapped children to play with 42 percent of the time and mixed groups of handicapped and non-handicapped children 39% of the time. The type of play in which the children were involved did not change when the non-handicapped children were involved with handicapped children. Although non-handicapped children played more frequently with other non-handicapped peers, they did engage in play activities with the handicapped children to some extent.

Guralnick and Groom (1988) examined whether mildly developmentally delayed differed in their peer related social interactions in mainstreamed and segregated settings. The social play interactions of eleven handicapped four year old boys were observed in a mainstreamed play setting five days a week for two hours for four weeks and in a segregated one, three weeks after being observed in the mainstreamed environment. Children were observed a total of 100 minutes in the mainstreamed environment and 80 minutes in the segregated setting. Children's play was observed in order to record their social participation and cognitive play. Children's social and cognitive play was compared between the two settings. The results showed that there were significant differences between the two settings on two variables: transition (moving from one activity to another) and adult directed (an activity with and adult). As far as cognitive play was concerned, dramatic play rarely occurred in either setting. Proportions of constructive play were considerably higher when children were in the mainstreamed play groups. Guralnick and Groom reported that the measures of social behavior for individual children with developmental delay, were higher in mainstreamed rather than in segregated settings.

There have been some reports in the literature that the play level of handicapped children in mainstreamed settings is positively influenced by interactions with non-handicapped children. (Dunlop, Stoneman and Cantrell, 1982; Frederlien, 1981; Guralnick, 1981; Ispa and Matz, 1978). In contrast, Fenrick, Pearson and Pepelnjak (1984) observed significantly less play behavior in the integrated setting than in the segregated environment for five of six handicapped children in this sample. They also reported a trend towards more cooperative play in the segregated setting.

Communication in play between handicapped and non-handicapped children has been another factor that has been of interest to researchers. It has been reported that in instructional and free play settings, non-handicapped children's speech was generally less frequent, less complex, and less diverse when they communicated with their handicapped peers (Guralnick & Paul-Brown, 1977, Guralnick, 1980). Non-handicapped children have been observed to adjust their patterns of communication so that they are understood by others. In Fenrick's, et. al (1984) study of handicapped children attending both integrated and segregated settings, the children exhibited the same amount of language in both environments, and did not imitate the language of their regular peers in the integrated settings.

Practitioners and researchers have thought that one way to overcome social skill deficits among special needs preschool children would be to deliver services to these youngsters in a non-segregated environment. In fact, social integration has been a powerful justification for mainstreaming. Positive outcomes of integration are the hypothesized development of friendships among children, improvement in the self-concept of the handicapped child, and the observation and imitation of non-handicapped children's language and other skills by the special needs youngster.

Young children with special needs are served in a variety of situations: in segregated programs where all the children are handicapped; in reversed mainstreamed settings, where 50 percent or more of the children have a handicapping condition, and the rest are non-handicapped; in community based day care centers and nursery school programs. Little is known about how these settings affect children's actions and interactions. In an effort to compare preschool environments serving handicapped and non-handicapped children, Bailey, Clifford and Harms (1982) rated 25 classrooms for the handicapped and 56 classrooms for the non-handicapped in North Carolina and Missouri. They reported lower environment ratings for programs for handicapped children.

Programs did not differ significantly in the quality of personal care routines, language reasoning experiences, fine and gross motor activities, and adult needs. However, there were differences in the areas of room arrangement for interest centers and relaxation and comfort, creative activities, and social development. In the programs for special needs children there were fewer art materials, fewer blocks, and no play and storage place for them, there were no provisions for sand, water, or dramatic play and few storage areas which encouraged independent use of materials.

In conclusion, there have been contradictory findings about the experiences handicapped children have with their peers in different types of preschool environments. It is still not clear what specific variables affect children's behaviors in the early childhood program. The questions of whether children's play is enhanced by the quality of the environment and different compositions of groups of children is the major focus of the chapter. The next section will discuss a study which focused on special needs children's play participation in four different types of community-based early childhood settings.

Method

Sample

This study was conducted in early childhood programs located in a large Canadian city. A sample of 20 programs was chosen: 5 segregated, 5 reversed mainstreamed, 5 day care centers and 5 nursery schools. Data were collected on two developmentally delayed preschool children per classroom. The children were between 4 and 5.10 years of age with a mean age of 5 years, 2 months. An attempt was made to match the children on their types of disability, age, gender and socio-economic backgrounds.

Instruments

The Free Play Classification Scale (Higginbotham, Baker and Neill, 1980) was used in order to observe children's social participation and cognitive play. This scale combines Parten's (1932) sequence of social play of preschool children (solitary, parallel, associative, cooperative, onlooker and unoccupied) with Smilansky's (1968) developmental sequence of cognitive play behavior (functional, constructive, dramatic) into clearly defined format. The scale was developed keeping in mind that play follows and order and organization and that children's abilities in problem solving, language processes and concept formation are all reflected in their play modality. (Table 8.1)

Table 8.1   Time Sampling Observation

CHILD

Free Play Classification Scale

SOLITARY Functional		
Constructive		
Dramatic		
PARALLEL Functional		
Constructive		
Dramatic		
ASSOCIATIVE Functional		
Constructive		
Dramatic		
COOPERATIVE		
Constructive		
Dramatic		
UNOCCUPIED		
ONLOOKER		

In order to obtain a measure of the quality of environments available for preschool handicapped children, The Early Childhood Environment Rating Scale (ECERS) (Harms and Clifford, 1980) was used. This scale consists of 37 items which yield a classroom profile based on seven sub-scales: personal care, furnishings display, language reasoning experiences, fine/gross motor, creative activities, social development, adult needs.

The instruments were piloted in two different types of settings: a day-care center and a mainstream after school program for five-year-old children. Two nonhandicapped children were chosen to assess their free play behaviors using the Higginbotham, Baker and Neill (1980) Free Play Classification Scale in the day-care center. An event sampling observation technique was used first for thirty minutes per child. Children were observed for five seconds followed by twenty five seconds for recording. This continued for a thirty minute time period. Children were observed for thirty minute segments over a three day period, generating one hundred and eighty "windows" of type of social/cognitive play for each child. This time sampling observation procedure was used in programs where two special needs children were observed. The pilot revealed that both scales were appropriate for these classrooms and that observers could use them as directed.

Procedure

Two observers were trained in the use of the instruments. Prior to the data collection inter-observer agreement was assessed on a video tape of a program for preschool children with special needs, a program not observed in the study. A research assistant received 40 hour of training. An 80% agreement on all items coded was obtained before actual data collection began.

Forty children were observed during "free play" time for 30 minutes, during three consecutive days. The type of social/cognitive play or non-playful activity observed was recorded. The number of times each child was observed in each category was computed. Each of the twenty early childhood settings received a total score on The Early Childhood Environment Rating Scale.

Results

A 4 (types of centers) x 5 (types of social play) x 5 (centers within types) repeated measures analysis of variance was used to assess the inter-action between types of centers and social play considering centers within types. There were main effects for social play (F = 23.79, p < .001).

However the play categories did not interact with type of center. There was a significant difference between centers within types ($F = 1.78$, $p < .05$). The same design was used to assess the interaction between types of centers and intellectual play. There were main effects for intellectual play ($F = 23.74$, $p < .001$). Type of play did not interact with type of center. There were also significant differences in the intellectual play scale between centers within types ($F = 3.14$, $p < .001$). It was speculated that this large difference among centers inhibited a significant statistical difference between types for both the social and intellectual play scale. Post hoc Scheffe tests of mean differences between types of social and intellectual play and all pair-wise contrasts were statistically significant at the $<.05$ level (Tables 8.2 and 8.3).

Developmentally delayed children engaged in high rates of solitary play both in the segregated and day care settings. Special needs children in day care settings played mostly in a solitary and parallel mode. The results revealed that very low percentage of time was spent by children in cooperative play. The intellectual play of handicapped children reflected low levels of complexity. The children played more constructively in the segregated, reversed mainstreamed and nursery school setting than children in day cares where they exhibited more functional play. Dramatic play occurred very infrequently in all types of environments. We can note that the social and cognitive play behavior of special needs children was qualitatively low in all settings.

Table 8.2   Percentage of Time (Means) Children Spend in Types of Social Play by Type of Preschool Center

Type of Center	TYPE OF SOCIAL PLAY				
	Solitary	Parallel	Associative	Cooperative	Inactive
Segregated	.33	.21	.24	.07	.14
Rev. Mainst.	.24	.30	.27	.03	.15
Day care	.30	.39	.23	.04	.10
Nursery School	.24	.43	.19	.01	.12
Composite Means	.28	.32	.24	.04	.13

CRITICAL VALUE FOR SCHEFFÉ TEST FOR COMPOSITE MEAN DIFFERENCES:
$\hat{C}_i \pm .0034$
ALL PAIRS OF MEANS EXCEED THIS VALUE AND ALL DIFFERENCES ARE SIGNIFICANT.

Table 8.3   Percentage of Time (Means) Children Spend in Types of Social Play by Type of Preschool Center

	TYPE OF INTELLECTUAL PLAY			
Type of Center	Functional	Constructive	Dramatic	Inactive
Segregated	.27	.48	.10	.14
Rev. Mainst.	.36	.40	.09	.15
Day care	.50	.32	.08	.10
Nursery School	.32	.48	.08	.12
Composite Means	.36	.42	.09	.13

CRITICAL VALUE FOR SCHEFFÉ TEST FOR COMPOSITE MEAN DIFFERENCES:
$\hat{C}_i$ ± .0066
ALL PAIRS OF MEANS EXCEED THIS VALUE AND ALL DIFFERENCES ARE SIGNIFICANT.

Scores on the Early Childhood Environment Rating Scale for day care centers (X = 156.40) were significantly lower (F = 10.37, p < .001) than those of segregated centers (X = 225.00) reversed mainstreamed centers (X = 212.40) and nursery schools (X = 191.40). The scores for the sub-scales revealed the same pattern. A one-way analysis of variance revealed statistically significant differences between the scores of day care centers and both segregated and reversed mainstreamed centers on the personal care routine scale (F = 5.80, p < .05), furnishings and display (F = 5.03, p < .01), fine and gross motor activities (F = 7.13, p < .005), creative activities (F = 5.71, p < .01), social development (F = 8.03, p < .005). In addition, day care centers were significantly lower than the segregated, reversed mainstreamed, and nursery schools on language reasoning experiences (F = 8.57, p < .005). The adult needs subscale analysis of variance showed that mean differences tended in the same direction and approached significance (F = 2.78, p < .08). (See Table 8.4)

Discussion

It is interesting to note that in this sample, scores obtained in the ECERS by segregated centers (X = 225.00) and reversed mainstreamed programs (X = 212.40) were significantly higher than those in the day-care centers (X = 156.40). Traditionally, special needs children have attended programs geared to meet their needs in segregated settings. Mainstreaming became a strategy for program implementation after segregated special education practices came under severe attack and the right to education in the least restrictive environment became widespread. (Dunn, 1968; Wolfensberger, 1972). Integration in preschool settings has come to connote a desirable setting with opportunities for higher levels of social development and complex communication patterns. Educators have wanted to show that by exposing special needs children to normally developing peers they will become involved with other children in increasingly more intricate systems of sociodramatic play which will increase social competency. The fact that mainstreamed day care centers in the study obtained a significantly lower rating for quality of the environment implies that children in these programs are not provided with the extra support needed to ensure that they participate in a range of learning experiences which will help them develop optimally.

Table 8.4   Analysis of Variance of Early Childhood Environment

Rating Scale for Type of Preschool Center

ECERS		Segregated (S)	Reversed Mainstreamed (RM)	Day Care (DC)	Nursery (N)	Post Hoc Results
		TYPE OF PRESCHOOL CENTER				
Personal	x̄	28.60*	30.00*	22.20	24.20	S>DC
Care (35)[1]	S.D.	1.51	4.00	2.77	4.50	RM>DC
Furnishings	x̄	27.80*	26.80*	21.00	25.80	S>DC
Display (35)	S.D.	4.09	2.05	2.34	3.11	RM>DC
Language	x̄	26.60*	24.60*	16.00	22.40*	S>DC
Reasoning (28)	S.D.	1.94	2.40	2.34	5.85	RM>DC
Experiences						N>DC
Fine/Gross	x̄	38.20*	36.80*	28.40	32.60	S>DC
Motor (42)	S.D.	3.27	2.17	3.79	5.02	RM>DC
Creative	x̄	42.60*	38.40*	29.80	35.80	S>DC
Activities (49)	S.D.	5.90	1.81	3.90	6.87	RM>DC
Social	x̄	37.40*	33.20*	23.60	30.20	S>DC
Development (42)	S.D.	4.16	4.81	3.43	5.63	RM>DC
Adult	x̄	23.80	22.60	15.40	20.40	
Needs (28)	S.D.	3.50	6.30	3.13	6.10	
Total	x̄	225.00*	212.40*	156.40	191.40	S>DC
(259)	S.D.	19.31	20.14	13.08	28.01	RM>DC

* SIGNIFICANT AT $A = 0.05$

[1] (MAXIMUM POSSIBLE SCORE)

As noted, measures of children's social and cognitive play showed that there were large differences in the results from site to site within the same type of program. However, no significant statistical differences were obtained between segregated, reversed mainstreamed, day care centers and nursery schools on child-child interaction. Although this study did not allow for a different characterization of children's play between each type of program, it suggests that a program label itself should not necessarily carry a connotation of specific types of experiences and interactions with other children.

Some researchers have reported that handicapped children play less with other children, as they do not elicit interaction from others. However, the play of handicapped children is positively influenced by interacting with normally developing peers when they are involved in a setting which is more responsive to social initiatives and more supportive peer social competence. (Beckman, 1983; Dunlop, Stoneman and Cantrell, 1980; Guralnick, 1981, 1988; Ispa and Matz, 1978; Novak et. al, 1980; White, 1980)

In this sample, children's play did not seem to be strongly influenced by the proportions of special needs and non-special needs children in the centers. Peer availability did not make a difference when comparing styles of play in different types of programs. Whether all children in a program were special needs children or there was a heterogeneous group made no difference in the children's play modality. The composite means of social and intellectual play of special needs children revealed that the greatest percentage of time was spent in parallel play (32 percent) followed by solitary play (28 percent) and associative play (24 percent). Cooperative play was extremely rare (4 percent). Constructive (42 percent) and functional play (36 percent) were the most frequent cognitive types of play while dramatic play was very low (9 percent). Thus we can note that the levels of play complexity for all developmentally delayed children were affected regardless of the play setting. These children lack the ability to attempt to play in group structures organized to achieve a common goal and to play in a symbolic fashion. The ability to make believe, to give and take, and take turns with other peers is missing.

Adult interaction and intervention (encouraging, playing, modeling, questioning) with the children was observed infrequently during "free play" time. This finding has important implications for the preparation of early childhood educators who work with special needs children. Specific attention must be given to consider ways of structuring the interpersonal environment and the play activities for special needs children in order to help them become engaged in higher levels of play.

The findings suggest that developmentally delayed children experience a wide variation in the opportunity to play with other children and that there are differences in the types of children's play across all settings. Furthermore, all programs do not serve the children equally well, as large within type of variations exist in the settings. Segregated centers in this sample emerged as providing higher overall quality of care for the special needs child while the mainstreamed day care centers obtained the lowest ratings. No significant difference in the patterns of children's play appeared between centers. Thus the study confirms the inconclusiveness around the issues of the effectiveness of mainstreaming young children with special needs.

This observational study documented children's behavior in a free play activity where no specific manipulations of any classroom features were observed. Several studies have suggested that planned designs are important for increased social peer interactions. If as a society we are committed to integrating handicapped children with their nonhandicapped peers in effective programs we need to look at ways of programming and adapting early childhood environments to help achieve social integration.

Conclusion

Incorporating special needs children into regular community based early childhood programs is a relatively recent development. Although the debate on the effectiveness of integration of exceptional students with nonhandicapped students is inconclusive, community programs are increasingly accepting the notion that the mainstreamed preschool environment offers special needs children a good possibility for success. Play is being recognized as an important avenue for learning for the special needs child. Two key factors need to be considered in both research and program implementation: a) developmentally delayed preschoolers engage in play activities that are less sophisticated than their nonhandicapped peers; and b) play is not enhanced by just bringing handicapped and nonhandicapped children together. Opportunities for children to engage in exploration, construction, discussions, problem solving, creativity, dramatization, experimentation and organization with others need to be structured. Strategies for enhancing social competency and social responsibility need to be incorporated into the curriculum. Teachers should modify preschool activities to encourage, guide, model, and reinforce opportunities for social interactions and prosocial behavior of special needs children and incorporate them into the daily activities. Integration of handicapped and nonhandicapped preschool children will be more successful as the quality of the environment is enhanced by these strategies.

Additional information is needed on new methodologies required to develop appropriate play skills in the young special needs child. Is the lack of cooperative and dramatic play in children with cognitive impairments associated with the development of abstract and imaginative modes of thinking? Could this situation be altered if teachers and program organizers structure the environment differently? Future studies need to address the relationship between a high quality program of a preschool environment and children's play. One could hypothesize that integrated high quality day care settings would provide more opportunities for language and social development than segregated settings in terms of positive peer interaction. More information is needed on the techniques that would increase social and cognitive play behaviors in the context of the classroom setting and the amount of adult interaction necessary to sustain the behavior. Data on the variations in program quality and children's functioning would help find the best ways to plan preschool environments for children with handicaps. Research also needs to address questions concerning which environmental manipulations facilitate maintenance and generalization of social interaction skills.

REFERENCES

Apolloni, T., & Cooke, T. P. (1975). Peer behavior conceptualized as a variable influencing infant and toddler development. *American Journal of Orthopsychiatry, 45,* 4-17.

Allen, E. (1981). Curriculum models for successful mainstreaming. *Topics in Early Childhood Special Education, 1* (1), 45-55.

Bailey, D., Clifford, R., & Harms, T. (1982). Comparison of preschool environments for handicapped and non-handicapped children. *Topics in Early Childhood and Special Education, 2* (1), 9-20.

Beckman, P. (1983). The relationship between behavioral characteristics of children and social interaction setting. *Journal of the Division for Early Childhood, 7,* 69-77.

Bricker, D. (1978). Current concerns of early childhood educators. *Education and Training of the Mentally Retarded, 17,* 114-119.

Burstein, N. (1986). The effects of classroom organization on mainstreamed preschool children. *Exceptional Children, 52,* (5), 425-434.

Cooke, T., Ruskus, J., Apolloni, T., & Peck, C. (1981). Handicapped preschool children in the mainstream: Background outcomes and clinical suggestions. *Topics in Early Childhood Special Education, 1* (1), 72-83.

Clune, C., Paolella, J., & Foley, J. (1979). Free play behavior of atypical children: An approach to assessment. *Journal of Autism and Developmental Disorders, 9* (1), 61-72.

Dunn, L. M. (1968). Special education for the mildly retarded—is much of it justifiable? *Exceptional Children, 35,* 5-22.

Dunlop, K., Stoneman, Z., & Cautrell, M. (1980). Social interaction of exceptional and other children in a mainstreamed preschool. *Exceptional Children, 47,* 132-141.

Fenrick, N., Pearson, M., & Pepelnyck, K. (1984). The play, attending and language of young handicapped children in integrated and segregated settings. *Journal of the Division for Early Childhood, 8* (19), 57-67.

Field, T. (1980). Self, teacher, toy and peer-directed behaviors of handicapped preschool children. In T. Field, S. Goldberg, D. Stern, & A. Sostek (Eds.) *High risk infants and children.* New York: Academic Press.

Fredericks, H., Baldwin, V., Grove, D., Moore, W., Riggs, C., & Lyons, B. (1978). Integrating the moderately and severely handicapped preschool child into a normal day care setting. In M. Guralnick (Ed.) *Early intervention and the integration of handicapped and non-handicapped children.* Baltimore, MD: University Park Press.

Guralnick, M., & Paul-Brown, D. (1977). The nature of verbal interactions among handicapped and non-handicapped preschool children. *Child Development, 48,* 254-260.

Guralnick. M. (1978). *Early intervention and the integration of handicapped and non-handicapped children.* Baltimore, MD: University Park Press.

Guralnick, M. (1980). Social interactions among preschool children. *Exceptional Children, 46,* 248-253.

Guralnick, M. (1981) Peer influences on the development of communicative competence. In P. Strain (Ed.) *The utilization of classroom peers as behavior change agents.* New York: Plenum.

Guralnick, M., & Groom, J. (1988). Peer interactions in the mainstreamed and specialized classrooms: A comparative analysis. *Exceptional Children, 54* (5), 415-525.

Harms, T., & Clifford, R. (1980). *The early childhood environment rating scale.* New York: Teachers College Press.

Higginbotham, J., Baker, B., & Neill, R. (1980) Assessing the social participation and cognitive play abilities of hearing impaired preschoolers. *The Volta Review, 82,* (5), 261-270.

Hill, P., McCune-Nicolich, L. (1981). Pretend play and patterns of cognition in Down's Syndrome children. *Child Development, 52,* 611-617.

Ispa, J., & Matz, R. (1978). Integrated handicapped preschool children within a cognitively oriented program. In M. Guralnick (Ed.), *Early intervention and the integration of handicapped and non-handicapped children.* Baltimore Md: University Park Press.

Jenkins, J., Speltz, M., & Odom, S. (1985). Integrating normal and handicapped preschoolers: Effect on child development and social interaction. *Exceptional Children, 52* (1), 7-17.

Karnes, M. & Teska, J. (1978). Early Childhood. Reston Va; The Council for Exceptional Children.

Kohl, F., & Beckman, P. (1984). A comparison of handicapped and non-handicapped preschoolers' interaction across classroom activities. *Journal of the Division for Early Childhood, 8* (19), 49-56.

Krakow, J., & Kopp, C. (1983). The effect of developmental delay on sustained attention in young children. *Child Development, 54,* 1143-1155.

Kugelmass, J. (1989). The "Shared Classroom:" A Case Study of Interactions Between Early Childhood and Special Education Staff and Children. *Journal of Early Intervention,* Vol. 13. No. 1, 36-44.

Novak, M., Olley, G., & Kearney, D. (1980). Social skills of children with special needs in integrated and separate preschools. In T. Fields, S. Goldberg, Stern, D., & Soslek, A. (Eds.) *High risk infants and children.* New York: Academic Press.

Peterson, N., & Haralick, J. (1977). Integration of handicapped and non-handicapped preschoolers: An analysis of play behavior and social interaction. *Education and Training of the Mentally Retarded, 12,* 235-245.

Pol, R., Crow, R., Rider, D. & Offner, R. (1985). Social interaction in an integrated preschool: Implications and applications. *Topics in Early Childhood Special Education, 4* (4), 59-76.

Rogers, S. (1988). Cognitive characteristics of handicapped children's play: a review. *Journal of the Division for Early Childhood,* Vol 11. No. 2, 161-168.

Rogers, W., Ruggles, L., Peterson, N., & Cooper, A. (1981). Playing and learning together: Patterns of social interaction in handicapped and non-handicapped children. *Journal of the Division for Early Childhood, 3,* 56-63.

Smilansky, I. (1968). *The effects of sociodramatic play on disadvantaged preschool children.* New York: John Wiley & Sons.

Strain, P., & Odom, S. (1968). Peer Social Initiations: Effective Intervention for Social Skills Development of Exceptional Children. *Exceptional Children*. Vol. 52, No. 6, 543-551.

Tawney, J. (1981). A cautious view of mainstreaming in early education. *Topics in Early Childhood Special Education, 1* (1), 25-36.

White, B. (1980). Mainstreaming in grade school and preschool: How the child with special needs interacts with peers. In T. Field, S. Goldberg, D. Stern, and A. Soslek (EDS.) *High-risk infants and children: adult and peer interaction*. New York: Academic Press.

Wolfensberger, W. (1972). *The principles of normalization in human services*. Totonto: National Institute of Mental Retardation.

9

Social and Non-Social Play of Infants and Toddlers in Family Day Care

Miriam K. Rosenthal

As research into the effects of daycare has shifted its paradigm from comparisons of home-reared children and those enrolled in daycare to the analysis of the effects of program quality (Clarke-Stewart & Fein, 1983), it has tended to derive its hypotheses from a "global" model of the nature of environmental action (Hunt, 1979). In this view, a high-quality environment is assumed to facilitate all aspects of development, whereas poor-quality childcare is assumed to inhibit all aspects of development. These assumptions have ignored an increasing body of evidence which suggests that different aspects of development are sensitive to different aspects of the environment (Wachs & Gruen, 1982; Wachs & Chan, 1986).

Family daycare is of particular interest for the examination of these effects. It is the most common form of child care for infants and toddlers in many countries. The home-like environment, with its fairly limited space and equipment and small, mixed-age group, present an interesting social setting for the exploration of theoretical issues relevant to the study of child-environment interaction. The effects of the specific features of such a setting on both social and nonsocial play merits exploration beyond the examination of the effects of the global quality of care offered (Howes & Stewart, 1987).

Dimensions of Family Day-Care Environments and their Possible Effects on Social and Non-Social Play

Two aspects of the environment are said to influence children's behavior and development: the social, or interpersonal aspects, and the physical features of the environment (Wohlwill, 1983). Each of these environmental dimensions are expected to have differential influences on the play behavior of children (Wachs and Gruen, 1982). In an educational setting such as childcare, another dimension that may have a differential effect on the children's play behavior is the educational emphasis in the daily program.

The social environment is composed of two elements: the peer group and the caregiving adult. Both social and also nonsocial play are likely to be influenced by the presence and play behavior of other children in the same small group. For example, the general level of play with objects is likely to be higher for every child in a group with predominantly older children.

163

Peer Groups in Family Day Care

The presence of children of varied levels of competence may have a different effect on the play of younger and older children (Brownell, 1982). Older children have more sustained sociable interchanges and engage at a higher level of social play (Sarafino, 1985). Lange et al. (1977) report that social interaction and verbal communication were least frequent in younger same-age dyads, intermediate in mixed-age dyads and most frequent in older same-age dyads. The authors conclude that the two types of social experience (same and mixed age dyads) may serve different functions in children's development.

The National Day Care Home Study (Stallings & Porter, 1980) found that the age composition of the group influenced several types of behavior that are relevant to children's play activity. For example, toddlers were more independent in homes with infants, and spent more time interacting with other children, and in dramatic play. In homes with more toddlers, younger children spent less time in exploration and older ones in less anti-social activity. Fein & Clarke-Stewart (1973) concluded on the basis of data available at the time that preschool children in heterogeneous age groups showed less verbal and physical aggression, more social contacts, and more imaginative behavior than children in same-age groups. Bronson (1975) found that toddlers playing with age mates were more likely to show agonistic interaction than when playing with non-age mates. On the other hand Stallings & Porter (1980) reported that toddlers in a more heterogeneous age group exhibited more distress, spent more time alone, showed affection and sought the attention of the caregiver. Preschoolers in these heterogeneous groups tended to interact more with other children, and to spend less time in educational activities.

The sex composition of the group is also likely to affect social play. Preschoolers of both sexes engaged more frequently in positive social interaction when playing with girls (Roopnarine, 1984). Since boy toddlers play more aggressively than girls (Fagot, 1980), more agonistic social interaction can be expected in groups with more boys than in groups with more girls. No other sex differences in children's play have been reported. Further, because the child's family background has an effect on his play behavior and development in the child-care setting (Howes and Stewart, 1987; Phillips et al., 1987) it is likely that children's play will be influenced by the background of other children in the group.

Thus, this study explores the effects of SES, age and sex characteristics of the peer group on children's social and nonsocial play.

Caregiving Adults in Family Day Care Homes

The caregiving adult forms a very important part of the social environment of the child. All studies investigating the effects of quality care on children's development in childcare highlight the contribution of the caregiver's interaction (Clarke-Stewart and Fein, 1983; Phillips et al., 1987) have shown that the effect of quality of care on social development in childcare is largely attributable to the nature of caregiver-child interaction, and the "structural" features (group size, caregiver-child ratio, caregiver training) that influence this interaction. We expect to find that children in the care of caregivers who frequently interact positively with them would display more frequent positive social interaction themselves.

The belief system of caregivers in family day care has not yet been adequately studied. A caregiver's beliefs concerning the child's development, the methods of socialization, and the extent to which she attributes to herself any influence over this development are expected to reflect the professional attitude she has toward her role (Hess, 1981; Rosenthal, 1991).

It was therefore expected that caregivers who attributed more influence to themselves than to parents would expect early achievement of developmental goals, and would adhere to less authoritarian socialization techniques. Thus, these caregivers would display more positive and less restrictive interactions with the children. Children in their care were expected to play more competently with both objects and peers, displaying more frequent fine-motor play with objects and more positive social interactions with peers.

The Educational Quality of the Daily Program and the Physical Environment

The nature of the educational program has been shown to influence preschoolers' cognitive play, although it was not related to social play (Tizard et al., 1976; Johnson, 1980). In programs with greater emphasis on direct teaching, children engaged in more constructive play, while those in programs emphasizing free play engaged in more functional play (Smilansky, 1968; Johnson, 1980). In this study, the emphasis on directed educational activities comes from the sponsoring agencies, although the caregiver is responsible for implementing the educational program in her own home. The emphasis on educational content in the daily routine was expected to be associated with the caregiver's beliefs and behavior, and also with the educational quality of the physical environment.

Two major characteristics of the physical environment may determine its educational quality: the amount and variety of play materials, and the amount of space and its organization. These have been shown to affect the play behavior of preschoolers (Prescott, 1981). Johnson (1935) reported that in settings with more play material, there is more gross motor activity, more play with materials, more social play, and less agonistic behavior. While it is quite clear that the amount and variety of toys and play equipment encourage exploration and sensorimotor play with objects (Yarow, Rubenstein & Pederson,

1975), their effect on social play among infants and toddlers has been the subject of some debate. There is a general consensus that children's interest in play-objects precedes their interest in peers. Maudry and Nekula (1939) found that most of the play encounters they observed in infants aged 6-18 months incorporated objects. Similarly, Meuller and Lucas (1975) have suggested that toddlers' first social interactions appear in the context of play around common objects. It is claimed that the way one-year-olds relate to objects encourages social exchanges such as giving, taking, resisting or sharing (Mueller & Vandell, 1979). Jacobson (1981) reported that longer peer interaction occurred for 14-month-olds when they played with a common object. However Eckerman and Whatley (1977) have argued that it is the nature of the peers' actions on the objects which is the major source of their attraction to other infants, rather than the objects per se. Vandell et al. (1980) found more social interaction in the absence of toys, and suggest that toys may be competing with peers for the infant's attention. Lewis (1975) takes yet another position and claims that toys are irrelevant to social play.

Space arrangement that allows "space to be alone" (to be used freely by the children and which is different from Time Out used for disciplinary purposes) is considered one of the variables defining "good space" by Prescott (1981), i.e., space that contributes to positive interactions with both objects and peers. Others have stressed the importance of such "stimulus-shelter" corners for sensory-motor development (Wachs et al., 1979). However these conclusions might not be generalizable to all age groups and for all care settings. Thus, for example, Legendre (1985) found that infants under the age of 21 months tended to stay in close proximity to the caregiver, and implies that at that age infants do not go to the "stimulus shelter corners."

Another consideration regarding the space arrangement is its crowdedness. Prescott (1981) reported that in conditions of high density, children were less involved in play. McGrew (1970) also reported that preschoolers in highly crowded settings spent less time in contact with each other. By contrast, Bates (1972) reported that in crowded conditions, preschoolers tended to interact more frequently with each other but also more aggressively. Rohe and Patterson (1974) however, have argued that sufficient amounts of play materials can alleviate the negative effects of high density.

In light of these findings, a number of hypotheses were generated regarding the effects of the social environment, the content of the daily program, and the educational quality of the physical environment on the child's play activity in FDC.

1. The parameters of the educational quality of the daily program and the physical environment would influence play behavior directly as well as through the social mediation of the caregiver and peers (Wachs & Gruen, 1982; Wohlwill & Heft, 1987).

2. Physical environmental parameters may contribute to the variance observed in both social and non-social play behavior even after quality of the caregiver's interaction is taken into account.

3. The characteristics of the child-care environment would be better predictors of children's play in these settings than their personal or home background, even after controlling for FDC selection.

4. Children in FDC settings with better educational quality (daily routine, amount and variety of play materials) would show a higher mean level of play with toys.

5. A daily program organized around educational activities, as well as play materials, would tend to bring the infants and toddlers more frequently into joint themes of activity (object, story, event) and would afford more opportunity for social engagement, and thus to a higher frequency of social interaction.

6. Space organization (crowdedness, space to be alone) would mainly affect social play. In crowded space children were expected to be in close proximity to each other, having more opportunities for interaction, including agonistic interactions as well. Areas designed as "space to be alone," on the other hand, would distance them from each other, unless the space arrangement, play materials, and the program were used to bring them together into contact and joint themes of activity.

Method

Sample

Forty-one FDC homes (and caregivers) were sampled out of the 97 homes which operated in Israel at the time of data collection. Due to the growing concern about the effects of out-of-home care on infants, only homes that had at least one infant were included in the sample. In each of the other six locations where FDC functioned, two homes were sampled randomly. These locations were all in rural communities in central Israel. All the caregivers agreed to participate in the study.

The average number of children in each home was 5.17 (S.D. = .83). Eighty-nine percent of the children were under the age of three and 44 percent were in heterogeneous-aged groups where the age difference between the youngest and oldest child was greater than one year.

Eighty-two children were sampled, two in each FDC home. One child was always the youngest in the home and the other was selected randomly from

among the other children. The sample consisted of 49 boys and 33 girls. The
mean age was 23.54 months (S.D. = 4.81). The mean age of entry into FDC was
13.04 months (S.D. = 12.25). Sixty-four percent of the children had stayed in
FDC for longer than 10 months at the time of the study. 57 percent were first born
and 22 percent were third born or of a higher birth order.

Only 71 of the 82 mothers of the children in the sample were interviewed.
Two refused to be interviewed, two participated as caregivers, and the rest had
moved and could not be traced.

Ninety-four percent of the families were intact. 75 percent of the mothers
placed their children in FDC because they were working, and in 25 percent
"social problems in the family" was the reason for child placement. The mean
level of parental education was 13.18 years (S.D. = 3.25).

Procedure
―――――――

Data were obtained for each FDC home through both observations of the
day care and through structured caregiver interviews (CI) and mother interviews
(MI). The observations of children and caregivers were conducted by four
trained observers and the interviews by three trained interviewers. Observers
used three different collection procedures.

The time-sampling procedure utilized predefined recording sheets and
followed a prescribed routine and recording rules. During an observation day,
size time-sample periods of five minutes each were taken of the behavior of the
caregiver and each target child, in a fixed sequence of Target Child A-Target
Child B-Caregiver. Behavior was observed for 10 seconds and then recorded for
10 seconds, yielding altogether 90 time sampling units of behavior for each target
subject. Each observation unit also provided information on the context of
behavior. At the end of each five minute period, the observer filled in a short
questionnaire describing that period and then shifted to the next target subject.

The *daily log* was used to recorded continuously the activities of the group,
and the duration of each group activity, throughout the day. These activities were
categorized as "directed educational activities," "free play," "physical routine
care" and others.

An *environment rating questionnaire* was adapted from the Day Care
Environment Inventory (Prescott, Kritchevsky and Jones, 1972) and the Family
Day Care Rating Scale (Harms and Clifford, 1984) to the Israeli setting. It was
completed by the observer at the end of the observation day.

Observers recorded the children playing with objects and playing with
peers. Play with objects included the following: fine motor play (such as
threading objects or playing with Leggo) and gross motor play (crawling or
walking for infants, climbing, throwing a ball for toddlers). The "mean level of
play with objects," rated on a scale devised by Rubenstein and Howes (1979).

This 5-point scale rates increasing the complexity of play with objects, from oral contact (which is rated as 1) through active manipulation (rated as 3) to the exploitation of the object's properties in a creative way (a rating of 5). The rating was recorded at the end of each 5 minute observation period.

Observers also recorded and coded the children's play with peers using the following definitions: *Positive interaction* with peers included smiling and another child and *agonistic interactions* included struggling with or attacking another child. *Joint peer play* refers to those episodes when the child joins into a play activity constructed by the children themselves. The children engage in repetitive, rhythmic activity, typically involving vocal exchanges smiles or laughter (Budwig, Strage & Bamberg, 1986). The occurrence of this activity was recorded once at the end of each 5 minute observation period, thus yielding a maximum score of six.

Level of play with peers was rated on a 5-point peer-play scale (Howes, 1980). Level refers to parallel play with no mutual awareness, while levels 2-5 refer to social play with turn-taking structure, complementary and reciprocal play. The occurrence and level of play was recorded during each 10 second unit of observation. The measure is therefore the number of 10 sec units during which these levels of play were observed. The *context of play* includes: The frequency with which the child is observed alone or in a group, and the frequency with which a child is observed using language. All these measures were based on data gathered during observations (OBS).

Child and Family Measures

All child and family measures were derived from interviews with the mothers (MI). Child characteristics included age (in months), sex, birth order, age of entry into FDC (in months), and the ease with which the child separated from his/her mother. The last measure was rated on a scale of 1 (difficult) to 3 (easy).

Family characteristics were parental education level (years) and the reason for child's placement in FDC. These two generated an indication of the family's socioeconomic status. Family background was also characterized by maternal beliefs about child development, which included the mother's *attribution of influence to herself*. The mothers ranked their own influence relative to that of the caregiver and the father on 11 items relating to child development (1 = least influential; 3 = most influential). Mothers also indicated their *developmental expectations for their children,* an average of the mother's responses to items stating the age of achievement in the domains of cognitive and social development (in months). Mothers' average of responses to questions on 17 episodes of misbehavior and disobedience were used as indicators of the mothers preferred *socialization techniques.* Six responses were possible,

ranging from "permissive" (1-2), through "authoritative" (3-4), to "authoritarian" (5-6). A higher average indicates a belief in more severe socialization
techniques.

The Child-care Setting

Several measures were generated from the demographic information
about the children and their families: group age mean (months) and age mix
(standard deviation), and mean level of parental education of the children in the
group (years). Age heterogeneity of the group was further assessed by a measure
of age span which described the age difference between the youngest and oldest
child in the group (less than six months; 7-12 months; 13-24 months and more
than 25 months.)

Two sets of measures were used in collecting information on the caregiving
adult in the group. Caregiver's *spontaneous interactions* with the children
included *Positive Interaction,* which was a composite measure of the ratings of
positive affect, frequency of positive responsiveness, frequency of one-to-one
interaction, the positive use of language; the direct involvement with the
children, and encouragement. Cronbach standardized item Alpha for the composite score is .66. *Restrictions* were considered a measure of the frequency of
the caregiver's attempts to control the children's behavior, i.e., diverting
attention, warning or scolding (OBS).

The caregivers' beliefs were derived in a similar assessment to that of the
mothers and focused on the same issues: attribution of influence to self,
developmental expectations in the cognitive and social domains and the types of
socialization techniques which the caregiver endorsed. These were derived from
interviews with the caregivers (CI).

The Educational Quality of the FDC Physical Environment
and the Daily Program

Physical aspects of the family day care home included the following:
Crowdedness, defined in terms of the ratio of the number of children to a rating
of the available space; *Space to be alone* (or stimulus shelter) usually behind
curtains closing off a small space such as a corner of the room or the space
underneath the high infant cots (high = such space is available); *Amount of play
material* is defined in terms of the amount of different toys and other play
materials available to the children (1 = small amount; 3 = large amount). All these
measures are based on the ERQ.

The educational quality of the daily program is defined in this study as a
composite score based on (a) the proportion of daily activities categorized as

"directed educational activities" (in the daily log), and (b) the use by the caregivers of various routine care activities for educational purposes (as recorded in the Environment Rating Questionnaire).

The inter-observer reliability for all measures based on observations was calculated as percent agreement, and ranged from 69 percent to 90 percent.

Results

An Overview of the Children's Play Behavior

From Table 9.1 it is clear that infants and toddlers in FDC spend more time in positive interaction with each other than in fine motor or gross motor play. They spend very little time in agonistic interaction (Table 9.1)—less than one tenth of the time they spent in positive interaction—despite the fact that they spent twice as much time in a group as they did alone.

Most children played with toys at the manipulative level (level 3 on the Rubenstein & Howes (1979) scale), with a relatively narrow distribution around this mean. When children played next to each other with the same or similar toys, they did not appear to be aware of each other (level 1 on the Howes (1980) scale).

Table 9.1   Play Behaviors of Children (N = 82)

	MEAN	S.D.	OBSERVED RANGE
Play with Objects			
Fine Motor	19.13	11.26	0–46
Gross Motor	6.61	6.65	0–24
Mean Level	3.00	.75	1.5–5.0
Play with Peers			
Positive Interaction	29.60	11.41	1–61
Agonistic Interaction	2.02	2.31	0–13
Joint Play*	2.59	1.96	0–6
Level 1	44.57	32.32	0–90
Levels 2–5	6.89	7.47	0–34
Context of Play			
Child Alone	14.34	9.69	0–47
Child in Group	30.60	14.84	2–62
Use of Language	15.43	10.67	0–52

*THE POSSIBLE RANGE FOR ALL SCORES IS 0–90 WITH THE EXCEPTION OF "MEAN LEVEL OF PLAY WITH OBJECTS" (RANGE: 1–5) AND "JOINT PLAY" (RANGE: 0–6).

Table 9.2 Relations Between Children's Play Behaviors (N = 82)[1]

	PLAY WITH OBJECTS			PLAY WITH PEERS					CONTEXT OF PLAY		
	Fine Motor	Gross Motor	Mean Level	Positive Interaction	Agonist Interaction	Joint Play	Level 1	Level 2–5	Child Alone	Child in Group	Use Language
Play with Objects											
Fine Motor	x	-.22*	.29**			-.18*	.17				-.28**
Gross Motor		x		.29**	-.17		-.29**	.19*	-.45***	.40***	.20*
Mean Level			x								
Play with Peers											
Positive Interaction				x		.40**	.34***	.41***	-.51***	.57***	.60**
Agonistic Interaction					x				.37***	-.31**	
Joint Play						x	.25**	.18*	-.19*	.27**	.31**
Level 1							x	-.41***	.45***	-.38***	-.27**
Level 2–5								x	-.41***	.43***	.61***
Context of Play											
Child Alone									x	-.86***	-.41***
Child in Group										x	.51***
Use of Language											x

1. ONLY R > .16 ARE PRESENTED   *p < .05   **p < .01   ***p < .001

On the average they were observed in joint-play in 2.59 out the six observation episodes. Table 9.2 reveals several consistent patterns in children's play behaviors.

Children who frequently engaged in fine motor play with objects also played with them at a higher level. They spent less time in gross motor play, more time in joint play with peers, less time alone, and used language more frequently. A high level of play with objects was also related to a high level of play with peers, and to frequent positive interaction.

Not only were the categories of play with objects related to the categories of play with peers, but the various indicators of play with peers were also interrelated. Children who played at a higher level with peers also engaged more frequently in positive interactions, and in joint play, whereas children who engaged more often in agonistic interactions tended to interact with peers at a lower level. In fact, joint play was associated with both a high and low level of play with peers. It is interesting to note that positive and agonistic interactions were independent of each other, i.e., children who spent more time in positive interactions did not necessarily spend less time in agonistic interactions (Table 9.2).

The social and linguistic contexts of play measured the child's competence in interacting with the environment. Children who spent more time alone played at a lower level with both objects and peers. They engaged less frequently in positive interactions and in joint play, and more frequently in agonistic interactions (Table 9.2). However, children who used language frequently evidenced a higher level of play with both objects and peers. They engaged more frequently in positive interactions and in joint play, and spent less time in gross motor play or in being alone (Table 9.2).

Since "being alone" and "being in a group" were almost mutually exclusive ($r = -.86$), only "being alone" appears in the following analyses. Similarly, as level 1 and level 2-5 of peer play are complementary, only the latter was used as an assessment of the child's level of play with peers.

The Influence of Childrens' Characteristics on Their Play Behaviors

With the exception of the somewhat obvious correlation between age of child and age of entry into child care ($r = .47$; $p<.001$), child characteristics were not inter-related. Difficulty of separation from mothers was related to one family characteristic and to one feature of the social environment. Children of parents with less education ($r = .25$ $p <.05$) and children in the homes of caregivers who believed in more severe methods of control ($r = -.37$, $p<001$) were reported by their mothers to have greater difficulty in separating from them in the morning.

A hierarchical regression model was used to determine the extent to which variation in play behavior was explained by two groups of independent variables. Individual characteristics were entered in the first equation, and factors related

Table 9.3 Hierarchical Regression of the Child's Play Behavior on the Child's Characteristics[1]

	Age	Sex	R-square	Birth Order	Age Entry	Ease Separate	R-square Change	Final R-square	Adjusted R-square
Play with Objects									
Fine Motor	.04	.03	.03	.17	.21	.08	.06	.08	.01
Gross Motor	-.17	-.12	.04	-.01	-.09	-.24*	.05	.10	.02
Mean Level	.19	-.10	.04	.03	-.10	-.02	.01	.05	-.03
Playing with Peers									
Positive Interaction	.48***	.21	.17**	-.18	-.04	.12	.05	.22	.16
Agonistic Interaction	-.03	-.27*	.07	.01	.03	.00	.00	.07	.00
Joint Play	.16	.15	.03	-.08	-.06	-.02	.01	.04	-.04
Level 2–5	.33*	.10	.12**	-.05	.12	.23*	.06	.19	.12
Context of Play									
Child Alone	-.09	-.17	.03	.03	-.02	-.08	.00	.03	.04
Use of Language	.35**	.30*	.14**	-.12	.05	.16	.04	.18*	.12

1. THE TABLE PRESENTS BETA VALUES FROM THE FINAL EQUATION *p < .05   **p < .01   ***p < .001

to the child's life experience in the second and final equation. Table 9.3 shows that the child's age was related to his or her social and communicative skills rather than to his or her play with objects. Older children used language more frequently, had more frequent positive interactions with their peers and played with them at a higher level. Similarly, girls used language more frequently, and engaged less frequently in agonistic interactions with peers.

Variables describing the life experience of the child contributed very little to the variance in his/her play behavior. No significant effect was found for birth order or age of entry, although ease of separation did affect the child's play behavior. Children who had some difficulty separating from their mothers in the morning spent more time in gross motor play with objects, and less time in a higher level of play with peers.

Two types of family characteristics were assessed: SES level, indicated by parental education level and the presence of social problems in the family as a reason for the child's placement in FDC, and maternal beliefs concerning child development and her influence over it.

Some of the variables comprising these two measures were interrelated. Parental education was negatively related to social problems as a reason for the placement of the child in FDC ($r = -.42$; p<.001). Mothers who had early expectations of developmental achievement in the cognitive domain also expected early achievement in the social domain ($r = .71$; p <.001). Mothers who attributed more influence over the child's development to themselves expected earlier achievements in the cognitive domain than did mothers who perceived themselves as less influential ($r = -.21$; p<.05).

Less educated mothers of those in families with social problems expected later achievements in the cognitive domain ($r = -.32$ and $-.31$ respectively; p<.01) and believed in more severe methods of control ($r = -.35$; p<.001 and $-.31$; p<.01 respectively). Mothers' beliefs were also related to the sex of their child. Thus, mothers of girls attributed more influence to themselves than did mothers of boys ($r = .20$; p<.05), and they had earlier expectations in the social domain ($r = -.21$; p<.05).

Previous research has suggested that because parents select child-care programs for their children, and selection biases may vary with program characteristics, it is important to control for program selection when examining the influence of the child-care environment on children's behavior and development (Phillips et al., 1987). It has further been suggested that selection biases may vary across samples or cultures (Kontos, 1991).

This study followed a data analysis procedure similar to that used by the Bermuda study (Phillips et al. 1987). All family background variables (parental education level, reason for placement in FDC, maternal developmental expectation and preferred methods of socialization and self-attribution of influence) were entered into a stepwise multiple regression for each of the child-care setting variables (group composition, caregiver's interactions, the educational quality of the physical environment and the daily program), in order to identify the specific family background measures that showed the strongest relation to the child-care setting variables.

The two best predictors that emerged from this analysis were family SES (mostly parental education but also reason of placement) and maternal expectation in the domain of social development. Children of better educated parents were more likely to be found in homes that were more crowded (Beta = .42, p<.001), that placed greater emphasis on educational content in the daily routine (Beta = .31, p<.05), and that had other children of better educated parents (Beta = .68, p<.001). They were less likely to be found in highly heterogeneous age groups (Beta = −.43, p<.001). Children from families with social problems tended to have more restrictive caretakers (Beta = .28, p<.01). Mothers who believed that children attained social development goals at an earlier age tended to have their children in groups where space to be alone is available (Beta = .36, p<.05) and with more girls (Beta = −.40, p<.001).

These relationships cannot be interpreted simply as "center-selection" biases. In fact, the relationship between crowdedness and parental education probably reflects the policy of placing children from lower SES in homes where they could get more individual attention and "enrichment." If so, these goals were not realized, (Rosenthal, 1990) as these homes in fact had less emphasis on educational content in their daily program, and their caregivers tended to be more restrictive. Obviously, enrichment could not be achieved without sufficient guidance to the caregivers.

While some of the relationships may suggest that parents have some influence over the program and the caregivers' behavior, the relationship between the number of girls in the group and maternal social expectation cannot reflect a selectivity bias. Whatever their source, these relationships indicate the need to control for family background when examining the effects of either group composition and/or program characteristics.

Once again, a hierarchical regression analysis was used to determine the relative contribution of these family characteristics on play behavior. Since social problems in the family correlated with parental level of education and showed similar correlations to other variables, a composite index of family SES was generated for the regression analysis.

Table 9.4 shows that, on the whole, family characteristics did not explain much of the children's play behavior, although some surprising correlations did emerge.

Children of higher SES families spent less time in gross motor play and more time in joint-play with peers. Contrary to expectations, their level of play with objects was lower than that of children of lower SES parents.

The relationship between mothers' developmental expectations and children's play was also contrary to common sense expectations. The children of mothers who expected early achievement in the cognitive domain spent more

Table 9.4 Hierarchical Regression of Children's Play Behavior on Family Background[1]

	FAMILY		MATERNAL Dev. Expectations		BELIEFS				
	SES	R-square Change	Cognitive	Social	Self-Influence	Social-ization	R-square Change	Final R-square	Adjusted R-square
Play with Objects									
Fine Motor	−.20	.05*	.31	−.35*	−.07	−.09	.08	.13	.06
Gross Motor	−.38**	.15***	.03	−.07	.00	.03	.00	.15*	.09
Mean Level	−.31*	.05	−.18	.06	−.14	−.08	.03	.08	.00
Play with Peers									
Positive Interaction	.02	.02	−.36*	.29	−.03	−.11	.06	.08	.01
Agonistic Interaction	.09	.00	.22	.00	.06	.13	.05	.05	−.02
Joint Play	.34*	.15***	−.23	.22	−.06	−.01	.03	.18*	.11
Level 2–5	−.08	.00	−.15	.24	.07	−.11	.04	.04	−.03
Context of Play									
Child Alone	.00	.00	.14	−.06	−.10	.00	.02	.02	−.05
Use of Language	.13	.05	−.08	.12	.02	−.18	.03	.08	.00

1. THE TABLE PRESENTS BETA VALUES FROM THE FINAL EQUATION *p < .05 **p < .01 ***p < .001

time in social interactions, while the children of mothers with expectations of early achievements in the social domain spent more time in fine-motor play with objects. Children spent less time in positive interactions with their peers if their mothers attributed more influence to themselves over their development.

The Influence of the Child Care Setting and the Social Environment on Childrens' Play

Table 9.5 presents the interrelations between various aspects of the child care setting, including the group composition, the caregiver's beliefs and behaviors, and the educational quality of the physical environment and the daily program. Each of these aspects will be discussed first in relation to the other elements of the setting, and then in relation to children's play behavior.

Table 9.5 shows that heterogeneous age groups were typically composed of older children, with a low SES group mean. Group mean characteristics were related to the characteristics of individual children and their families, so that younger children were in groups with a lower mean age (r = .64, p<.001), girls were in groups with more girls (r = .44, p<.01) and children of better educated parents were in groups with a higher mean educational level (r = .75, p<.001). Group characteristics were also related to the educational quality of the daily program. Thus, groups with older children and groups with children of more educated parents were in programs with a greater emphasis on educational activities (r = .40, p<.01, respectively) (Table 9.5).

Because of these covariations between groups characteristics and child and program characteristics, a hierarchical regression model was used in which the program characteristics were entered in the first equation, followed by the child and family characteristics in the second equation, and the specific group characteristics under investigation were entered in the third and final equation. The model was computed separately for each of the play behaviors, as well as for the context of play.

Table 9.6 presents the change in R-square at each step of the regression analysis and the Beta values for each of the group composition variables.

Table 9.6 shows that most of the individual differences in play behavior that were a function of age, sex or family SES (as seen in Tables 9.3 & 9.5), did not emerge on the level of group characteristics. Contrary to the effect of parental SES level on the *individual* child, joint-play was observed less frequently in *groups of children* from higher SES background. Similarly, while the individual child's age was not related to the level of play with objects, children in groups with a higher mean age did play with objects at a higher level. As may be expected, the frequency of joint-play was lower in more heterogeneous age groups, especially when these groups included both infants and preschoolers.

Table 9.5 Relations Between Child-Care Setting Characteristics[1] (N = 41)

	GROUP COMPOSITION				CAREGIVER'S DEV'L. BELIEFS				CG. BEHAVIOR		EDUCATIONAL QUALITY OF SETTING			
	Age Mean	Age Mix	Sex Mean	Mean Educ.	Cog. Exp.	Soc. Exp.	Self-Influ.	Social-ization	Pos. inter.	Rest-rict	Crowd-edness	Pri-vacy	Play Mat'l.	Edu. Prog.
Group Composition														
Age Mean	—	.36*											.26	.40**
Age Mix		—		-.49**										
Sex Mean			—				.32*	.27						
Mean Education				—				-.27			.27			.40**
Caregiver's Beliefs and Behavior														
Dev'l expect:Cognitive					—	.66***								
Dev'l expect:Social						—				.29				
Self-Influence	.26						—		.50***	.34*		-.27		
Socialization								—				-.28	.27	-.27
Positive Interaction									—	.35*				
Restrictions										—		-.46**	-.26	
Educational Quality of Setting														
Crowdedness											—	-.46**		-.28
Privacy												—	.40**	.49**
Play Materials													—	.44**
Educational Program														—

1. ONLY R > .26 ARE PRESENTED   *p < .05   **p < .01   ***p < .001

Table 9.6 Hierarchical Regression of Children's Play Behavior on Child-care Group Characteristics

	Educat'l Quality of Setting R-square	Ch. & Fam. characteristics R-square Change	Group		Composition[2]		R-square Change	Final R-square	Adjusted R-square
			Group Sex Mean	Group Age Mean	Group Age Mix	Parental Education			
Play with Objects									
Fine Motor	-.31***	.05	-.03	-.02	.11	.11	.01	.37***	.27
Gross Motor	-.22***	.10*	.02	-.07	-.15	.10	.02	.34**	.23
Mean Level	.02	.10	-.10	.34*	-.10	.21	.07	.18	.04
Play with Peers									
Positive Interaction	.05	.14*	-.02	.13	-.09	-.12	.02	.20	.07
Agonistic Interaction	.03	.06	-.06	.02	-.21	-.10	.03	.12	-.02
Joint Play	.31***	.01	-.04	.10	-.36**	-.29*	.10*	.42**	.32
Level 2–5	.02	.12*	.01	.19	.02	-.07	.03	.17	.03
Context of Play									
Child Alone	.02	.08	.06	-.25	.13	.06	.04	.14	-.00
Use of Language	.08	.12*	-.16	.19	-.12	.17	.05	.26*	.14

1. TABLE PRESENTS BETA VALUES FROM THE FINAL EQUATION
2. THE GROUP-MEANS WERE CALCULATED *WITHOUT* THE SCORES OF THE TARGET CHILD

*p < .05   **p < .01   ***p < .001

Table 9.7 Hierarchical Regression of Children's Play Behavior Caregivers Beliefs and Spontaneous Interactions with the Children[1]

| | CAREGIVER'S BELIEFS | | | | | CG'S INTERACTIONS | | | | |
	Dev'l Expectation: Cognitive	Social	Self-Influence	Socialization Technique	R-square Change	Positive Inter	Restrictions	R-square Change	Final R-square	Adjusted R-square
Play with Objects										
Fine Motor	-.40**	.38**	.12	-.26*	.18**	.20	.05	.03	.21**	.15
Gross Motor	.34*	-.18	.14	.22	.17**	-.08	.15	.01	.18**	.12
Mean Level	-.19	.23	.02	-.01	.03	.18	.02	.03	.06	.02
Play with Peers										
Positive Interaction	-.22	.40**	-.16	.10	.09	.26*	-.03	.04	.13	.06
Agonistic Interaction	.14	-.28	.00	.11	.05	-.11	.11	.01	.06	-.01
Joint Play	-.02	.05	-.10	.32**	.13*	.05	.06	.01	.14	.07
Level 2–5	-.04	.18	-.14	-.20	.07	.04	.06	.00	.07	.00
Context of Play										
Child Alone	.28*	-.55***	.11	.10	.16**	-.12	.04	.01	.17	.10
Use of Language	-.03	.19	-.25	-.12	.05	.20	-.24	.05	.10	.02

1. THE TABLE PRESENTS BETA VALUES FROM THE FINAL EQUATION *p < .05 **p < .01 ***p < .001

Other studies (Stallings & Porter, 1980) have suggested that the age mix of a group may have different effects on younger and older children in the group. An analysis of variance examined the effects of four levels of age heterogeneity (Age Span) on the play behavior of children younger than two, and on children older than two. These levels of Age Span were: (1) most homogeneous—less than six months between youngest and oldest child in the group; (2) fairly homogeneous—7 to 12 months between the youngest and oldest child; (3) fairly heterogeneous—13-24 months between youngest and oldest child; (4) most heterogeneous—more than 24 months between the youngest and oldest child. The analysis confirmed the findings reported above for the main effects of mean age and age mix. In addition however, interaction effects were found for the three variables assessing children's play with objects. The younger children spent the greatest amount of time in gross-motor play in the most homogeneous age groups and in fine-motor play in fairly heterogeneous groups. It was in these heterogeneous (13-24 month span) groups that the younger children played with objects at the highest level. Children more than two years old were less affected by the age mix of the group. They generally spent little time in gross motor play, and did so least often in the most homogeneous groups. The older children displayed more fine-motor play in either the most homogeneous or most heterogeneous groups.

The Influence of the Caregiving Adult on the Childrens' Play

Two major aspects of the caregiver's behavior were investigated: her stated beliefs concerning child development and her role in influencing it, and her spontaneous interactions with children, as recorded by the observer. Caregivers' beliefs were consistent with each other, with their behaviors, and with the characteristics of the child-care environment they provided in their home (Table 9.5). The following correlations were statistically significant:

1. Caregiver's developmental expectations in the cognitive and social domains were inter-related.

2. Caregivers who attributed more influence to themselves over the child's development had more frequent positive interactions with the children, and used restrictions less frequently, than did caregivers who attributed less influence to themselves.

3. Caregivers who were more restrictive also stated that they believed in using more authoritarian methods of socialization, and were less likely to provide the children with "space to be alone."

4. Caregivers who had more girls in their groups tended to attribute more influence to themselves, just as their mothers did.

As might be expected, children of caregivers who spent more time in positive interactions with the children, engaged more frequently in positive social interactions with peers (Table 9.7). Table 9.7 shows that of the various beliefs and interactions we examined, caregivers' developmental expectations and beliefs concerning socialization techniques were the best predictors of children's play behavior.

Children in the care of caregivers who expected them to attain cognitive skills earlier spent more time in fine-motor play and less time in gross-motor play or alone. This is in marked contrast to children of caregivers who expected early attainment of social skills, who spent less time in fine-motor play and in positive interaction with peers and more time alone. Children with caregivers who believed in using more authoritarian socialization techniques engaged less frequently in fine-motor play with objects, and more frequently in joint-play with peers.

The Influence of Caregivers' Spontaneous Interactions, the Physical Environment and the Daily Program on Childrens' Play

FDC homes that placed greater emphasis on educational content in their daily routine had more play materials and were more likely to provide "space to be alone" (Table 9.5). Those FDC homes with "space to be alone" also tended to have more play materials and were less crowded.

To examine the effects of the educational quality of the FDC setting on the children's play behavior, a hierarchical regression model was again used. The two family background characteristics that were found to be the best predictors of the educational quality of the FDC setting, parental SES and maternal social development expectations, were entered in the first equation to control for possible biases generated by family background.

In order to account for the correlations between spontaneous caregiver-child interactions with the educational quality of the physical environment and the daily program, we entered spontaneous interactions in the second equation of the hierarchical regression analysis, and aspects of the educational quality of the physical environment and the daily program in the final equation.

Table 9.8 shows that the educational quality of the physical environment and the daily program were by far the best predictors of children's play behavior.

Children in more crowded FDC homes spent less time in gross-motor play and more time in joint-play with peers. In homes where there was "space to be alone," children spent more time alone, engaged less frequently in positive interaction or joint-play, and more often in agonistic interactions with peers. They spent less time in gross-motor play and played with objects at a lower level.

In homes where there were more play materials, we observed more frequent fine-motor play. Similarly, in homes that placed a greater emphasis on the educational content of the daily program, children engaged more frequently

Table 9.8 Hierarchical Regression of Children's Play Behavior on the Characteristics of the Child-Care Environment and Educational Program

	Family characteristics: SES & Dev'l exp. Social R-square	Caregiver's Interaction: R-square Change	CHILD-CARE ENVIRONMENT AND PROGRAM				R-square Change	Final R-square	Adjusted R-square
			Crowded-ness	Space to be alone	Amount Play Material	Educat'l Program			
Play with Objects									
Fine Motor	.06	.05	-.03	-.04	.28*	.45***	.34***	.45***	.37
Gross Motor	-.18**	.02	-.32*	-.41**	.17	-.30	.19**	.38***	.30
Mean Level	.05	.02	-.17	-.58***	.06	.08	.16*	.23*	.12
Play with Peers									
Positive Interaction	.03	.05	-.01	-.55**	.11	.24	.18*	.26*	.16
Agonistic Interaction	.01	.01	.10	.41*	-.21	.11	.12	.14	.02
Joint Play	.13**	.18***	.30**	-.39**	-.07	.31**	.22***	.54***	.47
Level 2–5	.02	.03	.11	-.19	.07	.10	.04	.09	-.03
Context of Play									
Child Alone	.00	.04	.15	.63***	-.09	.00	.23**	.27**	.17
Use of Language	.06	.01	.18	-.10	-.11	.15	.05	.12	-.00

in fine-motor play, and less frequently in gross-motor play, and spent more time in joint-play with peers. Altogether this equation explained more of the variance in children's play behavior than any of the previous analyses.

Discussion

Two key aspects of young children's play were investigated in this study: play with objects and play with peers (Howes and Stewart, 1987). The sensori-motor interaction of children with objects was classified as fine-motor and gross-motor forms of play. Their social interactions were coded as positive, agonistic and a form of joint-play that is characterized by group participation with repetitive sounds and laughter (Budwig et al., 1986). Both aspects of children's play were rated on a scale that assessed their level of complexity (Howes and Stewart, 1987). The social and linguistic contexts of play were studied in relation to each type of children's play.

Although the two forms of play were inter-related, both reflecting the competence level of the child, they were affected somewhat differently by the child's background and by the child-care setting. The child's characteristics (age, sex and separation difficulties) affected social play, rather than play with objects. It is likely that level of play with objects was not sensitive to age differences mostly because of the very small variance in this measure. Experience with peers or with siblings was unrelated to the children's play behavior. While other studies have also found that experience with siblings did not influence play behavior of children with child-care experience, experience with peers has been cited as an important determinant of children's play (e.g., Howes, 1988). However, age-of-entry (while controlling for its confound with age) in this study, did not explain any of the variance in children's play behavior. Since all children had spent already more than four months at the FDC home and 64 percent had more than 10 months of FDC experience, it could be that this experience was sufficient to eliminate possible individual differences in play behavior which are related to this variable.

Family background was mainly related to characteristics of the care environment, rather than to the child's play behavior. In particular, children of better educated parents were more likely to be found in age homogeneous homes with a greater stress on educational content in the daily routine, while children of lower SES parents were found in less crowded homes.

These findings cannot be explained simply in terms of "center selectivity" concepts (Phillips et al, 1987; Kontos, 1991). First, it seems that the placement policy of the sponsoring agency intervened so that children from low SES homes were placed in less crowded homes with more heterogenous age groups. Second, and perhaps even more important, caregivers seem to respond to the type of population they serve: those working with children of better educated parents placed more emphasis on educational content in their daily program while those working with more children from "distressed families" used more restrictions. Whatever their source, it was obvious that we had to control for these indirect effects of home background in order to examine the effects of the child-care environment on children's play.

Family background had very little direct effect on the children's play behavior, although two somewhat puzzling findings emerged. First, children of better educated parents played with objects at a lower level of competence that those of less educated parents. One explanation of this result might be that children of higher SES parents do not find the FDC environment challenging enough; they spend more time in "aimless activity" (Rosenthal, 1990). Secondly, we found that children of mothers who had early developmental expectations in the cognitive domain (and presumably offer more experiences at home related to this domain) spent more time in social play, while children of mothers with early developmental expectations in the social domain spent more time playing with objects. This finding suggests that children may be using the FDC setting to complement aspects of the home environment, and that while in the day-care setting, they engage in those activities that are not stressed at home.

Though these findings may be specific to this sample, they point at the need to examine the effects of the interface between home and child-care environment at a level which is more subtle and complex than the simple "center selectivity" hypothesis may suggest. It is interesting that such young children spent more time in social interaction than in play with toys. This is possibly a result of the context of their play, which was predominantly a group interaction context that brought them into close contact with each other.

Perhaps the most striking finding of this study is that even when the family background effects are taken into account, children's play behavior is mainly influenced by factors in the child-care environment. Three major elements of this environment were considered: the social environment, the educational content of the daily program, and the educational quality of the physical environment. The social environment included peer group and the adult caregiver characteristics.

Both the mean age of the peer group and the age homogeneity of the group affected the competence level of children's play. However, while all children, regardless of age, played at a higher level in groups with a higher age-mean, only young children (under 2) were affected by the age mix of the group. In moderately heterogeneous age groups (13-24 months between the youngest and oldest child), young children played more competently with both toys and peers than they did in more homogeneous or more heterogeneous groups. Only the fine-motor play of older children were affected by the age heterogeneity of the group, which they displayed more frequently in either extremely homogeneous or extremely heterogeneous groups. The results of this study suggest that while the presence of older children facilitated high level of play in younger children, the presence of younger children did not have an effect of the competence in play of older children.

Two aspects of the caregiver's attitudes and behavior influenced the nature of the children's play: positive interactions and developmental expectations. Children seemed to be influenced by the caregiver's positive interactions with them: those in homes with caregivers who frequently engaged in positive interactions with the children spent more time in positive interactions with their peers than did children in homes with less frequent positive interactions with caregivers. Moreover, children in the homes of caregivers with early expectations in the cognitive domain spent more time in fine-motor play with objects and less time in gross motor play or alone. It is likely that the caregiver's expectations indirectly affected children's play with objects by mediating the physical environment and daily program she provided in her home. However, it seems that caregivers with early expectations in the social domain did not know how to "translate" these expectations into their daily program. The children in their homes spent more time alone and less time in social play or in fine-motor play with objects.

The educational quality of the physical environment and the daily program were the best predictor of variation in children's play behavior. An emphasis on educational content in the daily program, and on more varied play equipment, resulted in more frequent fine-motor play with objects.

It is this form of play with objects that brings children into close contact with each other, providing them with joint themes and leading to more frequent joint-play. Moreover, although crowdedness limits the children's opportunity to engage in gross-motor play with objects, it does create more opportunities for social contact resulting again in more frequent joint-play. Thus, fine motor play with objects, rather than gross-motor play, is obviously regarded by the caregiver as being most important for cognitive development. Although psychologists and education experts generally highlight the importance of "stimulus shelter" (Wachs et al., 1979) or "space to be alone" (Prescott, 1981) for the well being and sensorimotor development of children, our findings for this age group in FDC setting highlight their effect on social play. It seems that space to be alone in a small, mixed age group of infants and toddlers, in a home-like environment tends to distance children from each other. They spent more time alone or in agonistic interaction rather than in positive social interaction or joint-play, and played with objects at a lower level of competence.

Joint-play is an interesting form of social interaction among young peers which, although very distinct and easily identifiable, has not been the subject of very much research. The findings of this study suggest that it is related to the child's general sociability and communicative skills, and tends to come at the expense of the child's fine-motor play with objects. It was not related to any of the child's or child family's characteristics. It tended to appear in more homogeneous age groups, regardless of the child's age, with a lower mean SES level, and in crowded homes of caregivers who believed in more authoritarian socialization techniques, who placed greater emphasis on the educational aspects of the program, and who did not provide "space to be alone." It seems that the type of space and time organization that brings children of similar ages and play competence into continuous close contact with each other facilitates this form of social interaction.

This study was conceptualized within the general framework of an ecologic-systemic approach to child development (Bronfenbrenner, 1979). We have found that in order to understand individual differences in the play behavior of children, it is misleading to search for a linear relationship between one aspect in the child's life and his play competency. Instead, this study has demonstrated that it is the nature of the setting in which the child spends so much of his waking hours that affects his play behavior in that setting, rather than the direct and indirect effects of his personal and family background.

REFERENCES

Bakeman, R., & Adamson, L. B. (1984). Coordinating attention to people and objects in mother-infant and peer-infant interaction. *Child Development, 55,* 1278-1289.

Bates, B. C. (1972). *Effect of density on the behavior of nursery school children.* Eugene, OR: University of Oregon Center for Environmental Research.

Brenner, J., & Mueller, E. (1982). Shared meaning in boy toddlers' peer relations. *Child Development, 53,* 380-391.

Bronfenbrenner, U. (1979). *The ecology of human development.* Cambridge, MA: Harvard University Press.

Bronson, W. C. (1975). Developments in behavior with age-mates during the second year of life. In M. Lewis & L. A. Rosenblum (eds.), *Friendship and peer relations.* New York: Wiley.

Brownell, C. A. (1982). Effects of age and age-mix on toddler peer interaction. Paper presented at the International Conference on Infant Studies, Austin, Texas.

Budwig, N. S., A., & Bamberg, M. (1986). The construction of joint activities with an age-mate: The transition from caregiver-child to peer play. In J. C., W. A. & Streeck J. Cook-Gumperz, *Children's Worlds and Children's language.* (pp. 83-108). New York: Monton de Gruyter.

Clarke-Stewart, K. R., & Fein, G. C. (1983). Early childhood programs. *Handbook of child psychology* (4th ed.) (Mussen, P. H., Haith, M. M. & Campos, J. J.) (pp. 917-999). New York: Wiley.

Clarke-Stewart, A., & Fein, G. G. (1983). Early childhood programs. In M. Haith and J. Campos (eds.), *Handbook of child psychology: Vol. II Infancy and developmental psychobiology.* (pp. 917-1000). New York: Wiley.

Clarke-Stewart, K. A., & Gruber, C. (1984). Day care forms and features. In R. Ainslie (Ed.), *The child and the day care setting: Qualitative variations and development.* (pp. 35-62). New York: Praeger.

Eckerman, C. O., & Whatley, J. L. (1977). Toys and social interaction between infant peers. *Child Development, 48,* 1645-1650.

Fagot, B. (1980). The maintenance of aggression in toddlers. Paper presented at the meetings of the International Conference on Infant Studies, New Haven.

Fein, G. G., & Clarke-Stewart, A. (1973). *Day care in context.* New York: Wiley.

Garvey, C. (1977). *Play.* Cambridge, MA: Harvard University Press.

Hartup, W. W. (1983). Peer relations. In E. M. Hetherington (Ed.), *Handbook of Child Psychology: Vol. 4. Socialization, personality and social development.* (pp. 103-196). New York: Wiley.

Hess, R. D., Price, G. P., Dickson, W. R., & Conroy, M. (1981). Different roles for mothers and teachers: Contrasting styles of child care. In S. Kilmer (ed.), *Advances in Early Education and Day Care.* London: JAI Press.

Howes, C., & Stewart, P. (1987). Child's play with adults, toys and peers: An examination of family and child care influences. *Developmental Psychology, 23,* 423-430.

Howes, C., & Olenick, M. (1986). Family and daycare influences on toddlers' compliance. *Child development, 57,* 202-216.

Howes, C. (1988). Peer interaction of young children. *Monographs of the Society for Research in Child Development, 53* (1, Serial No. 217).

Howes, C. (1980). Peer play scale as an index of complexity of peer interaction. *Developmental Psychology, 16,* 371-372.

Howes, C., & Eldredge, R. (1985). Responses of abused, neglected and non-maltreated children to the behaviors of their peers. *Journal of Applied Developmental Psychology, 6,* 261-270.

Howes, C. (1987). Social competence with peers in young children: Developmental sequences. *Developmental Review*, 7, 252-272.

Hunt, J. M. (1979). Psychological development: Early experience. *Annual Review of Psychology, 30,* 103-143.

Jackson, D., & Angelino, H. (1974). Play as learning. *Theory into Practice, 13,* 317-323.

Jacobson, J. L. (1981). The role of inanimate objects in early peer interaction. *Child Development, 52,* 618-626.

Johnson, J. E., Ershler, J., & Bell, C. (1980). Play behavior in a discovery-based and a formal education preschool program. *Child Development, 51,* 271-274.

Johnson, M. (1935). The effect on behavior of variation in amount of play equipment. *Child Development, 6,* 56-58.

Kontos, S. J. Child care quality, family background and children's development. *Early Childhood Research Quarterly,* 6, 249–262.

Legendre, A. (1985). Influence of spatial arrangement on young children's social behavior. A paper presented at the 19th International Ethological Conference, Toulouse, France.

Lewis, M. Y., G., Brocks, J., & Michalson, L. (1975). The beginning of friendship. In M. Lewis & L. A. Rosenblum (Eds.), *Friendship and peer relations.* New York: Wiley.

Lieberman, A. (1977). Preschoolers' competence with peer. *Child Development, 48,* 1277-1287.

Lougee, M. D., Grueneich, R., & Hartup, W. W. (1977). Social interaction in same- and mixed-age dyads of preschool children. *Child Development, 48,* 1353-1361.

Maudry, M., & Nekula, M. (1939). Social relations between children of the same age during the first two years of life. *Journal of Genetic Psychology, 54,* 193-215.

McCartney, K. S., Phillips, D., & Grajek, S. (1985). Day care as intervention: Comparisons of varying quality programs. *Journal of Applied Developmental Psychology, 6,* 247-260.

McGrew, P. (1970). Social and spacing density effects on spacing density in preschool children, *Journal of Child Psychology and Psychiatry, 11,* 197-205.

Mueller, E., & Lucas, T. (1975). A developmental analysis of peer interaction among toddlers. In M. Lewis & L. A. Rosenblum (Eds.), *Friendship and Peer relations.* New York: Wiley.

Mueller, E., & Vandell, D. (1979). Infant-infant interaction. In J. D. Osofsky (Ed.), *Handbook of infant development*. New York: Wiley.

Mueller, E., & Brenner, J. (1977). The origins of social skills and interaction among playgroup toddlers. *Child Development, 48,* 854-861.

Pastor, D. (1981). The quality of mother-infant attachment and its relationship to toddlers' sociability with peers. *Developmental Psychology, 17,* 326-335.

Phillips, D. M., K., & Scarr, S. (1987). Child care quality and children's social development. *Developmental Psychology, 23,* 537-543.

Piaget, J. (1962). *Play, dreams and imitation in childhood.* New York: Norton.

Prescott, E. (1981). Relations between physical setting and adult/child behavior in day care. In S. Kilmer (Ed.), *Advances in Early Education and Day Care. 2* (pp. 129-158). London: JAI Press.

Rohe, W., & Patterson, A. H. (1974). The effects of varied level of resources and density on behavior in a day care center. In D. H. Carson (Ed.), *Man-Environment interaction*. Milwaukee, WI: EDRA.

Roopnarine, J. L. (1984). Sex-typed socialization in mixed-age preschool classrooms. *Child Development, 55,* 1078-1084.

Rosenthal, M. K. (1990). Social policy and its effects on the daily experiences of infants and toddlers in Family Day Care in Israel. *Journal of Applied Developmental Psychology, 11,* 85–104.

Rosenthal, M. K. (1991). Behaviors and beliefs of caregivers in Family Daycare: The effects of background and work environment. *Early Childhood Research Quarterly, 6,* 263–283.

Rubenstein, J. L., & Howes, C. (1979). Caregiving and infant behavior in day care and in homes. *Developmental Psychology, 15,* 1-24.

Rubenstein, J., & Howes, C. (1976). The effect of peers on toddler's interaction with mother and toys. *Child Development, 47,* 597-605.

Rubin, K. H., Maioni, T. L., & Hornung, M. (1976). Free play behaviors in middle- and lower-class preschoolers: Parten and Piaget revisited. *Child Development, 47,* 414-419.

Sarafino, E. P. (1985). Peer-peer interaction among infants and toddlers with extensive day care experience. *Journal of Applied Developmental Psychology, 6,* 17-29.

Schindler, M., & Frank. (1987). Time in daycare and social participation of young children. *Developmental Psychology, 23,* 255-261.

Smilansky, S. (1968). *The effects of sociodramatic play on disadvantaged preschool children*. New York: Wiley.

Stallings, J., & Porter, A. (1980). National Day Care Home Study: Observation Component (Final Report). Washington, DC: DHEW.

Tizard, B. P., J. & Plewis, I. (1976). I. Play in preschool centers, II. Effects on play of the child's social class and of the educational orientation of the center. *Journal of Child Psychology and Psychiatry, 17,* 265-274.

Vandell, D. L., Wilson, K. S., & Buchanan, N. R. (1980). Peer interaction in the first year of life: An examination of its structure, content, and sensitivity to toys. *Child Development, 51,* 481-488.

Verba, M. S., M., & Sinclair, H. (1982). Physical knowledge and social interaction in children from 18 to 24 months of age. In G. Forman (Ed.), *Action and Thought*. New York: Academic Press.

Wachs, T., & Gruen, G. (1982). *Early experience and human development*. New York: Plenum.

Wachs, T. D., Francis, J., & McQuiston, S. (1979). Psychological dimensions of the infant's physical environment. *Infant Behavior and Development, 2,* 155-161.

Wachs, T., & Chan, A. (1986). Specificity of environmental action, as seen in environmental correlates of infants' communication performance. *Child Development, 57,* 1464-1474.

Waters, E. W., J., & Sroufe, A. (1979). Attachment, positive affect and competence in the peer group. *Child Development, 50,* 821-829.

Wohlwill, J. F. (1983). Physical and social environment as factors in development. In D. Magnusson & U. L. Allen (Eds.), *Human development: An interactional perspective*. (pp. 111-129). New York: Academic Press.

Wohlwill, J., & Heft, H. (1987). The physical environment and development of the child. In D. Stokols & I. Altman (eds.), *Handbook of environmental psychology*. New York: Wiley.

Yarrow, L. J., Rubenstein, J. L., & Pederson, F. A. (1975). *Infant and environment: Early cognitive and motivational development*. New York: Wiley.

10

Play, Talk, Literacy, and the Ecology of Family Day Care

Hillel Goelman and Alan R. Pence

The study reported in this chapter attempted to relate two parallel foci in child development research. One focus is the relationship between symbolic play and the development of literacy. The second is the relationship between ecological features of child care and child language development. We begin this chapter with a brief review of these two distinct research literatures and then describe the conceptual and empirical bases for the study reported below.

Oral Discourse and Emergent Literacy

Literacy researchers have devoted increasing attention to the relationships between oral discourse in the preschool years and the child's subsequent development of literacy. The emerging consensus from studies reported by Wells (1985, 1986), Galda, Pellegrini and Cox (1989), Torrance & Olson (1984, 1985) suggests quite strongly that specific features of oral discourse in the preschool years predict emergent literacy. Three features of child talk in particular were found to be associated with overall levels of language development and early literacy. Based on Grice (1957), Olson and Pellegrini have argued, and reported data which support the view, that children develop a "literate" orientation in their oral language discourse. A major part of this literate orientation is the ability to reflect on language, to use language to describe language, to articulate a "metalinguisitc" view of thought and language. Both Olson and Pellegrini have shown that children's use of "psychological" or "metalinguistic" verbs such as "remember," "say," "mean" in both experimental and spontaneous situations appears to reflect this metalinguistic perspective.

A second feature of a literate bias in oral language is the use of certain cohesive devices which speakers use in tying together an articulate and meaningful conversation. Pellegrini (1982, 1985) referred to these devices as "endophora" while Torrance and Olson (1985) use the term "turnabouts." In using these devices speakers make explicit linguistic reference to their interlocutor's discourse in their own contributions to the conversation.

A third feature which Tizard and Hughes (1984) have identified is what they have called "cognitive demands." These are questions of increasing difficulty which adults tend to ask children in their later preschool years. As described in detail below, the "lower level" cognitive demands ask the child to come up with simple descriptions while more complex demands ask for the recall of sequences, explanations or specific questions referring to the mechanics of literacy (e.g. alphabet, word meanings).

In a series of papers Pellegrini and Galda (Pelligrini, 1982, 1985a,b; Pellegrini & Galda, 1982; Galds, Pellegrini & Cox, 1989) have argued that many of the critical and specific features of oral language which relate to the development of literacy are found in the language children use in their symbolic play behaviors. Pellegrini (1985a) identified the representational characteristics and narrative features of symbolic play and literate behavior. He points out that in both symbolic play and literate behavior children make use of decontextualized language to refer to, and to represent, non-present objects, people, and events. Similarly, the flow of children's symbolic play involves a temporal sequencing of events which maps onto the child's understanding of story structure.

The vast majority of studies of the relationship between oral discourse and metaliterate awareness has examined adult-talk in home environments (Wells 1985, 1986; Torrance & Olson, 1985), or nursery schools (Galda, Pellegrini & Cox, 1989; Corsaro, 1979; Cochran-Smith, 1984; Reeder, Shapiro, Watson & Goelman, in preparation; Pellegrini, 1985b; Tizard & Hughes, 1984). Research in this area has rarely examined children's talk in day care centers (Cross, Parmenter, Juchnowski & Johnson, 1984) or in family day care homes. (Goelman, 1986) in family day care settings. Thus, a major objective of the study reported below was to expand the study of the relationships between symbolic play and literate behavior by examining the adult-child discourse patterns in play settings in the most frequently used form of preschool child care in North America.

The Ecology of Family Day Care

The research reported in this chapter is part of a continuing investigation of the ecology of family day care (Goelman & Pence, 1988; Goelman, Shapiro & Pence, 1989; Goelman, Rosenthal & Pence,1990) the effects of family day care settings on child language development (Goelman, 1986; Goelman & Pence, 1987a,b) and the relationships between own-home and family day care home environments (Goelman & Pence, 1988a).

In Goelman & Pence (1987a) a model for examining the interaction of ecological features in day-care environments and the effects of this interaction on child language development was described. "Process" and "structure" variables in both own-home and day-care environments were seen to impact on children. Process own-home variables related to child-child and adult-child play interactions in the home environment. Structure variables in own-home settings included such socio-demographic variables as parental marital status, and parental levels of income, education, and occupation. Process variables referred mainly to the type of adult-child and child-child play interactions which occurred in day care. Structure variables in day care included the type of care, numbers of children, and levels of staff education and training.

In a study of licensed and unlicensed family day-care homes Goelman & Pence (1987a,b) "process" was assessed through time and event sampling observations of the children's spontaneous play. The major feature of the "structure" of the environment was program "quality," as measured by the *Day Care Home Environment Rating Scale—DCHERS* (Harms, Clifford & Padan-Belkin, 1983). These studies revealed that the licensing status and the overall programmatic quality of the family day-care homes were associated with both high scores on tests of language development and the frequency of facilitative educational activities in the children's play. In the better quality family day-care homes the children were more frequently observed in higher level interactive play activities which involved reading, information sharing, fine and gross materials. Lower quality family day-care homes were associated with lower levels of interactive play, test scores and more frequent television watching.

A series of follow-up studies of children's own-home and family day-care home environments (Goelman & Pence 1989; Goelman, Shapiro & Pence, 1990) examined the relationships between the levels of cognitive stimulation to which the child was exposed at home and in family day-care characteristics of social-emotional functioning in both environments, and the programmatic quality of the family day care environment. Cognitive stimulation was measured by Caldwell and Bradley's (1979) *Home Observation For Measurement of the Environment (HOME)* scale. The *HOME* scale addresses both structural features of the environment (e.g., amount of certain kinds of materials) as well as the process or social, learning and play aspects of the environment (e.g., type and frequency of certain kinds of interactions). A further measure of process was Moos's (1976) *Family Environment Scale (FES)* which is a self-report on the frequency of certain kinds of activities and interactions engaged in by the family. The scale is used to assess the social-emotional climate of family life and yield scores on such constructs as "organization," "responsibility," "religious orientation," "cohesion" and "conflict." This study was the first reported use of the *FES* and *HOME* scales in family day-care environments. Program quality was again measured by the *DCHERS* (Harms, Clifford & Padan-Belkin, 1983).

These studies revealed close relationships between the level of cognitive stimulation (*HOME*) and the programmatic quality in the family day-care environment (*DCHERS*). A factor analysis revealed an overall "quality" construct in which both *HOME* and *DCHERS* scores loaded significantly. Further, the overall quality scores were significantly correlated with specific aspects of the social-emotional dimensions of the family life of the family day-care provider. Specifically, quality correlated with the *FES* sub-scales on Organization, Independence, Active-Recreational activities, and Intellectual-Cultural orientations.

Taken together, these findings suggest a confluence of structure and process variables with contribute to the quality of family day care environments. Better family day-care environments tend, first, to be well-organized family environments in their level of cognitive stimulation, the physical organization of supplies and space, and in their social-emotional functioning. The family environment, revealed by the *HOME*, provides age-appropriate and facilitative interaction and activities. The *FES* data suggest that family life in better day care homes appears to be well organized and the needs of family members are recognized and addressed. The *DCHERS* data suggest that when family functioning is well-organized, a solid basis for an effective and high quality day-care environment can be designated and implemented.

The *HOME, FES,* and *DCHERS* data provide useful information on the content and context of family day-care environments. What they do not provide is detailed information on the precise nature of children's play in these settings. The *HOME* checklist is helpful in drawing the observer's attention to a pre-set list of materials and interactions. The *DCHERS* similarly provides a scale to determine the presence/absence of certain materials and the general frequency with which these materials are, in fact, used. Neither scale, however, allows for a detailed observation of the nature of children's spontaneous play in these settings and the ways in which these play patterns relate to developmental outcome measures.

The major purpose of the study reported in this chapter, then, is to expand on the information reported in earlier studies on the effects of the ecology family day care on play interactions. Towards this end, the major contextual factors which were used in this study were the *HOME* scores for the own-home and the family day-care home settings. As indicated above, the *HOME* was found to be a major factor in the composite "quality" factor derived in earlier analyses and, further, has been used extensively in numerous studies of home environments and has been identified as a significant predictor of cognitive development in children (ie Barnard, Bee & Hammond, 1984; Bradley & Caldwell, 1976, 1980; Gottfried, 1984; Johnson, Breckenridge and McGowan, 1984; Lamb, Hwang, Broberg & Bookstein, 1988).

While Goelman & Pence (1987a,b, 1988b) examined the frequency of different kinds of play activities, the current study was designed to go into further detail by examining on an utterance by utterance basis some of the specific features of the adult and child discourse patterns in play interactions. The current study also attempted to broaden the findings reported in previous studies of discourse patterns and emergent literacy by collecting data on psychological verbs and cohesion not just on child talk (as in the Torrance & Olson, 1984, 1985 and Galda, Pellegrini & Cox, 1989 studies) and on cognitive demands not just in adult talk (Tizard & Hughes, 1984) but in the ongoing flow of adult-child discourse produced by both conversational partners. Further, the data on both quality of the family day care home environments and discourse features found in adult and child talk were examined in the context of the children's overall levels of expressive and receptive language competence.

The major questions identified after examining the research literatures on emergent literacy and the ecology of day care and addressed in this study were the following:

1. What relationships exist between the levels of cognitive stimulation available to the child at home and in family day care (as measured by the HOME scale) and the child's levels of receptive and expressive language?

2. What relationships exist between the literate features of oral discourse found in adult and child talk at home and in family day care and the child's overall level of receptive and expressive language competence?

3. What patterns of similarity, complementarity of differences are there in the adult-child discourse at home and in family day care?

Method

Sample

The participants were recruited from lists of family day-care providers submitted by local licensing officials as well as from newspaper advertisement. Caregivers and parents of children in their care agreed to cooperate by being interviewed, allowing the children to be tested and by participating in the video-taped play settings.

The mean of the 12 girls and 8 boys in the study children was 46 months (SD = 10). On average, the children had been out of home care for the previous 28 months and had been in their current family day-care homes for the previous 20 months. The family day-care homes in which they participated has a mean size of 4.8 children. They were in these family day-care homes for 31.4 hours per week.

HOME and DCHERS

The preschool version of the *HOME* Scale is inventory designed to describe different features of a child's home environment which have been linked to children's cognitive development. The Scale generates both a Total Score as well as sub-scale scores on toys, games and reading materials; language stimulation; physical environment; pride, affection and warmth; stimulation of academic behavior; modelling and encouragement of social maturity; variety of stimulation; physical punishment. Within each of these areas the scale provides specific descriptors relating to either the presence of certain materials or the observation of certain interactions.

The Day Care Home Environment Scale (*DCHERS*) consists of 37 items grouped into seven sub-scales: personal care routines; furnishings and displays for children; language reasoning experiences; fine and gross motor activities; creative activities; social development and adult needs. Each item is accompanied by a descriptor of quality on a 7 point Likert-type scale with a score of 1 referring to poor quality, 3 as minimal, 5 as good and 7 as excellent.

Inter-rater reliability was obtained from two who agreed with one another over 85% of the time. All of the own-home and family day-care environments were rated on the *HOME* Scale and the family day-care homes were also rated on the *DCHERS*. Each observation was conducted in a 2-3 hour period.

Play Interactions

Pilot observations of child-child play activity in family day-care and nursery settings revealed a tremendous range of variability in the quantity and style of discourse among the children. One factor contributing to this variability was the availability of different kinds (and qualities) of play materials in different settings. A second critical factor was the availability of a play partner of appropriate gender, social, and linguistic competence. The language abilities represented among the five children in family day-care homes, ranging from infants to 12 year old school-aged children, varied tremendously in all of the family day care.

In an attempt to gain some measure of control and standardization, while retaining a large degree of ecological validity, it was decided to observe children interacting with a specific set of play materials with adult caregivers both at home and in family day care. The observation of adult caregivers with the children was based upon the empirical observation regarding the variability in language competencies of child language partners and the conceptual view that adult language provides the modelling and scaffolding which facilitates child language development. Specifically, the observation of adult-child interaction allowed us to examine the discourse for evidence of adults orienting their own, and the child's language, towards a literate bias or orientation. Observing both the child's adult caregiver at home in family day care would allow for comparisons of the degree of literature bias in the two adults' play interactions.

A semi-structured play situation was created both at home and in the family day-care setting. Based on Pellegrini's (1985) argument that symbolic play elicits certain literature features of oral discourse, we used play materials designed to be novel and to stimulate symbolic play. Children were shown a set of 12 finger puppets representing animals and fairy tale characters and a box of "poppoids," snapping plastic toys which fit together and which could be made into various constructions, creatures and people. The mothers and caregivers were told that the purpose of the video-taped session was to observe a typical mother-child play session. The adults were asked to interact with their children in as natural a manner as possible. The play sessions took approximately 20 minutes. The children were introduced to the play materials in their play sessions with their own mothers at home. The caregiver-child play sessions in family day care were held two to three weeks after the mother-child play sessions at home.

Coding Taxonomy

Three major coding categories were used in analyzing the adult and child talk. The coding taxonomy had been developed in earlier studies (Goelman, 1986a,b) and piloted on a sub-sample of 9 three year old children in a related project.

Psychological verbs

Psychological verbs were verbs which indicated a reflection on language ("say" "tell"), thought ("know," "believe," "forget") or affect ("feel") (Torrance and Olson, 1985; Galda, Pellegrini & Cox, 1989)

Cohesion

A number of different systems of cohesion were considered (Halliday & Hasan, 1976) and Pellegrini's (1982) definitions of endophora was adopted. While Pellegrini differentiated between anaphora, forward reference in a sentence ("*The car* is in good condition/*It's* only six months old") and cataphora, backward reference ("*He's* a great guy/ Yeah, *John's* number one"), in the current study anaphora and cataphora were conflated into one category of endophora.

Cognitive Demands

The five types of demands were: LABELLING ("What is that called?"); DESCRIPTION ("Tell me about this one"); RECALL ("What happened after that?"); EXPLANATION (How do you build this?") and THREE 'R ("What letter does your name start with?"). Of particular interest were the three more "advanced" types of demands with "Recall" demands seen as accessing children's sense of story, "Explanation" requiring children to articulate causal and linguistic linkages and "Three R" demands probing children's knowledge of the convention of literacy.

Coding Procedure

The video-taped interactions were transcribed onto floppy disk by one group of research assistants and the transcriptions were checked by independent raters who had not been involved in the initial transcription. Inter-rater reliability (agreements divided by disagreements) on 100 randomly selected utterances ranged from 85 percent to 92 percent. The final edited transcripts were then entered into a software program known as "Statistical Analysis of Language Transcripts" or "SALT" (Miller & Chapman, 1985). Every utterance in each transcript in SALT was then analyzed according to the coding taxonomy discussed above. The coded transcriptions were then analyzed on the SALT program which had been customized for purposes of this study. In addition, SALT generated default data including MLU for all participants in words and morphemes, were included in the data base for each dyad. Summary data for each dyad were then entered into mainframe computer for analysis purposes.

Measures of Language

Receptive language was measured using the *Peabody Picture Vocabulary Test—PPVT* (Dunn & Dunn, 1979) and expressive language was measured using the *One-Word Expressive Language Picture Vocabulary Test—EOWPVT* (Gardner, 1979).

Results

Total and sub-scale means for the FDC *HOME* Scale are found in Table 10.1. It should be noted that since the *HOME* is scored on a "yes/no" basis, indicating whether the target interaction was in fact observed or not, the means reflect the percentage of homes in the sample in which the targeted events were observed. There were no episodes (i.e., 0 percent) of physical punishments observed in any of the own-home or family day-care settings. For this reason the sub-scale on physical punishment was not included in any of the subsequent analyses.

As indicated in Table 10.2, the FDC *HOME* Total Score and the sub-scale on Toys, Games and Reading Materials both correlated significantly with the *EOWPVT*. The correlations between the *PPVT* and the Total Score ($r = .24$, $p < .10$), Variety of Stimulation (.27, .08) and Toys, Games and Reading Materials (.23, .11) approached, but did not reach significance.

Means on the own-home *HOME* total score and sub-scales are presented in Table 10.3. As indicated in Table 10.4, the *PPVT* (M = 102.16, SD = 11.5) correlated with the Total own-home *HOME* score as well as with the sub-scales on Physical Environment and Toys, Games and Reading Materials. The *EOWPVT*

($M = 112.96$, $SD = 16.0$) also correlated significantly with the sub-scale on Toys, Games and Reading Materials and approach significance in its correlations with Physical Environment ($p < .06$) and the Total Score ($p < .07$).

Table 10.1 Sub-Scale and Total Means of H.O.M.E. Scale in Family Day-Care Homes

FDC H.O.M.E.	MEAN % RESPONDING "YES"	SD
1. Stimulation Through Toys, Games & Reading Materials	89.89	16.50
2. Language Stimulation	97.50	8.42
3. Physical Environment	99.03	3.81
4. Pride, Affection	95.47	10.37
5. Stimulation of Academic Behavior	98.12	7.80
6. Social Maturity	78.12	35.78
7. Variety of Stimulation	68.75	20.86
9. Total	94.02	7.09

SUBSCALE 8 (PHYSICAL PUNISHMENT) NOT INCLUDED. NO INCIDENTS OF PHYSICAL PUNISHMENT WERE OBSERVED.

Table 10.2 Correlations Between FCD H.O.M.E. Scale and EOWPVT and PPVT Scores

FDC H.O.M.E.	EOWPVT	PPVT
1. Toys, Games, Reading	.39*	.23
2. Language Stimulation	.21	.26
3. Physical Environment	−.01	−.03
4. Pride, Affect	.07	.04
5. Academic Behavior	.14	−.16
6. Social Maturity	.08	.11
7. Variety of Stimulation	.17	.27
8. Total Score	.33*	.24

SUBSCALE 8 (PHYSICAL PUNISHMENT) NOT INCLUDED. NO INCIDENTS OF PHYSICAL PUNISHMENT WERE OBSERVED.
*$P < .05$

Table 10.3   Sub-Scale and Total Means of H.O.M.E. Scale
in Children's Own Homes

OWN-H.O.M.E.	MEAN % RESPONDING "YES"	SD
1. Stimulation Through Toys, Games & Reading Materials	83.46	20.94
2. Language Stimulation	99.40	3.15
3. Physical Environment	86.64	21.97
4. Pride, Affection	83.50	15.09
5. Stimulation of Academic Behavior	100.00	0.00
6. Social Maturity	73.21	25.39
7. Variety of Stimulation	68.75	20.86
9. Total	87.74	10.13

SUBSCALE 8 (PHYSICAL PUNISHMENT) NOT INCLUDED. NO INCIDENTS OF
PHYSICAL PUNISHMENT WERE OBSERVED.

Table 10.4   Correlations Between Own-Home H.O.M.E. Scale
and EOWPVT and PPVT Scores

OWN-H.O.M.E.	EOWPT	PPVT
1. Toys, Games, Reading	.36*	.37*
2. Language Stimulation	.00	−.03
3. Physical Environment	.29	.30*
4. Pride, Affect	−.06	.01
5. Academic Behavior	.16	−.06
6. Social Maturity	.19	.15
7. Variety of Stimulation	.01	−.05
9. Total Score	.29	.30*

SUBSCALE 8 (PHYSICAL PUNISHMENT) NOT INCLUDED. NO INCIDENTS OF
PHYSICAL PUNISHMENT WERE OBSERVED.
$*P < .05$

Correlations between the *HOME* scores in the child's home and his/her
family day-care home suggest certain continuities between the two settings,
particularly in the areas of stimulation and physical environments. As indicated
in Table 10.5, the Total *HOME* score and the Variety of Stimulation sub-scale
in the child's own home correlated with the sub-scale on Physical Environment
in the FDC home. Physical Environment in the child's own home correlated with

Social Maturity in the FDC home and with Physical Environment in the FDC home. The sub-scale on Variety of Stimulation in the child's own home also correlated with the sub-scale on Academic Stimulation in the FDC home, while the sub-scale on Toys, Games and Reading Materials in the child's own home correlated negatively with Variety of Stimulation in the FDC home.

A number of interesting consistencies were revealed in the mother-child talk and the caregiver-child talk and their respective correlations with the focal child's performance on the language measures. As in the mothers' talk, the frequency of endophoric references and "other verbs" in the caregivers' talk were positively correlated with the *EOWPVT* and the *PPVT* test scores. (See Table 10.6A).

In the child-caregiver talk (Table 10.6B), a similar pattern emerged in which discourse features argued to be facilitative of language development were positively correlated with test performance. Frequency of labeling demands were correlated with both *EOWPVT* and *PPVT* scores. The frequency of endophoric references and psychological verbs correlated significantly with the *EOWPVT*.

Table 10.5   Correlation Between FDC H.O.M.E. Scale and Own-Home Scale

Own H.O.M.E.	FDC H.O.M.E.							
	1	2	3	4	5	6	7	8
1. Toys, Games and Reading Materials	.003	.08	.11	−.02	−.08	.10	−.34*	.04
2. Language Stimulation	.17	−.06	−.03	−.09	−.05	−.11	−.18	−.02
3. Physical Environment	.17	.06	.51**	.20	.24	.35*	−.25	.20
4. Pride, Affection	.20	.13	.15	.05	.21	.13	.22	.25
5. Academic Stimulation	.23	.16	.53***	.19	.12	−.09	.21	.30*
6. Social Maturity	−.03	−.18	.17	−.15	.24	.11	.08	.007
7. Variety of Stimulation	.25	.09	.41**	−.03	.48**	.16	.13	.25
8. Total	.18	.09	.37**	.05	.20	.25	−.13	.16

SUBSCALE 8 (PHYSICAL PUNISHMENT) NOT INCLUDED. NO INCIDENTS OF PHYSICAL PUNISHMENT.

* < .05
** < .01
*** < .001

Table 10.6A Correlations Between Caregiver to Child Talk and Child EOWPVT and PPVT Scores

	EOWPVT	PPVT
Endophora	.49**	.52**
Psychological Verbs	.09	.01
Other Verbs	.51**	.47***
Labelling Demands	−.03	.37*
Describing Demands	.08	−.09
Recall Demands	.22	−.25
Explanation Demands	.04	.12
Three 'R Demands	−.07	−.03

Table 10.6B Correlations Between Child to Caregiver Talk and Child EOWPVT and PPVT Scores

	EOWPVT	PPVT
Endophora	.52**	.17
Psychological Verbs	.42*	.19
Other Verbs	.28	.02
Labelling Demands	.81***	.48**
Describing Demands	.00	.01
Recall Demands	.00	.00
Explanation Demands	−.05	−.175
Three 'R Demands	.00	

*p < .05
**p < .01
***p < .001

Table 10.7A Correlations Between Mother to Child Talk and Child EOWPVT and PPVT Scores

	EOWPVT	PPVT
Endophora	.25*	.22*
Psychological Verbs	.17	.39***
Other Verbs	.32**	.40***
Labelling Demands	.00	−.07

Table 10.7A   Correlations Between Mother to Child Talk
and Child EOWPVT and PPVT Scores (continued)

	EOWPVT	PPVT
Describing Demands	−.10	−.01
Recall Demands	−.04	−.06
Explanation Demands	−.21	−.01
Three 'R Demands	−.09	−.07

Table 10.7B   Correlations Between Child to Mother Talk
and Child EOWPVT and PPVT Scores

	EOWPVT	PPVT
Endophora	.16	.11
Psychological Verbs	.37**	.41***
Other Verbs	.13	.05
Labelling Demands	.33**	.10
Describing Demands	.13*	.01
Recall Demands	.27*	−.13
Explanation Demands	.25*	.05
Three 'R Demands	.23	−.13

*p < .05
**p < .01
***p < .001

Data analyses of the mothers' talk and the child's talk were conducted separately. In the mothers' talk, (see Table 10.7A) features related to both cohesion and total amount of language were positively related to children's test scores. The frequency of endophoric references and "other" (non-psychological) verbs were positively related to performance on the *EOWPVT* and the *PPVT*. In addition, the frequency of psychological verbs in the mother-child talk was positively correlated with the children's test scores on the *PPVT*.

A number of discourse features in the child's own talk (See Table 10.7B) correlated with their performance on the language measures. Frequency of psychological verbs was correlated with scores on the *EOWPVT* and the *PPVT*. It is interesting to note that while none of the cognitive demands in the mothers' talk were related to the childrens' test scores, all of the demands in the childrens'' talk were related to their performance on the *EOWPVT*.

Analyses of mothers' and caregivers' utterances to the children revealed a number of significant positive correlations in the frequency of cognitive demands addressed to the children. As indicated in Table 10.8, maternal requests for labels correlated with caregiver requests for labels. Maternal requests for descriptions correlated with caregiver requests for explanations and labels. Caregiver requests for labels correlated with maternal requests for both explanations and "Three 'R" questions. Further, caregiver requests for descriptions also correlated with maternal requests for knowledge from the children. These correlations suggest that home environments and family day-care environments share some aspects of the same type of linguistic environments, that is, in the kinds of verbal discourse in general and the kinds of cognitive demands in particular which are addressed to the children both at home and in care.

Table 10.8   Correlations Between Parent to Child Talk and Caregiver to Child Talk

| | PARENT-CHILD TALK | | | | | | |
Caregiver-Child Talk	1	2	3	4	5	6	7
1. Endophora	.02	−.23	.07	−.05	−.25	−.19	−.30
2. Psychological verb	.17	.18	.09	−.22	−.25	.35	−.16
3. Label	.22	.02	.48**	.34	.44**	.41*	.55**
4. Describe	−.25	.14	−.15	.02	.04	.13	.36*
5. Recall	.04	−.24	−.35	−.32	.00	−.04	−.28
6. Explain	−.11	.28	.14	.33	−.28	.11	.01
7. "3R"	−.24	−.37*	.12	.09	.10	.01	.00

$*p < .05$
$**p < .01$

Discussion

The data from this study (see Table 10.9 for a summary of findings) suggest that (a) ecological features of own-home and family day care home environments are related to overall levels of child language development, and (b) that specific literate features of adult-child discourse patterns in play interactions are also related to children's receptive and expressive language abilities.

The data from the own-home *HOME* scale reveal that the general level of cognitive stimulation, the physical environment and the presence of toys, games and reading materials were all associated with the child's language scored on measures of receptive and expressive language. Consistent with the own-home *HOME* scores, the Total score and the sub-scale scores for Toys, Games and Reading Materials from the FDC *HOME* scores were also linked to child language development. Thus, there appears to be a certain level of consistency in

Table 10.9   Summary of Correlations

OWN-HOME	PPVT	EOWPVT
HOME	TOTAL HOME	—
	Toys, Games, Reading	Toys, Games, Reading
	Physical Environment	—
OWN-HOME	PPVT	EOWPVT
Mother Talk	Endophoric	Endophoric
	Other Verbs	Other Verbs
	Psychological Verbs	—
Child-Mother Talk	Psychological Verbs	Psychological Verbs
		Labelling Demands
		Recall Demands
		Describing Demands
		Explanation Demands
		"3R" Demands
FDC HOME	PPVT	EOWPVT
FDC HOME	—	Total
	—	Toys, Games, Reading
DCHERS	—	Total
	—	Furnishings
	—	Language Development
	—	Learning Activities
	—	Social Development
Caregiver Talk	Endophoric	Endophoric
	Other Verbs	Other Verbs
Child-Caregiver Talk	Labelling Demands	Labelling Demands
		Endophoric
		Psychological Verbs

the overall levels of cognitive stimulation available to the child at home and in family day care.

However, in contrast to the own-home *HOME,* the FDC *HOME* scores correlated only with the measure of expressive language. This finding was interesting in light of the high correlation between the *PPVT* and the *EOWPVT* ($r = .73, p < .001$), and, second, because the own-home *HOME* scale correlated with both measures. It appears that the children in our sample (mean age = 45 months), their receptive language abilities were well-established by their home environments. On the average, these children had begun attending their current family day-care setting when they were about two years of age, by which time their ability to comprehend language and their ability to learn language were given a strong foundation by their home environments. It appears then that these children began care at approximately the age when children begin to make the transition from one-word utterances to two-word utterances and then subsequently, as three year olds, to begin creating more semantically and syntactically complex sentence structures.

The nature of adult-child language interactions were also linked to the outcomes on the language measures. This general pattern is consistent with Clarke-Stewart's (1988) observation that research has indicated "significant correlations between children's language gain and mothers' verbal input" (p. 63). In the mother's talk in our study three factors emerged: the amount of talk, the frequency of endophoric reference, and the frequency of psychological verbs. Amount of talk can be taken as an overall measure of language input and stimulation to the child. As Clarke-Stewart (1988) has pointed out "more motherese is not necessarily better" (p. 63). It is not just the increased amount of talk which is important, but the style and content of that talk as well.

The development of these aspects of language is likely contingent upon facilitative adult input and modelling and the data suggest that this modelling is provided both at home as well as in family day-care setting. Caregiver talk (endophoric references and psychological verbs) correlated with both expressive and receptive language, while only one feature of child-caregiver talk (labeling demands) correlated with receptive language and three features of child-caregiver talk (labeling demands, endophoric references, psychological verbs) correlated with expressive language.

The frequency of endophoric references indicates that the language tends to be explicit and self-referential. That is, as Pellegrini (1984) argues, language use is characterized by explicit linguistic identification of objects and assignment of roles in dramatic play. While including under the rubric of "endophoric" both "anaphoric" (forward referential) and "cataphoric" (backwards referential), these utterances demand a high level of attention paid to the discourse by one's conversational partner. The frequency of endophoric reference strongly implies a discourse pattern which is based upon clarity of meaning, clarity of reference, successful comprehension and accurate expression of one's intentions.

The frequency of psychological verbs suggests another aspect of conversational competence and precision. The use of these verbs implies a certain level of metalinguistic awareness in that the child appears to be differentiating between that which is explicitly stated (what is said) and that which is intended by the utterance (what is meant). For example, the growing awareness and appreciation of sarcasm, linguistically based "knock-knock" jokes, and puns, demonstrates that children at this age are receptive to language forms which interrogate their conventional understandings of word meaning, word boundaries, and sentence structure. Children's use of psychological verbs was also found to correlated with their levels of expressive and receptive language abilities. It was not just their mothers' tendency to use psychological verbs but the children's adoption of this style of talk as well which contributed to their level of language development.

The frequency of children's cognitive demands also correlated with their scores on the *EOWPVT*. This pattern suggests the child's interest in and attempts to elicit certain kinds of information from their mothers during free play situations. This finding adds to our knowledge on the use of cognitive demands in two ways. First, Tizard and Hughes' (1984) collected data only on mothers' and teachers' use of cognitive demands but did not collect data on the children's own use of cognitive demands. Second, it is interesting in this light to note that it was the frequency of cognitive demands in the child's language, not the mother's language, which correlated with their scores on the EOWPVT.

As in the mother-child talk, the caregiver-child talk is strongly associated with the child's level of language development. Further, there is similarity, consistency and, we would argue, complementarity and a mutually reinforcing dynamic in that the amount of talk and frequency of endophoric references at home and in family day care provide the child with enriched and facilitative language environments in both settings. The basic pattern then suggests that both own-home and quality family day care home environments provide the solid foundation in both expressive and receptive language development while the family day-care environments, precisely because they are consistent in style and content with the style found at home, continue to build on the basis in receptive language and provide a supportive environment for the continuing growth and development of expressive language.

Conclusion

The increasing numbers of children who are being cared for in family day-care settings are exposed to the influences of both their own home environments and their family day-care settings. Instead of trying to separate or isolate these two sources of influence from each other, our approach has been to try to assess the ways in which home and day care features together impact upon the child. The data reported in this paper suggest that critical features of the ecology of both own-home and family day-care environments contribute to the child's level of language development. Specifically, the data reveal that the levels of cognitive stimulation available to the child and features of adult-child language interactions in both environments are associated with overall language competence.

The data from this study also lend support to the growing body of research on the relationships between oral discourse patterns in the preschool years and the development of a literate orientation to language. Both children and adults were found to use features of a literate bias in symbolic play interactions, a finding predicted by Pellegrini's (1985a) hypotheses on the relationships between symbolic play and literate behavior. While previous studies have identified these features of language in own-home and nursery school environments, this is the first reported study which has focused on family day care. While there is a general perception that own-home environments are most facilitative of child language development and that the stimulating developmental programs of nursery schools are also encouraging of child development, there is a general perception that the care provided in family day care homes is of a more custodial and less facilitative nature. The data from this study, taken together with Goelman and Pences, (1987a,b) reports on the impact of quality in family day-care, suggest that these environments can also be of critical importance in the child's development of a literate orientation to language.

Useful follow-ups to this work would be to conduct longitudinal studies in this area in order to track children's subsequent success in their public school years, particularly in the areas of language growth and proficiency in reading. While these data suggest the mutual contributions of home and day care settings on children's language development, further work on children's emotional and social development would continue to inform our knowledge base on the interplay of home and family day-care dynamics on young children.

REFERENCES

Barnard, K., Bee, H. L., & Hammond, M. (1984). Home environment in a healthy, low-risk sample: The Seattle study. In A. W. Gottfried, (Ed.), *Home environment and early cognitive development.* (117-150), Toronto, Academic Press.

Bradley, T., & Caldwell, B. (1976). Early home environment and changes in mental test performance at 54 months: A follow-up study. *Child Development, 47,* 1172-1174

Bradley, R., & Caldwell, B. (1980). Home environment, cognitive competence and IQ among males and females. *Child Development, 51,* 1140-1148.

Caldwell, B., & Bradley, R. (1979). *Home Observation for Measurement of the Environment.* Little Rock: University of Arkansas.

Clarke-Stewart, K. A. (1988). Parents' effects on children's development: A decade of progress? *Journal of Applied Developmental Psychology, 9,* 41-84.

Cochran-Smith, M. (1984). *The making of a reader.* Norwood, NJ: Ablex.

Corsaro, W. (1979). Sociolinguistic patterns in adult-child interaction. In E. Ochs & B. B. Schieffelin, *Developmental Pragmatics.* New York: Academic Press.

Dunn, L., & Dunn, R. (1979). *Peabody Picture Vocabulary Test—Revised.* Circle Pines, MN: American Guidance Services.

Galda, L., Pellegrini, A. D., & Cox, S. (1989). A short-term longitudinal study of preschoolers' emergent literacy. *Research in the Teaching of English,* Vol. 23, No. 3, 292-307.

Gardner, M. F. (1979), *Expressive One-Word Picture Vocabulary Test.* Novato, CA: Academic Therapy Publications.

Goelman, H. (1986). The facilitation of language development in family day care homes: A comparative study. *Early Child Development and Care, 25,* 161-174.

Goelman, H., & Pence, A. R. (1987a). Effects of child care, family and individual characteristics on children's language development: The Victoria Day Care Research Project. In D. Phillips (Ed.). *Quality in child care: What does research tell us?* (pp. 89-104). Washington, DC: National Association for the Education of Young Children.

Goelman, H., & Pence, A. R. (1987b). The relationship between family structure and child development in three types of day care. In S. Kontos & D. Peters (Eds.) *Advances in applied developmental psychology* (Volume 2, pp. 129-146). Norwood, NJ: Ablex.

Goelman, H. & Pence, A. R. (1988a). The continuity of attitudes, beliefs and perceptions in three types of day care. *Canadian Journal of Research in Early Childhood Education,* Vol. 2, No. 2, 175–186.

Goelman, H., & Pence, A. R. (1988b). Children in three types of day care: Daily experiences, quality of care, and developmental outcomes. *Early Child Development and Care, 33,* 67-76.

Goelman, H., & Pence, A. R. (1989). Cognitive and social contexts of language development in home and family day care environments. Paper presented to the Annual Conference of the American Educational Research Association (March).

Goelman, H., Rosenthal, M. K., & Pence, A. R. (1990). Family day care in two countries: Caregivers, parents and children in Israel and Canada. *Child and Youth Care Quarterly,* (9) 19, 251–270.

Goelman, H., Shapiro, E., & Pence, A. R. (1990). Family environment and family day care. *Family Relations, 39,* 14-19.

Gottfried, A. W. (1984) (Ed.), *Home environment and early cognitive development.* Toronto, Academic Press.

Gottfried, A. W., & Gottfried, A. E. (1984). Home environments and cognitive development in young children of middle socio-economic status in families. In A. W. Gottfried, (Ed.), *Home environment and early cognitive development.* Toronto, Academic Press.

Grice, H. P. (1957). Meaning. *Psychological Review, 66,* 377-388.

Halliday, M. A. K., & Hassan, R. (1976). *Cohesion in English.* London, UK: Longman.

Harms, T., Clifford, R., & Padan-Belkin, E. (1983). *The Day Care Home Environment Scale.* Chapel Hill, NC: Frank Porter Graham Child Development Center.

Johnson, D. L., Breckenridge, J. N., & McGowan, R. J. (1984). *Home environment and early cognitive development.* In A. W. Gottfried, (Ed.). *Home environment and early cognitive development.* (151-196), Toronto, Academic Press.

Lamb, M. E., Hwang, C., Broberg, A., & Bookstein, F. (1988). The effects of out-of-home care on social competence in Sweden: A longitudinal study. *Early Childhood Research Quarterly, 3,* 379-402.

Miller, J. F., & Chapman, R. S. (1985). *Systematic analysis of language transcripts.* Madison: University of Wisconsin.

Moos, R. (1986). *Family Environment Scale* (2nd edition). Palo Alto, CA: Consulting Psychologists' Press.

Pellegrini, A. D. (1982). The construction of cohesive text by preschoolers in two play contexts. *Discourse Processes,* Volume 5, No. 8, 101-108.

Pellegrini, A. (1985a). The relaions between symbolic play and literate behavior: A review and critique of the empirical literature. *Review of Educational Research, 55,* 207-221(b).

Pellegrini, A. D. (1985b). Relations between symbolic play and literate behavior. In L. Galda and A. D. Pellegrini (Eds.), *Play, language and story: The development of children's literate behavior,* (79-97). Norwood, NJ: Ablex.

Reeder, K., Shapiro, J., Watson, W., & Goelman, H. (in preparation). Literate apprenticeships: The emergence of language and literacy in the preschool years. Norwood, NJ: Ablex.

Tizard, B., & Hughes, M. (1984). *Young children learning: Talking and thinking at home and at school.* London, UK: Fontana.

Torrance, N., & Olson, D. R. (1984). Oral language competence and the acquisition of literacy. In A. Pellegrini and T. Yawkey (Eds.) *The development of oral and written language in social contexts.* (pp. 167-182). Norwood, NJ: Ablex.

Torrance, N., & Olson, D. R. (1985). In D. R. Olson, N. Torrance, & A. Hildyard (Eds.) *Literacy, language and learning: The nature and consequences of reading and writing.* (256-284). Cambridge, UK: Cambridge University Press.

Wells, G. (1985). Preschool literacy-related activities and success in school. In D. R. Olson, Torrance, N., & Hildyard, A. (Eds.) *Literacy, language and learning: The nature and consequences of reading and writing* (229-255). Cambridge, UK: Cambridge University Press.

Wells, G. (1986). *The meaning makers: Children learning language and using language to learn.* Portsmouth, NH: Heinemann.

11

Conclusion: Emerging Ecological Perspectives on Play and Child Care

Hillel Goelman

*"A child knows his Nurse and his Cradle and by
degrees the play-things of a little more advanced Age."
(Locke, 1690)*

One cannot say for certain, of course, but it is possible that John Locke's comments in *An Essay Concerning Human Understanding* were among the earliest written observations of the effects of adult intervention, a stimulating environment, and age-appropriate play materials on children's developmental status. While one needn't go back 300 years to begin to explore children's play in child care settings, it does lend some perspective to realize that questions regarding how children come to "know" their world through interaction with their "Nurse" and "playthings" have a long and honorable history. It was in an attempt to further our understanding of children's play in child care settings that the papers in this volume were assembled. In this conclusion we review these papers by examining consistencies and differences among them and by placing them in the context of current and recent work in the field.

When examining the types of research questions which have been addressed in both the play and child care literatures, certain parallels are revealed in the definitional, conceptual, methodological, developmental and policy issues which have been raised in these respective research traditions. As noted by Ellen Jacobs in the introduction, in both play and child care research there have been extensive discussions regarding the definition and construct validity of the very phenomena under study. The play literature (i.e., Parten, 1932; Piaget, 1962; Vygotsky, 1967; Smilansky, 1968; Bruner, 1972; Sutton-Smith, 1979, 1980; Pellegrini, 1986) is replete with discussions on the definition of "play," the boundaries between "play" and "non-play" behaviors, the differentiations between the social and cognitive aspects of play and between the different types of social and cognitive aspects of play. In their excellent review article, Rubin, Fein and Vandenberg (1983) summarize these various approaches to the definition of play and proposed a working definition that "play" includes a number of features of child disposition and observable behavior and which occur in and are influenced by the nature of specific contexts. For example, Smith and Vollstedt (1985) examined raters assessments of different features of play behavior and concluded that raters' definitions of "play" were quite varied and were predicted by a combination of several different criteria. In this volume as well, different operational definitions of play have been used by the different authors yielding both consistencies and differences in their results.

"Child care" has also been subjected to numerous definitional and conceptual battles, and, as in the case of "play," child care is also now seen as a multi-faceted and heterogeneous phenomenon rather than a monolithic construct. The definitional battles about child care, in both the worlds of program implementation and research, are partly rooted in the historical paths which marked the evolution of early childhood education programs and child welfare/care programs (Fein, 1986). The worlds of child care have become even more complex with the multiplicity in forms of child care and the wide range of ways in which children experience child care.

As Clarke-Stewart and Fein (1983) point out, child care settings can be differentiated on the basis of organizational dimensions, underlying values, program orientation, the professionalism of the caregivers, and the nature of the sponsoring agencies. Day care centers can be operated by public agencies, non-profit societies or (large or small) private/commercial day-care operators and family day-care homes may be run as small private "cottage industries" or as part of a community-based networking system.

In the current volume, this multiplicity can be seen in a number of different ways. Children were observed in child care settings in four countries, Canada (Goelman & Pence; Tobias; Jacobs & White; Howe, Moller & Chambers), Israel (Rosenthal), Sweden (Lamb, Sternberg. Hwang & Broberg) and the United States (Field; Howes & Galluzzo; Roopnarine, Bright & Riegraf; Wittmer & Honig). Children's play was observed in family day-care homes and day-care centers which operated under different kinds of sponsorship and auspices. The characteristics of the children also varied. The experiences of the children in child care differ depending on such factors as age of entry, full-and part-time enrollment, age mixture of the children in care and other structural and process aspects of the child care settings. Children also participate in multiple child-care settings: home environments, preschool/day-care environments, shared custody arrangements with divorced or separated parents, school programs, after-school programs. As in the discussion of play, the boundaries between child care and nonchild care, and the different types of experiences which fall into the category of child care, create a complex, multi-dimensional phenomenon.

The complexity of understanding the nature of children's play in day care settings begins to ressemble the many possible combinations of a Rubik's cube. Play itself is as heterogeneous construct as is child care. Bronfenbrenner's (1979) framework of ecologically oriented child development research begins by acknowledging the complexity of children's lives and the interaction of systems which embed children's experiences. For these reasons, Bronfenbrenner has had a profound effect on research in both play and child care.

These effects can be seen in the increasing use of what Belsky and Steinberg (1978) first termed "model" rather than "modal" child care settings. In so doing, ecologically oriented researchers have examined children's play in what Howes and Unger (1989) have called specific "ecocultural" contexts. They directed their attention to the physical and human characteristics of child care settings and concluded that such features as caregiver training, caregiver facilitation of child-child interaction, the kinds of play materials, the organization of play space and the degree of familiarity with same-aged peers all contributed to social pretend play of toddlers in day care settings. Examples of this type of research are found in Holloway and Reichart-Erickson (1988) who reported strong associations between quality of the day care program (i.e. adult-child interactions, spaciousness, types of materials) and children's free play and social problem-solving abilities and Pellegrini (1986) who found that the language of social play among differently aged children in early childhood settings was affected by both the nature of the play materials and the presence/absence of an adult.

The three studies which examined children's play in family day care settings reported an interesting set of consistent and complementary findings. Goelman and Pence reported that the language development of 3-5 year old Canadian children was closely associated with both the quality of the day care environment (i.e., materials, program) and the nature of the caregiver-child verbal interactions. Lamb, Sternberg, Hwang and Broberg found that Swedish toddlers (as young as 16 months old) in family day-care homes demonstrated peer interaction and social skills which were also associated with the quality of the family day care environment. This finding is echoed, and extended, in Rosenthal's report of toddlers in Israeli family day-care homes. She reported that the quality of the environment and caregiver interactions contributed to the children's level of social interaction and play with peers.

The ecological orientation to human development has also encouraged the study of children's experiences not just in the immediate setting in which they may be observed, but in what Suransky (1984) has called the various "life spaces of the child." Child care researchers are beginning to examine the effects of family life on their children in nonparental child care arrangements. Howes and Stewart (1987), for example, reported associations between levels of nurturing in the child's family environments, quality of the child care arrangement and the child's level of competent play with objects and peers. Roopnarine, Church and Levy (1990) examined the relationships between parental behaviors, stress and companionship and their children's dramatic and functional play in child care. Goelman, Shapiro and Pence (1990) examined the social-emotional family dynamics of family day-care providers and the relationships between these aspects of the providers' lives and the quality of child care they were providing.

In the current volume the relationship of family background to children's play was included in a number of the studies. However, while findings of interest were reported within each chapter, there did not appear to be a clearly articulated resolution of this question across the different studies. Rosenthal found that parental background, assessed primarily through SES variables, helped to account for the choice of the specific family day-care home in which their child enrolled, but was not related to their child's play in the day care itself. Parental expectation levels for their children were also not related to the child's play. Taking a different tack, Roopnarine, Bright and Reigraf, built on their earlier work by examining specific features of family and marital dynamics. In finding that maternal marital relations was associated with children's play patterns, this paper draws our attention to the ways in which in-home family dynamics is one of the child's "life spaces" can contribute to the child's behavior and play interactions in another "life space." Resonating with this finding is the current chapter by Goelman and Pence which suggests that home language environments and mother-child discourse in the home, appear to complement and provide a basis for the language environments (and caregiver-child discourse) in a family day care environment. That home language environments were more closely associated with receptive language and day care environments more closely associated with expressive language would be consistent with children's general levels of language development in their infancy-toddlerhood and then in their preschool years. As demonstrated in Goelman, Shapiro & Pence (1990), contextual and affective features in a day-care setting are associated with child language development.

While caregiver interaction with the children was reported by numerous authors in this volume and elsewhere, Howes and Galluzzo report data which suggest a much less important role for caregiver "gatekeeping" or mediating in child care settings. They report low mediation levels among the caregivers and that children's level of peer play in day care were more closely associated with the number of play partners and frequency of play episodes outside of the child care setting.

At issue, then, would be not whether or not home environments contribute or affect children's play in child care settings, but, rather, to identify the specific features of home environments which impact on the specific types of play in which children are observed to engage.

A continuing question in both the play and child care research literatures focuses on the effects of each of these phenomena on child development. In the play literature the question is phrased frequently in terms of "competent" or "successful" play, the characteristics of such play and the impact of these types of play on a child's developmental status. Rubin, Fein and Vendenberg (1983) pointed out that while most theorists assumed a positive relationship between play and development, there was in fact little empirical work to support the assumption. Athey's (1987) review of a wide range of play researchers led to the conclusion that play was indeed influential in intellectual, language, social and emotional development and that these influences can be seen in infancy, early childhood, middle childhood, and adolescence. Bretherton (1989) has argued that some of the specific characteristics of make believe play (i.e., managing roles as playwrights and actors, blurring the boundary between play and reality, turn-taking, inventing plots) are facilitative of children's social, emotional and cognitive growth. Cannella, Berkeley, Constans and Parkhurst (1987) compared the play of at-risk and "typically developing" infants and reported that while children demonstrated early play and exploration behaviors in both groups, typically developing children exhibited a developmental pattern of decreasing exploration and increasing play behaviors. The at-risk children demonstrated increases in both types of behavior.

Questions of development and "at-risk ness" were raised in chapters by Field, by Jacobs and White and by Tobias. Field reports data from both a short- and long-term longitudinal study of infants who had been enrolled in infant day care centers. She reported no difference between early and late enrollees and that they demonstrated enhanced levels of play and social skills in their preschool years. In elementary schools a significant proportion of these children were placed in classes for "gifted children." Jacobs and White collected data on children in day care centers in their preschool years and then in kindergarten programs. These authors draw our attention in this kind of longitudinal research to the defining "quality" in child care in a careful and defensible manner, and are aware of variabilities and mitigating factors which can influence the results. They point out, for example, that while a substantial number of the children in their sample participated in "low quality child care centers," there was no apparent negative influence on them when they were observed in kindergarten a year later. They raise the point that the high quality kindergarten program may, in fact, have minimized if not negated the effect of the low quality day care center.

Specific ecological features of the day care setting is also a major focus on Eliana Tobias's examination of the play of special needs children in different kinds of preschool settings. On finding of educational and policy concern which she reports is that the special needs children were played with by nonhandicapped children very infrequently. While the goal of least restrictive environments and facilitating peer interaction remain laudable and defensible, these data suggest that the practice of integration in these sampled centers more often resulted in the handicapped children playing alone than with peers. Further, the specialized centres designed for the handicapped children received lower quality ratings than the other centers. It is of interest to note, however, that there was no main effect for setting type on any of the measures. That is, the types of play behaviors varied across all types of centers. Tobias argues that the "label" or "program" of a setting is far less relevant that an actual careful observation of the types of social interactions which are found in child care settings.

The relevance of play and child care to educational practice is receiving increasing attention. In the play literature researchers have directed their attention to questions regarding children with what have been described as "lower" levels of or "less competent" play. Curry & Arnaud (1987) describe a program in which the curriculum is determined by the special needs and interests of the individual child. They emphasize the value of play in meeting these needs and report on their own observations of play at a university demonstration preschool. If their observations they focused on the role enactment of children in play. They draw attention to the fact that, in spite of the claims of researchers that there is a natural progression in children from one stage of pretend play to another, there is also great variability from preschool to preschool in the amount of play, presumably because of differing emphases and opportunities provided by the teachers. Curry and Arnaud then go on to describe in some detail ways in which pretend play can be fostered in preschool environments. They point to rearrangements of the physical environment, acquisition of key toys and materials, and the role of the adult in facilitating play by actively helping children to negotiate and to interpret each other's behavior. They suggest that teachers may also play a role in channelling children's energies in a specific direction in play. They note that peers may also facilitate pretend play, and they make the suggestion that duplicate play materials be provided in order to lessen the difficulties of young children in sharing and turn-taking, and to provide opportunities for children to learn by imitation. They see a need for culturally relevant materials, and allude to cross-cultural research to support this idea.

Finally, they discuss the therapeutic value of play for children with specific emotional needs, and for children who have been traumatized, including groups of preschool children disturbed by an event occurring in the preschool itself. They also warn the reader that, in some cases, unhealthy or perseverative play may be a signal or consequence of disturbance in a child. In such cases, they add, attempts should be made to broaden the child's play experiences. Curry and Arnaud conclude that empirical evidence, including their own observational research, supports the idea of the developmental preschool in which play is a central activity.

While issues of educational policy and practices with young children derive from all of the chapters in this volume, they are addressed perhaps most centrally in the chapters by Howe, Mollar and Chambers and by Wittmer and Honig. Howe and her colleagues examined how specific aspects of the ecology of classroom design influenced the kinds of play engaged in by the children. The results indicated that when the classroom dramatic play centers were designed with the children's levels of developmental status in mind, by well trained and highly motivated individuals, the results included high levels of peer interaction. Certain specific features, however, (entry to and exit from a climbing structure) appeared to encourage the children to engage in more agonistic or solitary play.

Wittmer and Honig focused on how caregivers responded to children's initiatives. These one-to-one interactions took place most frequently in the context of story and song activities and least frequently in gross-motor activities. Almost half of the teachers' interactions were coded as "teaching" while fewer than 10 percent were either "negative controlling" or "ego boosting" (7.4 percent). The picture that emerges quite clearly, then, from the chapters by Howe, Mollar and Chamber, Tobias, and Wittmer and Honig is that both the design of classroom space and materials as well as the nature of appropriate adult interaction contribute to the kinds of play activities observed in child care centers.

The studies in this volume have in common a level of experimental rigor and a sensitivity to the kinds of ecological features which impact on young children. The commonalities and consistencies which emerge from the diverse methodologies and subject pools found in this collection of papers contribute to our understanding of the complex phenomena summarized too succinctly under the rubrics "play" and "child care." These studies also provide guidance to researchers wishing to establish reasonable experimental criteria for conducting observational studies of young children in child care settings. The differences in findings help to set the research agenda for continuing inquiries in this area.

REFERENCES

Athey, I. (1987). Contributions of play to development. In T. D. Yawkey & A. D. Pellegrini (Eds.) *Child's play: Developmental and applied.* Hillsdale, NJ: Erlbaum. pp. 9-27.

Belsky, J., & Steinberg, L. (1978). The effects of day care: A critical review. *Child Development, 49,* 929-949.

Bretherton, I. (1989). Pretense: The form and function of make believe play. *Developmental Review, 9,* 383-401.

Bronfenbrenner, U. (1979). *The ecology of human development.* Cambridge, MA: Harvard University Press.

Bruner, J. (1972). The nature and uses of immaturity. *American Psychologist, 27,* 687-708.

Cannella, G. S., Berkeley, T. R., Constans, T. M., & Parkhurst, S. A. (1987). Cognitive processes of at-risk and typically developing infants: Comparison of exploration, play, and problem solving. *Child Study Journal, 17*(4), 269-286. (ABS).

Caruso, D. A. (1988). Play and learning in infancy: Research and implications. *Young Children,* September, 63-70.

Clarke-Stewart, A., & Fein, G. (1983). Early childhood programs. In P. H. Mussen (Ed.), *Handbook of child psychology: Volume II, Infancy and developmental psychobiology,* 917-1000. New York: Wiley.

Curry, N. E., & Arnaud, S. H. (1987). Play in developmental preschool settings. In T. D. Yawkey & A. D. Pellegrini (Eds.) *Child's play: Developmental and applied.* 273-289.

Fein, G., (1986). The play of children. In G. Fein and M. Rivkin (Eds.), *The young child at play: Reviews of research,* Vol. 4, pp. vii-ix. Washington, DC: National Association for the Education of Young Children.

Holloway, S. D., & Reichhart-Erickson, M. (1988). The relationship of day-care quality to children's free-play behavior and social problem-solving skills. *Early Childhood Research Quarterly, 3,* 39-53.

Howes, C., & Unger, O. (1989). Play with peers in child-settings. In M. Block & A. D. Pellegrini (Eds.) *The ecological contexts of children's play,* pp. 104-117. Norwood, NJ. 423-430.

Parten, M. (1932). Social participation among preschool children. *Journal of Abnormal Psychology, 27,* 243-269.

Pellegrini, A. D. (1986). Play centers and the production of imaginative language. *Discourse Processes, 9,* 115-125.

Piaget, J. (1962). *Play, dreams and imitation in childhood.* New York: Norton.

Roopnarine, J., Church, C., & Levy, G. (1990). Day-care children's play behaviors. Relationships to their mothers' and fathers' assessments of their parenting behaviors, marital stress and marital companionship. *Early Childhood Research Quarterly, 5,* 335-346.

Rubin, K., Fein, G., & Vandenberg, B. (1983). Play. In P. Mussen & E. Hetherington (Eds.). *Handbook of child psychology: Volume 4, Socialization, personality and social development,* 693-774. New York: Wiley.

Smith, P. K., & Vollstedt, R. (1985). On defining play: An empirical study of the relationship between play and various play criteria. *Child Development, 56,* 1042-1050.

Smilansky, S. (1968). *The effects of sociodramatic play on disadvantaged preschool children.* New York: Wiley.

Suransky, V. (1982). *The erosion of childhood.* Chicago, Ill: University of Chicago Press.

Sutton-Smith, B. (1979). Epilogue: Play as performance. In B. Sutton-Smith
    (Ed.), *Play and learning,* pp. 295-322. New York: Gardner.

Sutton-Smith, B. (1980). Children's play: some sources for play theorizing.
    In K. Rubin (Ed.), *Children's play.* San Francisco: Jossey-Bass.

Vygotsky, L. (1967). Play and its role in the mental development of the child.
    Soviet Psychology, 12, 62-76.

Index

Author Index